Investigating Tree Archaeology
History and Technology of Woodland Management and Product Use

Edited by Ian D. Rotherham and Christine Handley

Supported and sponsored by:

With the European Society for Environmental History & The Vernacular Architecture Group

Landscape Archaeology and Ecology, **13**

Edited by Ian D. Rotherham and Christine Handley

ISBN: 978-1-904098-70-6

Black and white version; cover price £25

August 2020

Published by:
Wildtrack Publishing, Venture House,
103 Arundel Street, Sheffield S1 2NT

© Wildtrack Publishing and the individual authors 2020

All rights reserved. No part of this publication may be reproduced or transmitted in any form or by any means, electronic or mechanical, including photocopying, recording, or any information storage or retrieval system, without permission in writing from the publisher.

Front cover: photograph credit Ian D. Rotherham

Contents

Foreword 1

Chapter 1. Planting & Woodland Management – producing wood and timber for construction in pre-industrial England
Ian Rotherham
.... 3

Chapter 2. The Worked and Veteran trees of Brackenhurst Estate
Andy Alder
.... 31

Chapter 3. The Beetle Faunas of Ancient and Veteran Trees
Keith Alexander
.... 41

Chapter 4. Bishops' House
Ken Dash
.... 63

Chapter 5. Abbots, Barons and Trees – Five Centuries of Woodland Management in Two Yorkshire Dales
Ian G. R. Dormor
.... 69

Chapter 6. Bobbin Mills in the North of Scotland
Joanna Gilliatt
.... 91

Chapter 7. A Right Royal Forest: The woodland archaeology of Speech House, the Forest of Dean
Andrew Hoaen and Helen Loney
.... 109

Chapter 8. Marker and Marked Trees in Anglo-Saxon England and Continuing Tradition
Della Hooke
.... 125

Chapter 9. Tree Species & Uses from Documentary Evidence
Della Hooke
.... 143

Chapter 10. Managing Woodland in the Past for Constructional Timber – the Documentary Evidence from South Yorkshire and Ireland
Melvyn Jones
.... 155

Chapter 11. Managing trees in coppice-with-standards woodland
Melvyn Jones
.... 175

Chapter 12. From tree-rings to timber trade: dendrochronological evidence for woodland history in Scotland
Coralie Mills
.... 197

Chapter 13. Reading the past lives of working trees
Helen Read & Ted E. Green
.... 211

Chapter 14. Hidden woodland heritage in south-east Wales
Nicola Strange
.... 233

Chapter 15. Life and death of wooden artefacts: a review of the evidence for early medieval woodcraft
Kevin Tillison
.... 277

Chapter 16. Relict Woodlands in the South Pennines and Dark Peak – reconstructing the evidence from ecological indicators and archival sources
Ian D. Rotherham
.... 289

Chapter 17. A short introduction to the Oaks of Lincoln Cathedral
Andy Alder
.... 327

Short Contributions
.... 335

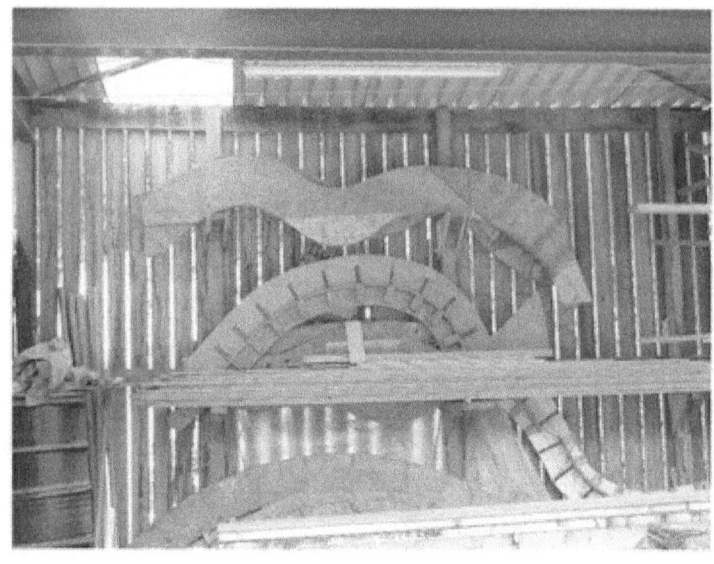

Wooden patterns and materials hanging in a woodworker's workshop, Ecclesall Woods Discovery Centre. Source: C. Handley (2016)

Foreword

This volume of papers arose from the 2-day conference *Investigating Tree Archaeology* that was held in Sheffield, and from associated events and activities. It was organised by the *South Yorkshire Biodiversity Research Group* and the *Landscape Conservation Forum* with Sheffield Hallam University supported by Historic England.

The main 2-day event brought together veteran tree specialists, dendrochronologists, archaeologists, vernacular building architects and technologists, ecologists and woodland historians to discuss the history and technology of woodland management, processes and products. It considered the various aspects of tree and woodland archaeology extending from the hedgerow / wood-pasture / wood [*process*] to final destination [*product*].

The conference considered issues around the legacy of veteran trees and the evidence of past management and technologies that exist in the transformed products, some of which are still found today. Whilst focussing on the UK, we welcomed speakers and contributors from other European countries with different and / or more recent traditions of management, production and process in woodlands.

The conference was one of the series of events in our programme of 'Wilder Visions- re-constructing nature for the 21st century'. The book is also a volume in our long-running journal series **Landscape Archaeology and Ecology**. Back issues can be downloaded from our website: www.ukeconet.org

Chapter 1. Planting & Woodland management – producing wood and timber for construction in pre-industrial England

Ian Rotherham
Sheffield Hallam University

Figure 1. Charcoal burner's hut New Forest 1800s (IDR)

Summary

Understanding how landscape resources have been used throughout history is central to the study of long-term environmental history. In this context, the relationships between vernacular buildings, other built structures, and natural resources are of particular interest.

Research into vernacular architecture for example, may set out to place structural timbers and other woodland products into the context of the buildings and other artefacts, but often the connection to the landscape is relatively limited. Experts in analysing, for example, timber *in situ*, may not be so knowledgeable about the processes involved prior to the delivery of materials onto site, or to the workshop of the craftsman. Furthermore, there may be only limited appreciation of the general environmental issues surrounding the management and conservation of woodland and the other demands placed upon its exploitation in pre-industrial societies. Competing demands historically included fuel extraction and processing for domestic and for industrial usage. There were also tensions between those requiring woodland or parkland timber for different structural uses – from local modest buildings, to higher status construction, and to other uses such as shipbuilding. The management and resolution of these issues is at the core of understanding ancient woodlands and trees in the landscape.

Finally, the 2017 annual meeting of the Vernacular Architecture Group at Leicester highlighted a need to understand better the dynamics of the interrelationships between the wood and the landscape producing the raw materials, the craftsman and others shaping the products, and the end uses in buildings or other construction.

Figure 2. High status building from local materials in middle England (IDR)

Planting & woodland management

Much of the interest ranges broadly from the early medieval period to the eighteenth century, up to and including the main period of parliamentary enclosures, a time of major transformation in the landscape. Indeed, in the build-up to enclosures, to agricultural revolution and to industrial revolution and urbanisation, attitudes to the countryside and its management began to change dramatically.

This paper provides a perspective on processes and issues of environmental change, and associated demands on woodland and related resources. I consider the management responses to the pressures and demands, and especially the competition for resources by different actors.

Woods and other 'tree'd' habitats provided 'timber' and 'wood' resources plus much else besides; often with competing demands between different stakeholders. Since from the early medieval period, with growing human populations across Europe and Great Britain, resources came under greater pressure, managers were forced or opted to approach the landscape differently. This utilisation might be to produce timber for building and other construction or generate fuelwood or to manufacture charcoal for industry. From the extensive wood-pasture landscapes and commons, woods and parks were enclosed and protected, and in the increasingly 'hedged' countryside hedgerow trees became significant too.

Figure 3. A scene from Sherwood Forest in the 1800s (IDR)

Vernacular histories & localisation

The uses of, and demands upon, natural resources for buildings vary over time. If we consider pre-industrial society in Great Britain specifically, we see also marked geographic variations and resulting character depending on the nature of the landscape. Additionally, as populations ebbed and flowed with climate change, diseases, conflicts, and economic fluctuations, the demands on resources fluxed and the choices of materials in buildings shifted with availability, cost, convenience, status and fashion.

Resources:
- Timber
- Wood
- Turf
- Peat
- Stone
- Clay
- Reed & sedge
- Bracken

Figure 4. Harvesting poles for the hop industry (IDR)

In the pre-industrial countryside many 'prime' resources were not available to most people, and almost all resources were carefully (and sometimes strictly) controlled. We see a separation between the resources and materials used for high-end prestigious projects and buildings (royal, aristocratic, and ecclesiastical uses), those of the wealthier peasants or in towns, those in commerce or crafts, and the poorer commoners and peasantry.

All these issues influenced and affected the way sites were managed and resources were harvested and utilised.

Seeing the wood in the trees......
Evidence of past usage of tree resources may be visible in the once-worked but now abandoned trees – so-called 'working trees' as they 'worked' for a living, and now are 'worked' or 'retired' veterans. This 'tree-archaeology' with coppices, shreds, stubs, pollards, and single- or multiple-stemmed open-grown standards, can be hugely informative about past management. Some of the multiple-stemmed, open-grown standards may be outgrown coppices selected on for specific uses, singled as individual trunks, or else merely abandoned.

It is also important to recognise the difference between 'wood' or 'underwood' (*boscus* in Latin medieval documents, or *le spryng bosci* combining French and Latin (Jones, 2009)) which was small diameter poles cut from coppice, pollards, shreds or scrub; and 'timber' which was large diameter material for major constructional work (referred to as *meremium* or *maerimium* in Latin medieval documents). Poles from coppice or other sources provided fuel, but also wood for lighter constructional work (such as wattles or light, supporting struts) on modest buildings and around farms or cottages. In some regions such as fenland areas, the products would be predominantly small-wood from willow or alder coppice and brushwood. Similarly, in many upland zones or areas such as the Western Isles for example, there was an acute shortage of larger timbers and therefore larger wood poles were important and prestigious.

Figure 5. Shielings on Jura in the 1700s, but note the exaggerated scale (IDR)

In order to understand the roles of woodland and trees in building construction, it is necessary to know about their history of both management and utilisation, and about how these were controlled. We need to know, who had the rights to what, where, and when?

Before Domesday, (1086), most British 'woodland' was in the form of 'wood-pasture' – with open, grazed grassland and heath populated by large 'open-grown', standard trees, and probably more-dense areas of close-canopy 'forest' and scrub. This was a large and expansive landscape with a relatively low density human population. Across much of the countryside there would have been only limited controls over what resources were available and to whom; perhaps related to 'tribal' ownership of resources and rights.

A key account and source of information is the Domesday record of the Saxon countryside researched and drawn up for William the Conqueror, the Norman overlord. There are two versions, the 'Little Domesday Book' which includes Norfolk, Suffolk and Essex and has less of a summary and greater detail than the 'Great Domesday Book' for the rest of the kingdom. As a document, it is perhaps less organised and some of the nomenclature differs too.

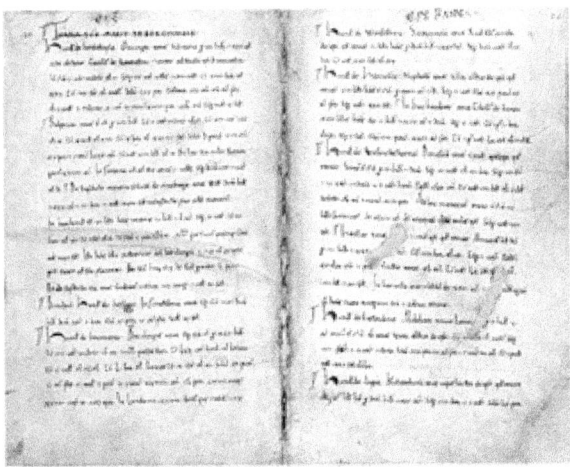

Figure 6. An entry from Essex from the Little Domesday book (IDR)

However, overall, the 'Great Domesday' account of 1086 provides detailed insight into woodland resources across much of England which it describes in four main forms:

1) *Silva* – simply woodland
2) *Silva modica* – not known exactly but perhaps some form of woodland with coppice
3) *Silva minuta* – meaning coppice
4) *Silva pastilis* – meaning wood pasture

Figure 7. A typical Domesday entry from Herefordshire (IDR)

At Domesday, documenting the former Anglo-Saxon landscape, although the countryside varies in terms of the extent of arable land *etc.*, there is generally an abundance of (4, *Silva pastilis*) wood-pasture, and less of the coppice types. This is typical for an extensive landscape of abundant resources and relatively few people. Interpreting distances and areas in Domesday can also be problematic with different measures applied at regional levels. However, the following are broadly accepted:

> **Acre, acra, ager:** A value of land assessment frequently applied to pasture, meadow, and woodland. Measurement of an acre was a multiple of 'hides' but this varies from region to region.
> **Hide, hida:** This was a measurement of land for tax assessment used outside Danelaw counties (for which 'carucates' were used) and was around 120 acres; dependent on local variations in the acre.
> **Carucate, carucata:** Derived from the Latin word *caruca*, meaning plough, it is a measure of land used in Danelaw (North and Eastern) counties in Domesday. This was equivalent to a hide and represented the amount of land which could be ploughed by one plough team.
> **League:** A measurement of distance, twelve furlongs, or about 1½ miles.

With the imposition of the Norman feudal system across England, this inherent flexibility in the countryside changed into very organised and largely fixed manors distributed with rights rigorously controlled from the Crown and gifted to those in the hierarchy below. Within this new organisation, rights and access to resources were strictly controlled and allocated through a mix of ownership and long-established traditions. However, there was a further twist in this situation, when, as acknowledged in the *Act of Commons* (1235), the various parts of the manor estate were fixed and allocated to diverse functions – the 'wood', the 'park', the 'common', the open fields, the heath, the bog, the fen, and more. Within this medieval countryside the role of timber and wood from hedgerows is often forgotten.

This act, also called *'The Statute of Merton'*, is regarded as the *'Magna Carta of the landscape'* and whilst it probably did not bring about the changes in the countryside it ratified processes occurring under the Norman feudal system. The extensive and often fluid rural landscape and its resources were increasingly fixed and regulated to supply the needs of growing populations and a source of revenue for the Lord and the State.

Furthermore, and important in terms of their maintenance, for the commoner and many of the poorer peasants, the resources from the unenclosed commons and heaths were vital for both fuel energy and for constructional works. As the human population grew steadily over the period from around 1100 to 1300 AD, the countryside became an increasingly disputed space and resources needed to be managed more rigorously in order to maintain the sustainable provision of vital materials. In some regions such as Norfolk and Suffolk for example, the increasingly hedged landscape became important in the supply of faggots of wood-fuel (often from pollard trees), and for timber trees too.

The emergence of managed 'woods':
One consequence of the shift noted above, from wood-pastures to coppice woods, was the development of protected 'woods', named and enclosed by a bank and ditch, a wall or a paling fence to keep out grazing livestock but also to demarcate the wood from the lands around. Most of today's 'ancient woods' derive from about this time of the Act of Commons, or in some cases, a little earlier. These are enclosed medieval 'woods' and were usually privately owned, by the Crown, an aristocrat, a manorial lord, or an ecclesiastical foundation; and a few were in common usage.

The management process:
Coppice: the coppice cycle to produce poles of varying ages and sizes dependent on the subsequent use – anything from a seven year to a 25-year cutting cycle. The relatively young growths are cut back to a stool at about ground level and allowed to 'spring' back with new growth.

This may be simple coppice with no over-storey of timber tees, or coppice-with-standards, which in effect has two cycles of harvesting intermeshed in the same area of land. The timber might be on a cycle of 80 to 120 years, but with 'thinnings' harvested at younger ages to allow the bigger trees to mature. Some coppice was cut at different ages from an individual stem, and this is most frequently seen in the Western Atlantic Oak-Hazel Woods but can be found in other woods too. The individual tree can be cut to provide the specific gauge of wood required for a particular job on a 'cut-and-come-again' system.

Figure 8. Ancient lime coppice (IDR)

Pollarding: The pollard cycle was similar to that of the coppice but at a height of up to several metres from the ground in order to raise the young sprouts above possible grazing by livestock, both wild and domestic. The harvest may be for wood-fuel, for light constructional work, or for leaf fodder; and the timing of the cut varies accordingly.

Shredding: The approach here was similar to pollarding except that the lateral branches were cut back to the stem all the way up the trunk. This system is still practiced in parts of Europe and was probably used in Britain too, though little documented.

Standards: These tall, woodland standard trees branchless to the first three to four metres in height were suited to conversion into structural timbers. Growth in the tight confines of closed canopy woodland encouraged tall, straight stems. In the more open conditions of parkland or hedgerow for example, a mature oak could send out major branches at maybe 1.5 metres to 2 metres height, and produce a massive, spreading crown of 25 metres or more in diameter. Such open-grown trees were less suited to the production of straight and uniform constructional timbers but might be selected for specific shapes required in certain buildings. These might even be specifically shaped over decades to fulfil a particular need. The best examples of this are the so-called 'guided pollards' found in parts of the Spanish Basque Country.

Figure 9. A Cumbrian pollard ash (IDR)

Oak was the main species for major constructional work. It is strong and resilient plus pliable and useable when 'green', in the period soon after felling, but hardening over the years to give strength to a building. Rackham (1986) suggested that around ninety percent of structural timbers in England were of oak, but noted that elm, ash, and aspen were also used in lower status buildings. Elm was especially useful in wet situations and was used for piles, conduits, pipes, and for example, weatherboarding. Ash was generally too pliable to take the strain of larger structures.

The industrial woodland cycle as evidenced in South Yorkshire from the 1600s and 1700s

According to Jones (2009), the following terms were applied to the standard trees in the coppice-with-standards managed woodland:

a) **Standards** – uncoppiced trees that remained throughout the coppice cycle and beyond.
b) **Wavers** – young trees in the early stage of the standards cycle.
c) **Black barks** – about 40 to 50 years old having grown through two coppice cycles of 20 to 25 years.
d) **Lordings** – older standard trees, maybe 70+ years old

The intention of this system was to produce a sustainable supply of both underwood (coppice) and timber based on two inter-linked cycles in the upper and lower canopies. The timber and wood were from mostly oak, but also ash, field maple, hawthorn, birch, rowan, hazel, lime, willow and holly. The larger woods were each divided into different compartments managed on a cyclical basis and these individual units often had names, sometimes as separate named 'woods'. The complex and carefully controlled industrial harvesting must have evolved from traditional woodmanship developed with local variants though the medieval period.

The medieval rights
Gifted by the Crown, and disseminated via the feudal system, land resource rights might be in the ownership of a Lord, perhaps an

aristocrat or one of the lesser gentry, or of an ecclesiastical foundation. From these 'owners' the lesser but more numerous commoners, serfs and un-landed poor had access to enough vital resources to at least survive. Such access to resources was recognised in rights such as:

a) **House-bote:** This is an allowance of necessary timber out of the landlord's woods, for the repairing and support of a house or tenement. This would belong as a common-right to any lessee for years or for life. House-bote is said to be of two kinds - *estoveriam aedificandi* (estovers) = a right allowed by law to tenants of land to cut timber for fuel and repairs, *et ardendi* = to burn.

b) **Hedge-bote:** This is the common-right to take wood to be used for repairing hedges or fences.

The wider context of these rights to resources was of a largely rural society with few urban settlements, and certainly very few with more than a few thousand inhabitants.

Estovers: Derived from the French word meaning 'necessary', a right of estover conferred the ability to take limbs of timber for minor works to buildings, for making farm implements and hurdles, and as deadwood for fuel, or to take bracken and heather for bedding. This was once a mainstay of rural communities.

In the medieval landscape, 'timber' and 'wood' were subject to different rules, ownership, rights, and access.

The wood, the common, the fields & lanes, and the park

Wood, timber and other building materials such as stone, clay, sand and gravel, turf, furze, and ling might be sourced from various parts of the manorial estate. However, in terms of wood and timber, the different areas supplied varying types and qualities of produce. A working 'wood' for example, produced abundant coppice 'wood' and timber up to a certain size, but for the massive timbers required for major constructional work, it is likely that these might be supplied from the manorial park. In the park landscape, big standard trees were grown alongside grazing animals as a multi-functional system. In some cases, trees were grown to a specific shape and destined for a particular use over a period of more than a hundred years – requiring vision and foresight on the part of the landowner. A particular example of this practice was the growing of so-called 'guided pollards' in the Basque country with trees grown and shaped for individual, specific purposes.

Figure 10. Outgrown hedgerow pollard in Norfolk (IDR)

Smaller wood was taken from wooded common and heath, and both wood and timber might be harvested from lane-side and field boundary hedgerows. Although in the latter cases, over-large specimens might not be tolerated because of their shading of arable crops.

Generally, from the common resources, peasant commoners with rights would be allowed to take or harvest the necessities for survival but not for commercial gain. The cottages and other buildings of the rural poor were a direct reflection of these resources available to them. Some buildings were long-lived permanent structures, but many were temporary or short-lived residences. Some were associated with transhumance and others with semi-nomadic rural crafts such as charcoal burning, clog making, potash burning, bodging, and barking.

The emergence of industry & commerce
Towards the later medieval and into the early industrial periods, the emergence of commercial harvesting of resources, such as wood and timber, probably resulted from the demands of the increasing urban centres of population and stimulated by other, major constructional projects that necessitated the purchase of valuable resources. The growth of commercial and industrial exploitation undoubtedly competed with traditional common utilisation. In woodlands owned, for example, by emerging coal and iron masters (such as the Duke of Norfolk and the Earl Fitzwilliam in South Yorkshire), these conflicts of interest might cause serious problems for those relying on access to such resources. One solution, with the landowners' help, would be a shift towards alternative building materials (for example from wood and timber, to brick and stone), or the re-location of communities from rural to urban (as commoners moved to the towns). In developing industrial regions such as South Yorkshire, North Derbyshire and the north-east, the commercial production of wood for charcoal and whitecoal, and poles for pit-props, or timbers for industrial construction, displaced other usage.

Relating to the latter, as common rights lapsed, commercial exploitation of the countryside resources took over. Around London for example, former wooded commonland was exploited commercially for fuelwood for the city. This intensive use of oak and beech pollards must have displaced common rights and also compromised the production of constructional timbers.

Figure 11. Fuelwood pollards at Burnham Beeches (IDR)

The distribution of resources

In the wider landscape, people, wealth, and resources are not distributed evenly, meaning that demand for and access to resources such as wood and timber were uneven across the countryside. Furthermore, the use of local resources for all but the highest status buildings, led to distinctive vernacular styles based on availability at regional and local levels. Within a particular region, the use of materials for construction differentiates between the needs and abilities of the different classes. In this case, to understand the constructional use of wood-based materials in buildings, it is useful to consider separately the social level of the end user.

In regions with abundant timber and wood, such as part of the English midlands, then building styles and structures reflected this availability of resources, and homes from quite moderate to high status would include big timbers. However, in extensive wetlands such as the pre-drainage fenlands, the Cumbrian or Pennine uplands, or the Scottish Islands, for example, large timbers would be very scarce indeed. In these situations, the common people would resort to building materials and structures that reflected local availability – in the fens, withies, turf or mud, and reeds, and in the uplands, birch poles on stone bases, supporting turf thatch and rushes or bracken. Highly-prized, large timbers would be reserved for manorial or ecclesiastical buildings.

A further potential limitation to the use of particular materials, such as large timbers for construction, would be the availability of the skills to manipulate and to prepare them. For a major or prestigious project such as a large ecclesiastical or aristocratic residence, the specialist labour could be imported, for others this might be an issue.

Conversion to timber
The living tree was often selected for a specific end purpose, and might be chosen *in situ* by the craftsman, often the master carpenter, responsible for the construction. The tree needed to be selected, payment and contracts agreed, and then prepared on site for felling and processing. Nothing in this economy was wasted so bark, branches, broken twigs (ramel), stumps and roots, were all accounted for. Sometimes the cut stump might be converted to coppice. Felling would normally be undertaken in winter when after leaf-fall the carpenter could best assess the size, shape, and structure of the tree. Additionally, the woodman might fell the tree with the least damage to the underwood adjacent. Sometimes felling would be delayed until the spring when the rising sap added value to the harvest of bark. After felling, the timber was next 'scappled' (roughly hewn into squared beams) for transportation.

Cutting the felled 'raw' tree into workable timbers was called conversion, and this involved various technical steps from squaring up with box hearting, to box halving and box quartering. The carpenter would make best use of the particular strengths and properties of wood relating to species, to position on the tree, and of course, to grain. A cut log might be split radially or sawn through. In England, it seems that the saw was introduced at some time around the twelfth century, and before that time, timber was worked with an adze. Again, a matter for experience, but it would be important for the carpenter to judge the smallest piece of timber able to do the necessary job as required. Availability and cost would be prerequisites.

With all these factors to take into account, most structural timber trees were harvested at a relatively young age – maybe from fifty to 150 years old. Much older than this and a tree may have succumbed to attack by beetles and by fungi, and even though they can live to a much older age, their usefulness and value were compromised.

Cutting at the sawpit would take place outside the wood for timbers but inside at smaller pits for underwood. With the beams and planks produced at this stage, they could be tidied up to varying degrees depending on the status of the building and the position of the timbers within that structure.

Work by Melvyn Jones in South Yorkshire (Jones, 2009) shows that many later medieval and early industrial stone-built buildings encased or enclosed an earlier timber-framed structure, and in many cases stone-work rests on a 'substantial framework of locally grown timber'. Stone only began to displace timber as the main material for construction in the seventeenth century, and even then, of course, the roof trusses remained timber-built.

Other examples
The management or exploitation of woodland and timber resources varies as described in pre-industrial and early industrial societies according to access, need, supply and demand. As the human pressures vary and the countryside resources differ, the detail changes. So, in Japan with the prevalence of large bamboo species, these materials were managed, harvested and used for construction at all levels of society. The bamboo forests provided a ready and adaptable resource for domestic building.

When European settlers colonised North America, they were faced with a super-abundant forest and timber resource. This could be harvested and utilised almost free for the taking and became the mainstay of the settlers' domestic construction.

Furthermore, the burning of brash and other materials to make potash as a cash harvest helped fund land improvement efforts. In this super-abundant landscape of excessive resources beyond demand, at least at first, there was little need to manage or maintain the resource. The forest could be clear-cut for harvesting and then the wave of settlers moved on to the next untouched area. The land cleared of trees could be converted to pasture, arable, or orchard. This must have borne similarities to the situation in pre-Domesday England except that it occurred more speedily and more thoroughly. Only as the human pressure increases and the natural resources reduce or become less available, is there an imperative to manage the forest sustainably.

The impacts of such exploitation, pressures and landscape transformations are eloquently expounded by Perlin in 'A Forest Journey' (1989), as he explores the role of wood and timber in the development of civilisation.

Building structures
There is an extensive literature on timber building forms and styles, and there is little need to repeat the information here. In England, by the medieval period, there were major regional schools of carpentry involved in the construction of timber-framed buildings. A major separation was between 'box-frame' buildings constructed as integral timber frames sitting on sills, and so-called 'cruck' buildings with an A-frame of two massive timbers, often from a single tree. In the latter case, which is not strictly a timber-frame as such, the weight of the building is carried directly to ground by the curved major timbers seated on padstones in the ground. A true timber-frame structure is a little like an old-fashioned Meccano set except much larger and in wood. A big advantage of the timber frame approach was that much of the structure could be pre-fabricated and then carried to the building plot for rapid assembly and erection. Proper timber-frame building was being adopted in England by around the thirteenth century. Cruck-framing has a remarkably northern and western distribution in Britain.

Figure 12. Typical 'cruck' construction (IDR)

The primitive

Alongside these higher status dwellings described above, were the low status, temporary or even portable dwellings of itinerant workers and the poorer peasants and landless poor. Often rough shacks of wooden poles supporting a covering of turf, bracken or ling, some of these persisted in the English landscape until the early 1900s; and are probably one of the oldest building types known. Whilst less is written on these traditional dwellings of the rural poor, they too depended on locally available natural resources, but often those taken from the common, heath, bog or fen.

Figure 13. Image from Thomas Pennant of a cottage on Islay in the 1700s (IDR)

Figure 14. An image of Sheffield charcoal burners from Addy (1898) (IDR)

Woodland crafts workers such as charcoal burners lived in primitive and ancient wigwam shelters and a photograph from Parkwood Springs in Sheffield shows such as building in the late 1800s. Each craft group (potash makers, barkers, charcoal-makers *etc*) had their own distinctive type of shelter.

Figure 15. The footings of a typical south Cumbrian potash-maker's hut (IDR)

Conclusions

Throughout history, wooded and forested landscapes have been contested spaces, and this applies to both stakeholder groups and between different products and demands. In an extensive landscape with abundant resources and relatively low-density human populations, timber and wood might be taken freely from the countryside. However, as human populations rose or resources became depleted, the forest or the wood had to be protected and managed through controls on usage or on access to exploitation. These rules were necessary in order to provide for the raw materials for essential domestic construction at every level, from the rich to the poor.

Conflicts arose through illegal harvesting or from competing uses - such as grazing animals in areas of managed 'woods', and later from commercialisation and industrialisation. As contested spaces, the woods and forests were under pressure for lordly or royal recreation (hunting), for the extraction of big timber for the construction of ships, especially warships, and for charcoal production especially for smelting metals. All these demands would have compromised the ability of the countryside to produce and provide material for domestic construction but these conflicts were spatially uneven and linked to factors such as proximity to major water-courses suitable for transportation of extracted timbers. The impacts varied with geography and through time.

With changing technologies, and socio-economic fluxes, the pressures also changed. So, with urbanisation and industrialisation, many commoners were displaced and migrated to emerging townships. Intensive industrial coppice management took over to provide 'wood' for metal smelting and mining, and other lands were converted to modern-style 'forestry'. Woodmanship and traditional woodland management continued extensively in the industrial woodlands until around the middle of the nineteenth century but declined thereafter. Additional pressures and conflicts arose as commons and manorial woods were moved into management for game and sport rather than the provision of locally-needed resources. Again, this is too big and complex an issue to address in detail here.

In the face of competition and problems of access, one solution to the domestic construction problem was to move to alternative materials, as was always the case in landscapes where wood and timber were inherently scarce. With industrialisation, the shift was towards mass-produced building materials such as bricks from clay. The poorer people made do with whatever they could find as so evocatively portrayed in books such as *'Home-Made Homes - Dwellings of the Rural Poor in Wales'* by Eurwyn Wiliam (1988). Sadly, these examples of basic rural and urban domestic architecture are generally poorly documented, and many examples were swept away during the passion for 'improvement' during the early- to mid-twentieth century. These buildings relied very much on immediately available natural resources from wood, forest and common, but when they were 'improved' little evidence of their origins and form remained.

Figure 16. A welsh mud house in the early 1900s from Eurwyn Wiliam (1988) (IDR)

It is clear that in England, 'management' of wooded landscapes to produce necessary resources of 'timber' and 'wood' for local consumption became a necessity in the post-Conquest period. Growth in the human population, reduction in immediately available resources, and conflicts between users and uses meant that at a manorial level, exploitation had to be controlled. This is reflected in the Act of Commons of 1235. Throughout the medieval, pre-industrial period, the careful allocation of essential timber and wood was via a mix of ownership and of common rights and this helped ensure that most people could at the very least survive. However, with modernisation, urbanisation, enclosure and 'improvement' came a further shift; this time away from local communities and towards commercial or industrial exploitation of 'woods', and then a combination of modern forestry and the conversion of landscapes to recreational and 'sporting' interests. This latter change is a part of the process termed 'cultural severance' (Rotherham, 2011, 2012) whereby local people become separated from their subsistence countryside which is converted to the twin uses of exclusive sport (as leisurely landscapes), and to industrial agriculture and forestry, or else abandoned. These processes can be witnessed in many other parts of the world, such as for example in North America subject to Western European colonisation.

In 1808, the Philadelphia Society for Promoting Agriculture noted how '......*Timber is wantonly because lavishly and unnecessarily destroyed; and becomes in a few years scarce, where its abundance was at first accounted a burden......Fencing, fuel, building, implements etc., call for timber - but it is distant or gone*'. Written in the early nineteenth century, this could just as easily have been about the post-Conquest colonisation of England.

Finally, from the productive countryside through the process of the craftsman, into the constructed buildings there is a trail of history, of archives and of archaeology that tells a story of resources, of people, and of architecture. The craftsmen have left a trail of worked trees, of humps and bumps in the woodland landscape as tangible heritage, and sometimes a cultural knowledge of traditional crafts and processes as intangible heritage. From within the built structures, there is the story in the crafted timbers and the tree–rings or carbon dates that informs our understanding of the craft processes and the landscape beyond. Even the problem insects which bore into constructional timbers of antique buildings originated in the ancient trees of forest, park and chase. All this is the subject we now call, '**tree-archaeology**'.

References & Bibliography

Addy, S.O. (1898) *The Evolution of the English House.* Swan Sonnenschein and Co., London.

Fowler, J. (2002) *Landscapes and Lives. The Scottish Forest through the ages.* Canongate Books, Edinburgh.

Grenville, J. (1997) *Medieval Housing.* Leicester University Press, Leicester.

Hayman, R. (2003) *Trees. Woodlands and Western Civilization.* Hambledon and London, London.

Jones, M. (1997) *Woodland management on the Duke of Norfolk's Sheffield estate in the early eighteenth century.* In: M. Jones (ed.) *Aspects of Sheffield: Discovering Local History, Vol.1.* Wharncliffe Publishing Ltd, Barnsley, 48-69.

Jones, M. (1998) *The rise, decline and extinction of spring wood management in south-west Yorkshire*. In: Watkins, C. (ed.) *European Woods and Forests: Studies in Cultural History*. CAB International, Oxford, 55-72.

Jones, M. (2009) *Sheffield's Woodland Heritage*. 4th Edition (revised), Wildtrack Publishing, Sheffield.

Muir, R. (2005) *Ancient Trees Living Landscapes*. Tempus Publishing Ltd, Stroud, Glos.

Perlin, J. (1989) *A Forest Journey: Role of Wood in the Development of Civilization*. The Countryman Press, Woodstock, USA.

Rackham, O. (1976) *Trees and Woodland in the British Landscape*. J. M. Dent & Sons Ltd, London.

Rackham, O. (1980) *Ancient Woodland; its history, vegetation and uses in England*. Arnold, London.

Rackham, O. (1986) *The History of the Countryside*. J. M. Dent & Sons Ltd, London.

Rasmussen, W.D. (1981) *Wood on the Farm*. In: Hindle, B. (ed.) *Material Culture of the Wooden Age*. Sleepy Hollow Press, New York.

Rotherham, I.D. (2007a) *The Historical Ecology of Medieval Deer Parks and the Implications for Conservation*. In: Liddiard, R. (ed.) *The Medieval Deer Park: New Perspectives*. Windgather Press, Macclesfield, 79-96.

Rotherham, I.D (2007b) The ecology and economics of medieval deer parks. *Landscape Archaeology and Ecology*, **6**, 86-102.

Rotherham, I.D. (2007c) The implications of perceptions and cultural knowledge loss for the management of wooded landscapes: a UK case-study. *Forest Ecology and Management*, 249, 100-115.

Rotherham, I.D. (2009) *Peat and Peat Cutting*. Shire Publications, Oxford.

Rotherham, I.D. (2011) *The Implications of Landscape History and Cultural Severance in Environmental Restoration in England*. In: Egan, D., Hjerpe, E. & Abrams, J. (eds) *Integrating Nature and Culture: The Human Dimensions of Ecological Restoration*. Island Press, Washington DC, 277-287.

Rotherham, I.D. (2012) *Traditional Woodland Management: the Implications of Cultural Severance and Knowledge Loss.* In: Rotherham, I.D., Jones, M. & Handley, C. (eds) (2012) *Working & Walking in the Footsteps of Ghosts. Volume 1: the Wooded Landscape.* Wildtrack Publishing, Sheffield, 223-264.

Rotherham, I.D. (ed.) (2013a) *Cultural Severance and the Environment: The Ending of Traditional and Customary Practice on Commons and Landscapes Managed in Common.* Springer, Dordrecht.

Rotherham, I.D. (ed.) (2013b) *Trees, Forested Landscapes and Grazing Animals: A European Perspective on Woodlands and Grazed Treescapes.* EARTHSCAN, London. 412pp

Rotherham, I.D. (2013c) *Ancient Woodland: History, Industry and Crafts.* Shire Publications, Oxford.

Rotherham, I.D. (2013d) *The Lost Fens: England's Greatest Ecological Disaster.* The History Press, Stroud.

Rotherham, I.D. & Handley, C. (eds) (2011) Animals, *Man and Treescapes: The interactions between grazing animals, people and wooded landscapes,* Wildtrack Publishing, Sheffield.

Rotherham, I.D., Handley, C., Agnoletti, M. & Samoljik, T. (eds) (2013) *Trees Beyond the Wood – an exploration of concepts of woods, forests and trees.* Wildtrack Publishing, Sheffield, 378pp.

Rotherham, I.D., Jones, M., Smith, L. & Handley, C. (eds.) (2008) *The Woodland Heritage Manual: A Guide to Investigating Wooded Landscapes,* Wildtrack Publishing, Sheffield.

Wiliam, E. (1988) *Home-Made Homes - Dwellings of the Rural Poor in Wales.* National Museum Wales Books, Cardiff.

Sherwood Oak, once open-grown and now shrouded. Source: Ian D. Rotherham

Chapter 2. The Worked and Veteran Trees of Brackenhurst Estate

Andy Alder
Woodscape Consultancy

Abstract

This paper profiles some of the worked and veteran trees of the Brackenhurst Estate, near Southwell, Nottinghamshire. It highlights research based upon the studies carried out by the author and students on the *BTEC National Diploma in Countryside Management* course. The work focused on recording trees in the landscape and exploring the landscape history of the estate.

Introduction

The Brackenhurst Estate was built in 1827 at Southwell, Nottinghamshire, the name Brackenhurst meaning the cleared parcel of land on a hill (Brack: land broken up for cultivation (Brak Old Norse) and Hurst: woodland clearing (Hyrst Old English) (Addison, W 1978)). "There is little evidence that there were any buildings on the site before the Hall was built. There was a group of closes or enclosed fields almost on the southern edge of the parish of Southwell. One of these fields was called Tower Wong Close and this was where the present house was built" (Train, K 2001). The area was called Brackenhurst as early as 1561 and in the Enclosure Period was known as Brackenhurst Closes, part of the old open field system of Southwell.

In 1947, the estate was sold to Nottinghamshire County Council and opened in 1949 as the Farm Institute, with a lecture hall. Laboratories and residential accommodation were in place by 1964. In April 1999, the College merged with Nottingham Trent University and is now part of the School of Animal, Rural and Environmental Science.

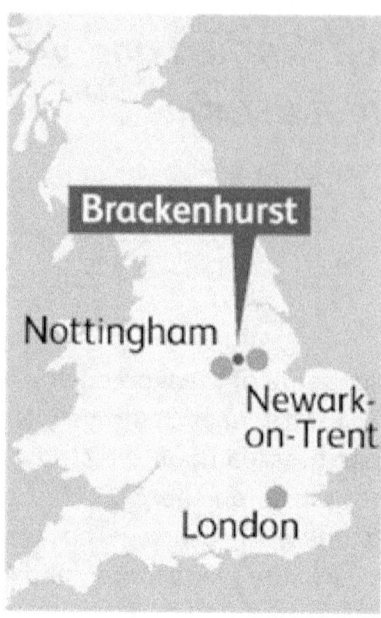

Figure 1. Position of Brackenhurst Estate (NTU Images)

The Estate

Figure 2. Brackenhurst: the cleared parcel of land on a hill (NTU Images)

There are three parks that surround Brackenhurst Hall, (known as First Park, Second Park and Third Park), the parks are divided from the formal Edwin Lutyens style gardens by a ha-ha. The 1919 Ordnance Survey map shows the parks with a wealth of parkland trees, an excellent setting for the dairy short-horn cattle that grazed there in the early half of the twentieth century. The 2013 survey, by the students, shows the number of trees lost and a large change in the landscape of the parks.

Figure 3. Brackenhurst Parks: changes in tree cover 1919 (above) and 2013 (below) (A. Alder 2013, based on 1919 OS map)

The avenue of Common Lime (*Tilia vulgaris*) that can be clearly seen in Figure 3 roughly laid out in a north-south alignment, was intended to line a new drive proposed by William Hicking (who lived at Brackenhurst Hall from 1899 to 1947). Due to a dispute with a neighbouring farmer, the drive was never built. The woodman statue was erected at the end of the line of Limes and formed a folly. The trees were felled, but in recent years, 34 Lime trees have been planted to replicate the avenue. The English Oak (*Quercus robur*) next to the woodman bears a cross with the name Timothy and three X's and shows the remains of an earlier plaque. It is believed to be the grave of a dog or a horse.

Figure 4: The woodsman at the end of the avenue and the grave tree (A. Alder 2013)

The western area of the Brackenhurst Estate sits alongside the Parish Boundary between Halloughton Parish and Southwell Parish. This old boundary contains a Gospel Oak (English Oak (*Quercus robur*)) which would have been visited during the beating of the bounds that took place in Rogationtide, just before Ascension Day. The local community walked in procession along the boundary of the parish, stopping at boundary stones and Gospel Oaks, where a passage from the Bible was read and land was blessed. The ceremony still exists at Brackenhurst but does not visit the Gospel Oak stopping in the centre of the campus on procession from Southwell Minster.

Figure 5. Gospel Oak on Halloughton / Southwell Parish Boundary (A. Alder 2013)

The Gospel Oak stands in the field known as Arnolds Field which is partly woodland that is now mixed coppice. It aptly stands on Stubbins lane and once again "stubs" of ash stand in the landscape.

Figure 6. Stubbins land sign and Ash "stubs" (A. Alder 2013)

There is also a Lime Tree (*Tilia vulgaris*) in Arnolds Coppice which is traditionally dressed by students on Tree Dressing Day (The first weekend in December). This links to the new tradition started by Sue Clifford and Angela King of Common Ground in 1990 to highlight our responsibility for looking after trees and remind us of their cultural heritage.

Figure 7. Decorated Lime Tree, Arnolds Coppice (A. Alder 2013)

Arnolds Field now also contains willow beds. The willow beds are worthy of note. R.C.L. and B.M. Howitt, the authors of the last County Flora for Nottinghamshire (1963) had by the late 1950s established a notable collection of willows at Farndon, near Newark, Nottinghamshire. This collection had fallen into disrepair until the site was purchased by Nottinghamshire Wildlife Trust and in a joint project with Mark Woods of Nottingham Trent University the Howitt collection was resurrected. The beds are now used on a three-year rotation for student craft projects (Figure 8).

Figure 8: Willow stool and wattle hurdle Arnolds Coppice (A. Alder 2013)

One other tree of importance stands in this small woodland. A cutting of the Arbor tree (*Populus nigra* var. *betulifolia*) from Aston on Clun, Shropshire, has been planted. The Black Poplar was planted in Aston on Clun to commemorate Oak Apple Day (29th May – coronation day of Charles II who hid in an Oak tree and escaped capture during the English Civil War). It was changed to Arbor day in 1786 to commemorate the wedding of the local Squire.

The Brackenhurst Estate contains three farms, Brackenhurst Farm, Home Farm, and Durdham Farm each with their own history ranging from medieval ridge and furrow to worked trees. Home Farm has a pair of veteran Hawthorns (*Crataegus monogyna*), one of which is being supported in its later years and stands opposite a possible marker stone. The Home Farm is in its more or less original layout and contains its own viewing gallery in the crew yard. This allowed the showing of "state of the art" farming machinery and livestock during the late nineteenth and early twentieth centuries.

Figure 9. Old Hawthorn at Home Farm (A. Alder 2013)

Figure 10. Willow Pollards on Durdham Farm Lane (A. Alder 2013)

The lane to Durdham Farm contains many willow pollards (*Salix fragilis*), brought back into production as part of a Countryside Stewardship Scheme and cut regularly by students on both countryside and horticultural courses. This is bringing a typical feature of the Trent Valley back into the landscape (Figure 10).

The numerous hedgerows that meander through the fields of Brackenhurst's farms contain many veteran trees including the coppiced Ash (*Fraxinus excelsior*) shown in Figure 11. This tree sits on a footpath that follows the line of the old Nottingham road and is a possible boundary, fodder or marker tree.

Ash marker tree

Figure 11. Ash coppice on Weirs Close hedgerow (A. Alder 2013)

Figure 12. Ash coppice at Ash Holt, Brackenhurst (A. Alder 2013)

Ash Holt (Holt: Old English for wood or copse) is a small remnant of an Ash woodland on the Estate. It was possibly planted for the supply of ash to repair the Estate's farm machinery, tools and gates, but could also have supplied poles for the Hop Ground along the River Greet. "The poles were supplied from ash coppice managed for this purpose. There are small ash woods bordering the River Greet which clearly show signs of former coppice management regimes" Carolan & Carolan (2006).

"In the first half of the 19th century, the growing of hops was still of considerable importance around Southwell. Early maps, notably Sanderson's (1835), the Tithe Commutation Map of 1841 and the first edition of the Ordnance Survey (one inch to one mile, 1837-8), all show hop gardens along the valley of the River Greet and the Hockerton Dumble" Carolan & Carolan (2006).

Figure 13. Tithe Commission map and hedgerow oak; location of the tree on the map is shown by the black line. (A. Alder 2013)

In the Brackenhurst archive is a copy of the Tithe Commission map from 1841-42. This gives us a wealth of information about the changes in field names and also field shapes. A fossil of the enclosures can be seen with the oak tree on the boundary of the enclosure fields of Sheepwalks and Bottom Meadow, but which now sits firmly in the middle of the later day field Sheep Walks East.

Conclusion

There is still much to discover for the landscape detective on the Brackenhurst Estate including recent research into Roman Brackenhurst (Clarke & Alder, unpublished). Having a labour force of willing students to do the work will help the studies to continue into the future.

Acknowledgements

Thanks to my National Diploma Students many of whom have become tree hunters.

References & Bibliography

Addison, W. (1978) *Understanding English Place Names*, Batsford, London.

Barnes, G. & Williamson, T. (2006) *Hedgerow History*, Windgather, Bollington.

Carolan, I. & Carolan, E. (2006) Alternative Farming: Hops and apples. In Chapman, S. & Walker D., (ed.) *Southwell, The town and its people*, Southwell & District Local History Society.

Clarke, A. & Alder, A. (ed.) (2011) *An Investigation into possible remnants of a Roman Road and alternative Parish Boundaries on the Brackenhurst Estate*, Unpublished

Field, J. (1989) *English Field Names*, Alan Sutton, Gloucester.

Filmer, R. (1982) *Hops and Hop picking*, Shire, Princes Risborough.

Lyth, P. (1984) *The Southwell Charter of 956 A.D.: An Exploration of its Boundaries*, Southwell District & Local History Society.

Muir, R. (2009) *Ancient trees, Living landscapes*, The History Press, Stroud.

Rackham, O. (2000) *The History of the Countryside*, Phoenix, London.

Train, K. (2001) *History of Brackenhurst*, Unpublished.

Chapter 3. The Beetle Faunas of Ancient and Veteran Trees

Keith Alexander
Independent Researcher

Abstract

Beetle remains have been found in a wide range of substrates. Their chitinised cuticles are very resistant to environmental degradation, and fragments may remain recognisable to species level for very long periods, depending on the medium in which they have been preserved. The ecology of most species is known to a basic level at least, and many have been subject to detailed scientific studies. Their presence in a site may potentially provide very useful information on the local conditions under which the deposit was made.

It is important to work with the species-specific knowledge when analysing assemblages rather than to make unfounded assumptions. For example, the presence of a large number of saproxylic (wood-decay) beetle species does not imply closed-canopy woodland conditions, as assumed by many palaeo-ecologists, but rather the availability of a wide range of saproxylic niches. The richest sites under modern conditions tend to be characterised by substantial numbers of large open-grown veteran trees. Only shade-demanding species should be used to imply closed woodland conditions and even these may potentially be found away from such situations. This chapter will provide examples of saproxylic beetle species which have been found in dated deposits, will discuss current knowledge of their precise habitat requirements, and how this knowledge provides evidence for the nature of the local tree-scapes at the time of deposition.

Introduction

Fragments of beetles and other insects have long been found in palaeo-ecological and archaeological deposits, but serious study of the species concerned, and their implications only really began in the 1960s and 1970s. It has now been demonstrated that study of this fauna can reveal important ecological data about the local environment of the time. Beetles have been at the forefront of this research for a variety of reasons (Buckland & Buckland, 2010):

- Relative ease of identification
- Niche specificity
- Apparent morphological and physiological stability

The specimens have typically been found in deposits of peat or organic silts. As a rule, all deposits that contain macroscopic plant remains also contain fossil insects (Coope, 1970). Saproxylic (wood-decay) beetles may be found in preserved timbers and this is useful in demonstrating that habitat associations have remained stable over time.

Russell Coope (1970) comments that one of the more outstanding facts to emerge from the study of Quaternary insect fossils is that those skeletal elements which possess distinctive features match precisely those of species that are still living today. Many of these fragments are specifically unique and leave no doubt that they are conspecific with existing species. No fossil has yet shown intermediate features between known species, even though many thousands of specimens have been investigated from several dozen Quaternary sites. A key conclusion to be drawn from the fossil evidence is that a great many species have maintained their specific integrity throughout the upper half of the Quaternary epoch, and that there is no fossil evidence of any morphological evolution among insects during this period. This is still the case today, after 50 years more research.

Coope (1970) also makes the very pertinent comment that only the specimens themselves constitute the indisputable facts of the fossil record and that extrapolation must always be a matter of interpretation. Interpretation has however been plagued by assumption based on prevailing hypothesis. Osborne (1965) was the first to recognise the important 'old forest' element in the fossil beetle faunas found in early to mid-Holocene samples – species which in the modern landscape are confined to remnant areas of the least disturbed tree-scapes, places such as Sherwood and Windsor Forests. However, he also reported on the effect of forest clearance on the distribution of the British insect fauna, fitting the subfossil beetle fragments into the prevailing hypothesis rather than asking the question: 'what does the presence of these particular species tell us about the landscape at the time?' *Rhysodes sulcatus*, *Ernoporus caucasicus* and *Dryophthorus corticalis* are referred to as 'woodland' species, which they are most certainly not (Figure 1). Under modern conditions they are associated with **trees** and occur in **situations with trees**, irrespective of whether those trees occur in woodland, open wood-pasture, parkland, hedgerows, *etc*. The underlying assumption is that trees only occur in woodlands, but we all know that this is not true today, so why would we think it so in the past?

Figure 1. Habitat for the rare saproxylic weevil *Dryophthorus corticalis* in Windsor Great Park [image by Ted Green]

The significance of a single saproxylic beetle species in describing vegetation structure

Rackham (2006) stated that practical observation should be our guide rather than unstable theory. Saproxylic (wood-decay) beetles have very precise habitat requirements. The presence of a single species can provide considerable information about the character of the vegetation around the site where it was found. *Dryophthorus corticalis* for instance lives within large volumes of humid brown-rotten heartwood, and so it needs the host trees to be of large girth. The host trees in Britain today are ancient open-grown oaks but subfossil material also comes from pine and the species is known from large old pines with brown-rotten heartwood on the European mainland. Both host trees are light-demanding species and only develop in open and well-lit situations, not in closed canopy, shady woodlands. Thus, the presence of a single specimen of this single species immediately implies the presence of open-grown trees within flying distance, and sufficient open-grown trees to support a viable population of this beetle. This is a significant amount of information about the local landscape.

In many ways, it is the oak that has been a focus for improving our understanding of the dynamic vegetation of British – and wider European - landscapes. The two native oaks in Britain are well-known to be light-demanding species, with new young trees only surviving under very open conditions (Ellenberg, 1974; Bobiec et al., 2018). A substantial part of the oak crop each year is carried away and cached by birds into open habitats, particularly - but not exclusively - by the Jay. Bobiec *et al.* (2018) go so far as to state that our two species of oak "are not typical components of the canopy layer of natural forests on mesic to eutrophic sites;" they are of course using a different meaning to 'forest', implying closed canopy conditions. They go on to state that the actual habitats fostering oak regeneration in temperate Europe are dynamic variegated landscapes, not a given type of habitat but rather an intricate complex of various habitats. The habitually accepted assumption that oaks are late-successional 'forest-marking' trees is based on the performance of adult trees, rather than on the whole life history. So, basically, expert knowledge of oak ecology is not consistent with closed-canopy conditions, or even near-closed-canopy conditions. Other light-demanding species include hazel and pine. Pollen from these three species feature strongly in the subfossil pollen record and – to a modern-day ecologist – clearly indicate widespread open conditions for seeding and establishment. They do not suggest closed woodland conditions, even 'intuitively' – the Bobiec paper describes "high deciduous forest" as "not an obvious oak habitat".

In conclusion, the mere presence of *Dryophthorus corticalis* is - in reality - evidence for an open mosaic vegetation structure, with sufficient open space for oak to be maintaining its presence, with a diverse age structure, with new generations of oak trees gradually increasing in girth and eventually becoming suitable for colonisation by the weevil, a process taking perhaps 400 or 500 years. There also need to be sufficient large old open-grown oaks to maintain a viable population of the weevil, i.e. such trees need to occur, or have occurred, at landscape scale. The presence of subfossil *Dryophthorus corticalis* on the Somerset Levels (Girling, 1984), Warwickshire (Osborne, 1965) and Thorne Moors, South Yorkshire (Buckland & Kenward, 1973), demonstrates that there has been continuity of this open mosaic type habitat across much of England in the distant past, as the weevil had to recolonise Britain after the last Ice Age, spreading across large areas of land in order to reach Somerset and Yorkshire. Practical observation and a few subfossil weevils have led to such a radically different interpretation of the vegetation structure to the assumptions being made.

But at the same time, statements made by Osborne (1965) in the very same paper are also correct. He acknowledges that *Dryophthorus corticalis* was widespread in Britain 5,000 years ago and that its modern range is seriously curtailed. He states that the once dominant forest element has become much restricted in range, although not much depleted in numbers of species. But he clearly viewed that 'forest' as 'climax forest' and 'woodland', rather than an open mosaic of trees of all ages, shrubs, and grassland or heath. Species like *Dryophthorus corticalis* have become rare and threatened through the loss of large old open-grown trees throughout the countryside, at landscape scale. Windsor Forest and Great Park supports the largest surviving population and has one of the most extensive areas of large old open-grown oaks in Britain today – this is no coincidence.

The terms 'forest' and 'woodland' are of course subjective, as they mean different things to different people. Very few authors ever state what they mean when using these words – scientific papers are unfortunately characterised by such unscientific language. Had Osborne travelled to Windsor and asked to be shown the habitat for *Dryophthorus corticalis* he might have realised that there was something wrong with the idea of climax forest.

Dryophthorus corticalis is just one example of a beetle species which can potentially provide extremely valuable insights into the local and wider landscapes in which it has been found. There are very many more.

The importance of tree condition

Figure 2. Modern landscape supporting the beetle *Prostomis mandibularis* (Cordillera Cantabrica, Northern Spain) [image by Keith Alexander]

A key problem has been that people have associated saproxylic beetles with tree species and / or dead wood *per se*, rather than tree condition. Girling (1982, 1984) - in her studies of the fauna associated with the Sweet Track on the Somerset levels – focuses on host tree species and compares this with the botanical evidence but shows no appreciation for the precise habitat requirements of the beetles concerned. *Dryophorus corticalis* is merely described as a 'dead wood borer'. *Prostomis mandibularis* is noted as predatory on the larvae of other wood-borers. She concludes that the fauna indicates "natural tree cover in the vicinity". She goes on to comment further on the presence of *Prostomis*, a species otherwise only known in Britain at that time from fossils found at Thorne Moor. She says it lives in damp decaying trees, especially oak, but does not appreciate that the species is an indication of much more than that, namely of the presence of large old oak at landscape scale (Figure 2). It develops in white-rotten heartwood – in contrast to the brown-rot association of *Dryophthorus* – and thereby demonstrates the presence of a second species of heartwood-decay fungus active in the old trees, and so effectively dramatically increases the number of individual large old oaks required in the surrounding landscape to support viable populations of both beetle species. So much useful ecological data is being overlooked through the blindness promoted by the prevalent, and dominant, closed woodland hypothesis. Buckland and Dinnin (1993) do note that specialisation in saproxylic beetles is towards a very particular microhabitat, rather than the species of tree. This is however swinging too much to the opposite end of the spectrum. In reality the situation is much more complex, with early successional saproxylic beetles being strongly associated with tree species, but this degree of association rapidly declines as decay progresses – while the specific features of the tree remain distinctive specialisation will reflect the species of tree, but as the wood structure is degraded it increasingly becomes of a similar nature across the tree species, and beetle species increasingly specialise in the type and degree of decay irrespective of tree species.

Prostomis mandibularis has subsequently proved to be one of the most frequent fossils in the Thorne Moors assemblage (Buckland & Dinnin, 1993) but is said to live in wet rotten wood (Dajoz, 1974). This is rather too vague to be useful ecologically: wet from rainwater or from a high water-table, or both? What volumes of decayed wood are necessary? Dajoz (2000) increases the confusion by describing the beetle as having a flattened body as an adaptation to living beneath bark but this appears to be a mistaken assumption as he later describes it as characteristic of tree holes, living in very damp wood mould rich in fragments of decaying wood, in chestnut trees. He does not mention the type of decay at all. The present author's only experience with the species was from moist, soft, white-rotten heartwood in a large fallen oak trunk; the flattened beetle was found living between the annual rings, the pectin causing them to stick together having been decayed by a specialist wood-decay fungus, almost certainly *Ganoderma australe* (D. Lonsdale, pers. comm.). The moisture making the rings soft appeared to be due to rain, mist or heavy dew, as the situation was on a high open hillside of the Cordillera Cantabrica in Northern Spain. The site is part of a very extensive area of common pasture with scattered open-grown trees. The flattened body is clearly well-adapted to the annual ring situation. This is a particularly interesting species case study as palaeo-entomologists cannot be expected to understand the ecology of this species if entomologists do not record the correct data for each record. Entomologists do tend to be remarkably poor at recording the key habitat features for records of rarer species.

Impacts of people on saproxylic beetle fauna

Dealing with archaeological deposits brings in additional problems with interpretation of course. People may have transported many species unwittingly through trade, imports of timber in particular affecting the range of saproxylic species which might be found in archaeological sites. Excavation of a Roman period refuse pit at Alcester, Worcestershire (Oborne, 1961) revealed a large number of the central and southern European longhorn beetle *Trichoferus fasciculatus*. The larvae of this species develop in twigs of a very wide range of tree species which are typically 1-4cm in diameter

(Sama, 2002). Eggs are usually laid on a living thin lateral twig near its base, the young larva feeding internally descending to the main branch where it digs a spiral girdle, which interrupts sap circulation and causes the drying of the twig. In the second year the larva feeds in a subcortical gallery. No fossils have been detected from natural situations about this time and it is thought unlikely that this species could have survived in natural populations outside human habitations under the climate of Roman Britain. The species must therefore have been imported but in what type of material is difficult to suggest without intimate knowledge of Roman importation practices. Could branch-wood have been cut for use as packaging around large fragile objects being shipped across to Britannia from the continental mainland and the Mediterranean in particular?

Significance of process – death and decay of woody plant tissues

The death of woody plant tissues may result from two broad processes:

1. Crown development in young trees results in increasing shade being cast over lower branches and the tree eventually withdraws nutrients from the most unproductive branches and they then die. A separate situation arises from crown retrenchment in aging trees, whereby the uppermost branches die back due to the annual rings becoming thinner as the trunk expands and a point being reached where water drawn up by the roots can no longer reach the outermost foliage in sufficient volume. Again, the tree eventually withdraws nutrients and the outer branches die – the tree becomes stag-headed. In both situations, death is under the direct control of the tree. The dead wood has been stripped of nutrients before it dies, providing habitat for a range of specialist decay-fungi and saproxylic invertebrates.
2. In contrast, wood that is killed suddenly - and outside of the control of the tree – is nutrient-rich. Sudden death may occur as the result of storm damage or cutting by people. The nutrient-rich dead woody tissues support a

very different range of wood-decay fungi and saproxylic invertebrates.

All of this is an over-simplification, but it is an important point to bear in mind when interpreting subfossil beetle faunas. Tree diseases may produce both types of situation, depending on the speed of damage caused to the tree concerned. Crown retrenchment can also result from damage to tree roots, arising from strong winds causing tearing, from pathogens, or soil enrichment caused by people.

Dinnin (1997) was one of the first palaeo-entomologists to acknowledge that there was a succession of beetles species exploiting trees as they died – for whatever reasons – although did not distinguish between decay processes in relatively young trees lacking heartwood decay, and larger, older trees with advanced heartwood decay. He was drawing on an unpublished manuscript which had been circulated widely (Alexander, 1994) which collated basic information about saproxylic invertebrates but did not go into process in any detail – this document was developed further and eventually formally published (Alexander, 2002). He went on to expand this approach to the whole of Britain and Ireland (Dinnin & Sadler, 1999) but was still trapped intellectually by the closed forest / woodland hypothesis and tried to interpret fossil beetle faunas into that landscape narrative. He did not appreciate that many of the beetle species found in fossil assemblages have a requirement for large, old, open-grown trees

Sudden death of timber and powder-post beetles *Lyctus* spp
Lyctus linearis develops in the freshly dead sapwood of hardwoods while the starch content is at the right concentration – the wood needs to be killed suddenly, so that the tree is unable to withdraw the starch before death; also the wood needs to be relatively large girth timber. The female only lays eggs if there is a 3% starch content in the sapwood; she is attracted to fresh-cut timber. The beetle only occurs in wood in its first few seasons after the wood was killed. The larva feeds on the cell contents, containing mostly starch, sugars and related substances together with a little protein. The cell walls cannot be digested. Moisture

content in the wood of 8-30% is necessary for feeding (Hickin, 1981). The larvae gradually reduce the timber to dust, leaving a thin veneer of sound wood on the outside.

The species has had a long history of exploiting wood that has been cut and fashioned by people. It used to be strongly associated with freshly-cut oak palings, used for fencing, and on hop poles in Kent. Another focus for the beetle was ash wood used for tool handles, gun-stocks, *etc*; but it also occurs in more natural situations associated with freshly split or damaged trees, especially of oak and beech (Fowler, 1890). As industrialization has progressed, the opportunities for the beetle have diminished.

Sub-fossil data (Buckland & Buckland, 2006) provide tantalising glimpses into these relationships. *Lyctus linearis* appears to have been attracted to the freshly cut and split timbers of Roman building across Britain: it is first detected in Britain from a Roman well in Warwickshire dated to about AD 64-80, from a defensive ditch around the fortress at Exeter dug AD 80-120, a Roman well at York of about AD 175-250, and also known from Roman Alcester (AD 200-300). It is also associated with another major phase of building arising from the Norman invasion some 700 years later, being found in a sample from the Norman motte and bailey fortification at Hen Domen in West Wales, dated to between the late twelfth and early thirteenth century. It was also present in a medieval friary near Leicester, dated to between 1250 and 1540, and in late fifteenth century Worcester. Moving into the historic (entomological) period, Stephens (1830) commented that it frequents dry oak wood and "delight especially in new palings". He stated that it was "very common in the neighbourhood of London, and I believe throughout the country: it abounds on palings, beneath bark, *etc*, especially of the oak." Of course, paling / wire fencing was a relatively new thing at the time, having been developed from the mid-1800s (Cameron, 1984). Fowler (1890) repeats much of this information, but describes its status as "local, but occasionally abundant where it occurs". It was then "common on hop poles" and "abounds in Birmingham in ash wood used for spade and other tool handles, gun-stocks, etc, and does immense damage to both the raw and finished materials".

This may be assumed to represent a record of continuous presence across lowland Britain since at least Roman times. Locally made fresh oak palings may have been commonplace in the Victorian countryside but have largely been replaced in recent decades by mass-produced and chemically treated posts and fences. This appears to have had a major impact on specialist saproxylics such as *Lyctus linearis* and *Xyletinus longitarsis*. Untreated freshly cut timber has become a rarity in the modern countryside – the beetle has been obliged to rely once again on its native habitat of naturally split trees, but there are now many fewer trees in the countryside than in times past and technological developments mean that people can remove freshly split trunks and branches soon after they appear. The species has now virtually disappeared from Britain. The evidence suggests that *L. linearis* may be a 'boom and bust' species. The data available to the present assessment indicates that *L. linearis* was last 'widespread but local' over 100 years previously, but that it had almost died out within its known range by the 1930s.

Attempts to analyse fossil beetle assemblages in support of the closed forest hypothesis

One of the most bizarre developments in palaeo-entomology has been the attempt to analyse beetle assemblages statistically into landscape types. Robinson (1991) suggested that 1% pasture/dung beetles in a particular fossil assemblage may be expected for closed woodland and 10% for a largely pastoral landscape. This would sound relatively plausible to a student of modern fauna, but he went on to suggest that up to 20% saproxylic representation suggests closed ancient woodland, although this may fall to 10% in early Holocene landscapes. Values of less than 2% wood and tree taxa have been interpreted as open, largely tree-less landscapes (Robinson, 1993). These figures are said to be intuitively rather than empirically derived, but the authors appear not to have consulted anybody with expertise on modern saproxylic faunas. This approach is completely at variance with practical observation of the same beetle species in the modern landscape, and yet it has been widely quoted and used in the interpretation of sub-fossil beetle assemblages. The richest places for saproxylic beetles under modern conditions are, however, the open pasture woodlands with their large old open-grown trees rather than closed woodlands with their stressed and suppressed trees which do not live long enough to develop heartwood decay.

Sandom *et al.* (2014) have used the newly developed BUGS database (Buckland & Buckland, 2006) to try and analyse the vegetation structure in which sub-fossil beetles must have lived. They collated evidence for all beetle species known from sub-fossil studies across Britain – over 500 species. They then used BUGS to categorise the beetle species by habitat associations but fell foul of the widespread assumption in palaeo-ecology that trees only ever occur in woodlands and categorised all saproxylic beetles and all canopy-living beetles as woodland species. They concluded that beetle assemblages in the early Holocene (10,000 – 5,000 years BP) indicate "mostly closed or semi-closed woodlands, or closer to the former". They clearly failed to consult anyone with a good knowledge of the ecology of those same species under modern conditions. The analysis was subjective, based on unproven hypothesis.

A new and more objective approach to beetle assemblage analysis has become available through Natural England as a result of the development of their ISIS (Invertebrate Species and habitat Information System) computer application (Drake *et al.*, 2007) which now forms part of their on-line PANTHEON application (Drewitt & Webb, 2017). The collated beetle data from Sandom's study has been entered into ISIS and a very different picture emerges, (Alexander *et al.*, 2018) Table 1.

Table 1. The proportional representation of different beetle assemblage types in peat deposits of different ages. Time periods are: Late Interglacial 132,000 – 110,000 years BP; Last Glacial 50,000 – 15,000 years BP; Early Holocene 10,000 – 5,000 years BP; Late Holocene 2,000 – 0 years BP

Assemblage type	Last interglacial	Last glacial	Early Holocene	Late Holocene
Grassland & scrub	35	69	28	44
Arboreal	18	10	13	11
Wood decay	34	0	47	34
Mineral marsh	4	9	3	3
Shaded field layer	0	0	2.5	2.5
Unshaded early successional mosaic	0	0	1	3

The Early Holocene category which Sandom et al. (2014) analysed as closed canopy woodland is clearly shown to be very open vegetation – grassland and scrub (28% of all beetle species detected) with scattered trees. The arboreal assemblage is relatively poorly represented but wood decay is the best represented assemblage type. This suggests a relatively low percentage cover of trees (13% of the beetles) but that these trees included a great diversity of wood-decay niches, i.e. these included many veteran trees. The only assemblage type which implies closed-canopy woodland conditions is the 'Shaded field layer' assemblage type which is so poorly-represented as to be verging on being invisible in this dataset. It is interesting that a very recent re-analysis of the pollen data from the same period (Fyfe, 2018) now also concludes that 35% of the landscape in the Early Holocene was covered in open-ground vascular plants. This is a very different conclusion from the conventional closed-canopy woodland hypothesis that has dominated palaeo-ecology since its inception. Is the closed-canopy woodland hypothesis now dead?

Figure 3. The next generation of old oak - a young oak which has established under the protection of thorn scrub within ancient wood-pasture at Hatfield Forest

Basically, it is becoming increasingly clear that the Early Holocene environment was more akin to ancient wood-pasture as a habitat, with large patches of open grazed grassland amongst the trees and shrubs (Figure 3). This presented people with a varied accessible landscape and one where it was relatively easy to move from a hunter-gatherer existence towards a more pastoral life-style, by exploiting the existing mosaic habitat features.

Figure 4. A cardinal click beetle *Ampedus cardinalis* – a species which develops in red-rotten heartwood in ancient oak trees in open wood-pasture situations; relatively poor mobility and confined to relict areas of ancient wood pasture [image from Nigel Reeve, with permission]

More evidence for an open wood-pasture type landscape over much of Britain is the fact that so few saproxylic beetle species appear to have become extinct during the Holocene. The mythology of the closed-canopy forest hypothesis would suggest that the change towards todays much more open landscape would have resulted in considerable loss of forest habitat and major extinction of the forest beetles (Figure 4). The facts are quite otherwise, with only 18 saproxylic beetle species known from sub-fossil remains but no longer extant in Britain. The present saproxylic beetle fauna comprises around 700 species, so 18 is a very small loss.

The four dimensions of saproxylic beetle ecology and site quality

There are four key factors which determine the species-richness of the saproxylic beetle fauna (Alexander, 2008, 2018):

- The age structure of the tree and shrub populations, which provide continuity of habitat for saproxylic beetles from each generation of trees to the next.
- The total number of available trees and shrubs, which affect population viability of the saproxylic beetles at a moment in time.
- The density pattern of the trees and shrubs, which enables saproxylic beetle species which depend on large old open-grown trees to live alongside more shade-demanding species.
- Continuity over time, as many saproxylic beetle species are relatively poorly mobile and take a relatively long time to spread across landscapes and are also poor at crossing large expanses of unsuitable habitat – areas where habitat suitability has been maintained over centuries tend to be the most species-rich.

The species composition of the saproxylic beetle assemblages reflects these four factors and so subfossil remains from palaeo-ecological and archaeological contexts can be interpreted within this framework. This is evidence-based knowledge rather than unproven hypotheses. Site quality is not about volumes of deadwood, but rather a successional supply of a wide variety of saproxylic features and their condition.

Figure 5. A larva of the cobweb beetle *Ctesias serra* – a species primarily associated with ancient trees but relatively mobile and fairly common and widespread in suitable sites

Figure 6. The net-winged beetle *Erotides cosnardi* - a beetle with relatively poor mobility and confined in modern Britain to just two areas of remnant medieval forest; tolerant of closed-canopy situations

Continuity over time is a key factor for the less mobile species. There is a wide spectrum of mobility represented in the rich saproxylic fauna. Highly mobile species have better abilities to find suitable habitat within landscapes (Figure 5). Species with relatively poor mobility become increasingly confined to pockets of old growth habitat through fragmentation and isolation (Figure 6). Old growth species are assumed to have evolved under conditions of large-scale continuous habitat and with little or no selective pressure for higher mobility (Figure 7). They were able to slowly spread across what is now Britain as trees and shrubs recolonised after the last glacial period, but they have become threatened with extinction as people have increasingly modified the landscape into modern times. Today they are special features of the remaining fragments of the medieval forests, historic parklands and ancient wood-pastures generally. This special fauna was first reviewed by Harding & Rose (1986) and has been updated (Alexander, 2004). The mere presence of such species can indicate habitat continuity at a particular site back into the past. Knowledge of these species can be very informative to palaeoecology and archaeology.

Basically, all saproxylic beetles are not the same ecologically, and past attempts to treat them so has led to serious error in interpretation of past faunas. There is a richness of information available through intelligent analysis of sub-fossil specimens and assemblages.

Figure 7. A darkling beetle *Pseudocistela ceramboides* which develops amongst accumulations of fine wood mould in the base of large cavities in large old, generally open-grown trees

Conclusions

The remains of beetles found in dated deposits can be extremely useful in extrapolating information about the environments in which they lived. Reliable interpretation has unfortunately been held back by the persistence of the unproven closed-canopy forest hypothesis and the reluctance of researchers to examine data objectively, using knowledge of the ecology of those beetle species from modern environments. The rich biodiversity of the Holocene landscapes was associated with open wood-pasture type conditions not closed forest. This has been clearly demonstrated by the ISIS analysis of the subfossil beetle data and it appears that palynologists are now tending in the same direction.

References

Alexander, K.N.A. (1994) *An annotated checklist of British lignicolous & saproxylic invertebrates.* Unpublished manuscript.

Alexander, K.N.A. (2002) The invertebrates of living and decaying timber in Britain and Ireland – a provisional annotated checklist. *English Nature Research Report*, **467**, 142 pp.

Alexander, K.N.A. (2004) Revision of the Index of Ecological Continuity as used for saproxylic beetles. *English Nature Research Report*, **574**, 60pp.

Alexander, K.N.A. (2008) Tree biology and saproxylic Coleoptera – issues of definitions and conservation language. *Revue d'Ecologie (Terre et Vie) Supplément*, **10**, 9-13.

Alexander, K.N.A. (2018) Tree abundance, density and age structure: the key factors which determine species-richness in saproxylic invertebrates. In: Çolak A.H., Kirca, S. & Rotherham I.D. (eds) *Ancient Woodlands and Trees: A Guide for Landscape Planners and Forest Managers.* IUFRO World Series, Volume 37.

Alexander, K., Allen, M., Butler, J., Green, T. & Woods, R. (2018) Britain's natural landscapes – promoting improved understanding of the nature of the post-glacial vegetation of lowland Britain. *British Wildlife*, **29**(5), 330-338.

Bobiec, A., Reif, A. & Öllerer, K., (2018) Seeing the oakscape beyond the forest: a landscape approach to the oak regeneration in Europe. *Landscape Ecology* https://doi.org/10.1007/s10980-018-0619-y

Buckland, P.C. & Dinnin, M.H. (1993) Holocene woodlands, the fossil insect evidence. In: Kirby, K.J. & Drake, C.M. (eds) *Dead wood matters: the ecology and conservation of saproxylic invertebrates in Britain*. English Nature Science, No. 7.

Buckland, P.C. & Kenward, H.K. (1973) Thorne Moor: a Palaeo-ecological study of a Bronze Age site. *Nature*, **241**, 405-406.

Buckland, P.I. & Buckland, P.C. (2006) *Bugs Coleoptera Ecology Package*. www.bugscep.com.

Buckland, P.I. & Buckland, P.C. (2010) Species found as fossils in Quaternary deposits. In: Duff, A.G. (ed.) *Checklist of Beetles of the British Isles. 2nd Edition*. Pemberley Books, Iver.

Cameron, D.K. (1984) *The Cornkister Days. A Portrait of a Land and its Rituals*. London: Victor Gollancz Ltd.

Coope, G.R. (1970) Interpretations of Quaternary insect fossils. *Annual Review of Entomology*, **15**, 97-120.

Dajoz, R. (1974) Les insects xylophages et leur role sans la degradation du bois mort. In: Pesson, P. (ed.) *Ecologie Forestiere*, Ganthier-Villars, Paris, pp 257-307.

Dajoz, R. (2000) *Insects and Forests*. Intercept.

Dinnin, M. (1997) Holocene beetle assemblages from the Lower Trent floodplain at Bole Ings, Nottinghamshire, UK. *Quaternary Proceedings*, **No. 5**, 83-104.

Dinnin, M.H. & Sadler, J.P. (1999) 10,000 years of change: the Holocene entomofauna of the British Isles. *Quaternary Proceedings*. **No. 7**, 545-562.

Drake, C.M., Lott, D.A., Alexander, K.N.A. & Webb, J. (2007) Surveying terrestrial and freshwater invertebrates for conservation evaluation. *Natural England Research Report*, NERR005.

Drewitt, A.L. & Webb, J. (2017) An application of Pantheon to a Windsor Forest dataset. *The Coleopterist*, **26**, 103-113.

Ellenberg, H. (1974) Zeigenwerte der Gefässpflanzen Mitteleuropas. *Script geobotanica*, **9**, Göttingen.

Fowler, W.W. (1890) *The Coleoptera of the British Islands*. Reeve, London.

Fyfe, R. 2018. 'Natural' vegetation in Britain: the pollen-eye view. *British Wildlife*, **29**(5), 339-349.

Girling, M.A. (1982) Fossil insect faunas from forest sites. In: M. Bell & S. Limbrey (eds) *Archaeological Aspects of Woodland Ecology*. Symposia of the Association for Environmental Archaeology. *BAR International Series*, **146**, 129-146.

Girling, M.A. (1984) Investigations of a second insect assemblage from the Sweet Track. *Somerset Levels Papers*, **10**, 78-116.

Harding, P.T. & Rose, F. (1986) *Pasture-woodlands in Lowland Britain*. Institute of Terrestrial Ecology, Huntingdon.

Hickin, H.E. (1981) *The Woodworm Problem*. Rentokil Library, Hutchinson, London.

Osborne, P.J. (1965) The effect of forest clearance on the distribution of the British insect fauna. *Proceedings of the XIIth International Congress of Entomology, London, 1964*, 456-457.

Rackham, O. (2006) *Woodlands*. Collins New Naturalist, London.

Robinson, M.A. (1991) The Neolithic and Broze Age insect assemblages. In: Needham, S. (ed.) *Excavation and salvage at Runnymede Bridge, 1978: the Late Bronze Age Waterfront site*. British Museum, London.

Robinson, M.A. (1993) The pre-Iron Age environment and finds, the scientific evidence. In: Allen, T.G. & Robinson, M.A. (eds) *The prehistoric landscape and Iron Age enclosed settlement at Mingies Ditch Hardwick-with-Yelford, Oxon. Thames Valley Landscapes: the Windrush Valley 2*. Oxford University Committee for Archaeology, Oxon, 120 -123.

Sama, G. (2002) *Atlas of the Cerambycidae of Europe and the Mediterranean Area. Volume 1: Northern, Western, Central and Eastern Europe. British Isles and Continental Europe from France (excl. Corsica) to Scandinavia and Urals*. Nakladatelství Kabourek, Zlín.

Sandom, C.J., Ejrnaes, R., Hansen, M.D.D. & Svenning, J.-C. (2014) High herbivore density associated with vegetation diversity in interglacial ecosystems. *PNAS*, **111**(11), 4162-4167.

Stephens, J.F. (1830) *Illustrations of British Entomology. Volume III Mandibulata*. Baldwin & Cradock, London.

Carved oak chair, cupboard and wooden yoke displayed in Bishops' House, Meersbrook, Sheffield. Source: C. Handley (2018)

Chapter 4. Bishops' House

Ken Dash

Friends of Bishops' House

View of Bishops' House looking west. Source: C. Handley (2018)

Bishops' House is one of very few timber-framed buildings to survive from the Tudor period in Sheffield, and the only one with unlimited public access to the whole building. It is situated at the southern end of Meersbrook Park, 147 m above sea level. The House is situated in what was once the tiny Derbyshire village of Norton Lees, which became part of Sheffield in 1903 when the county boundary was moved.

Initial attempts at dating Bishops' House in 1976 and 1977 placed the origins of the building in the 1500s, but without a good understanding of the sequence of its construction. A survey undertaken between 2011 and 2014 and a dendrochronological survey undertaken in 2017 have at last given a clear understanding of the sequence of construction and dating of the building.

The name Bishops' House can be traced to the late nineteenth century when the House's antiquity was being researched. Two of the Blythe family, who farmed the land and lived locally, John and Geoffrey, became bishops in the late fifteenth and early sixteenth century. However, John died in 1499 and Geoffrey in 1532, dates which the 2017 survey confirmed are well before the House was built. The name, however, has stuck.

In its earliest phase, Bishops' House was built in 1554 as a three-bay, two-storey oak built king-post truss fully timber-framed building aligned north-south. Two of the bays survive from this time, the north bay being demolished in 1630 (see below). If, the north bay was the same length as the other two bays then the building would have been about 12.5 m long, 5.3 m wide and 7.0 m high.

In 1580, a single-storey two-bay king-post truss building, 11.0 m long, 6.5 m wide and 7.2 to 7.5 m high was added at right-angles to the east of the original structure, effectively as a cross-wing. This had a flagstone floor but no upper floor until one was inserted in about 1630. Its purpose remains somewhat of a mystery.

Access to the upper floor was via a steep ladder-type staircase, some evidence for which survives in the middle bay. The original floor survives upstairs and several of its timbers provide evidence of having been re-used. During the 1977 dendrochronological survey, one of these timbers was dated to 1446.

The recent dendrochronological survey provides strong evidence that for the 1554 and 1580 phases, timber was felled at the same time from the same stand of woodland on each occasion. Unfortunately, the evidence cannot say where that woodland lay.

The Blythe family, who owned the surrounding land and most probably lived in Bishops' House, were not only farmers but were heavily involved in making agricultural tools: sickles and scythes. In fact, Norton parish, in which Bishops' House lies, was the principal community for sickle and scythe making in the north of England in the sixteenth century.

In about 1630, the north bay of the original 1554 building was demolished and replaced with a stone-built structure on two floors. It is 4.1 m N-S by 7.0 m E-W and 7.2 to 7.6 m high. Part of this new structure joined with the 1580 building, providing a grand staircase which replaced the original ladder staircase. This phase of the building is contemporary with William Blythe (1608-1665) and a surviving wall panel bears the inscription 'WB 1627'. Now lost, except in a photograph, is an overmantel with the inscription 'WB 1655'. At this time, or shortly after, a chimney was added at the south east corner of the 1554 building and another between the two bays of the 1580 building. The entire structure was clad in a thick stone wall up to first floor level. The stone wall provided the structural strength for a massive framed floor to be added to the 1580 building, giving it two floors. Whatever the original purpose, it seems that this part of the building now acquired a more domestic use. In about 1665, an internal partition at the east end of the upper floor of this building created a new room.

The last of the Blythes to live in Bishops' House was Samuel Blythe (1673-1735). On his death, the building passed out of the ownership of the Blythe family. The 1580 building was further divided by an internal partition wall in the mid to late eighteenth century and the whole building was let out to tenant farmers. A narrow second staircase was inserted at the north east corner of the 1580 building so that each household could have its own access to the upper floor. The land, no doubt including Bishops' House, passed through a succession of owners – the Roebuck family from 1757 to 1783 and the Shore family from 1783 until 1843, when that family became bankrupt. However, there was enough money left within the family for the House to remain in tenanted occupation until, in 1886, Sheffield Corporation acquired the land.

The earliest of the tenant farmers that we know of are the Wilde brothers, George and Thomas, who lived there with their families from at least 1779 to 1816. Joseph White and later his son James and their families lived in Bishops' House from at least 1841 until 1886. The farmers were then removed to an adjacent cottage and a series of park keepers and gardeners lived in Bishops' House until 1974 when the last of them left. Sheffield City Council renovated the building in 1975 and 1976, removing the partition wall and internal plasterwork and replacing timber that had rotted.

The House opened to the public as a museum in July 1976. As a result of funding cuts, Museums Sheffield pulled out of managing the building in 2011 and since then, Sheffield City Council have continued to maintain Bishops' House with management of public opening conferred to The Friends of Bishops' House. In addition to making significant advances to our historical and structural knowledge of the building, the Friends have also successfully hosted many events, school visits and weddings.

Sources
Arnold, A. and Howard, R. (2017) *Bishops' House Norton Lees Lane, Norton Lees, Sheffield. Tree analysis of timbers*. The Nottingham tree-ring dating laboratory, University of Nottingham, Nottingham.
West, B.A. (1998) *Listed Buildings in Sheffield*. The Hallamshire Press, Sheffield. (Bishops' House is p 26-7).
Beswick, P. (1976) *Bishops' House*. Sheffield City Museums Information Sheet 16, Sheffield City Museum, Sheffield.
Morgan, R. (1977) Dendrochronological dating of a Yorkshire timber building. *Vernacular Architecture*, **8**, 809-814.

Investigating Tree Archaeology

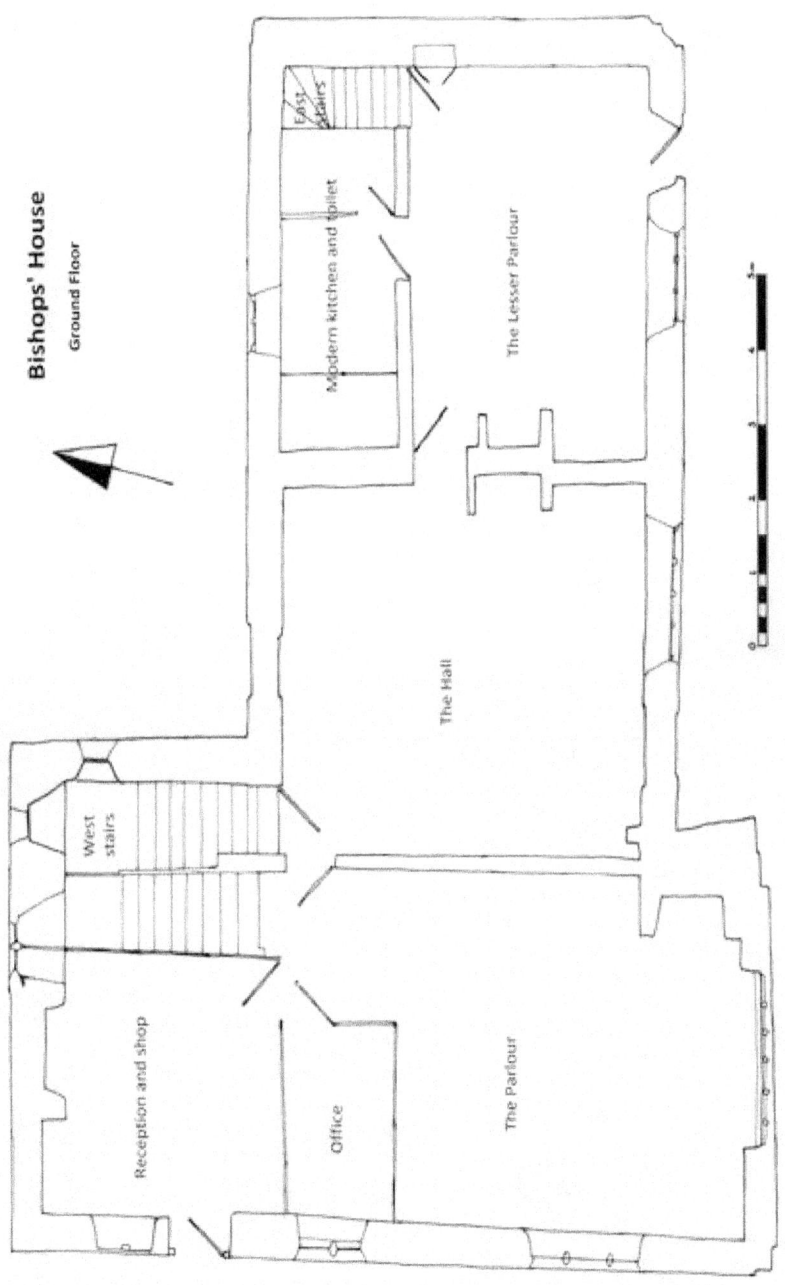

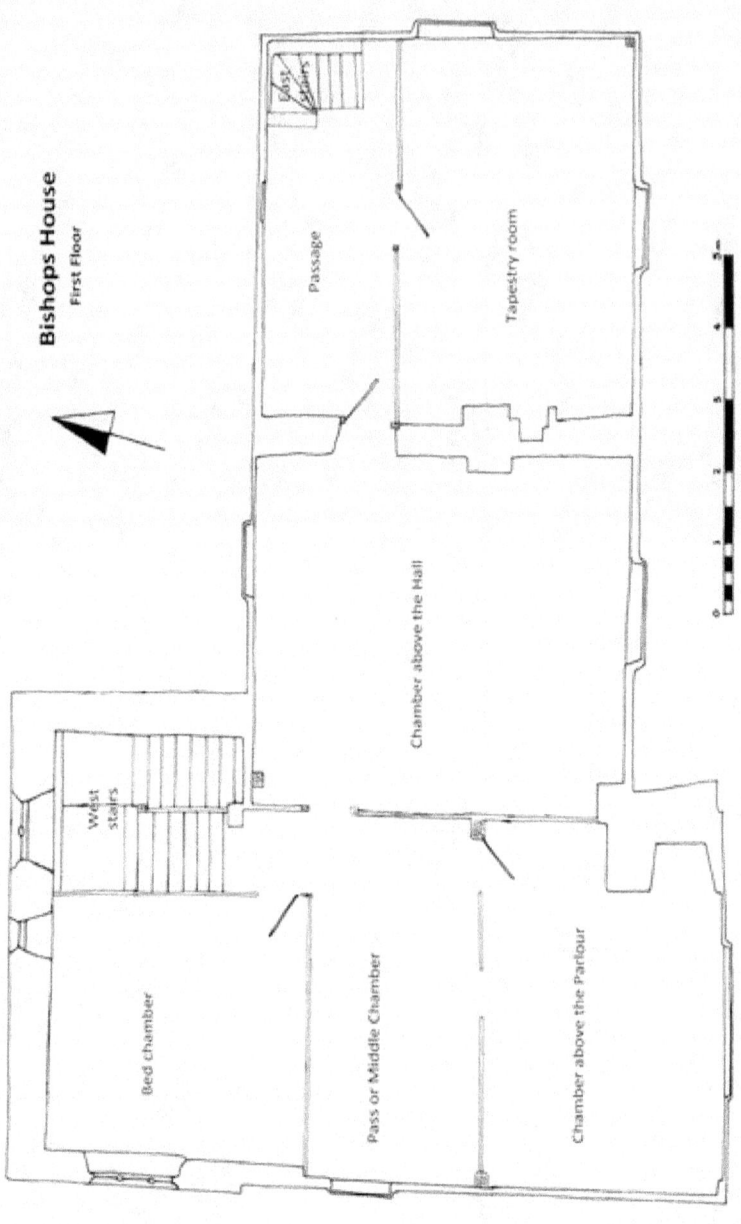

Chapter 5. Abbots, Barons and Trees
Five centuries of woodland management in two Yorkshire Dales

Ian G. R. Dormor

PLACE (People, Landscape & Cultural Environment Education & Research Centre), York

Abstract

This paper explores the woodland management traditions that were practised in two neighbouring Yorkshire Dales over a period of 500 years. In Nidderdale, coppice woodland was a widespread feature of the land-use framework put in place by the Cistercians of Fountains Abbey. Whilst in Wensleydale, seigneurial tenure resulted in large tracts of land being set aside for deer hunting. In Nidderdale, the monks of Fountains Abbey were engaged in extensive lead-mining and smelting activities which were reliant upon charcoal derived from managed coppice woodlands on the Abbey's satellite granges where access to those woodlands by tenants was strictly controlled. By contrast, in mid-Wensleydale a profusion of deer parks on the lordly estates around Middleham and Wensley gave rise to a form of land-use that favoured wood-pasture over coppice. In essence, the functions of woodland differed markedly in two discrete areas over the same time period.

Following the Dissolution of Fountains Abbey in 1539, there was a gradual transition from the intensive monastic coppice regime to amenity and plantation forestry practice by the Ingilby Estate on former monastic land. Two sixteenth century valuations of former monastic woodland have been interpreted by the writer to provide an insight into the composition and management of the monastic woodlands prior to their transfer to secular ownership. On the Bolton Estate in Wensleydale, woodland was initially regarded as a means of addressing the estate's financial shortcomings. However, a remodelling of former parkland wood-pasture into plantation woodland, which took place within the space of a few years during the late eighteenth century, can be seen to have influenced the rise of commercial forestry in the North of England. This process has been revealed by the writer's fieldwork together with a study of estate archives. The characteristics of present-day woodland are in many cases related to past management which is itself a function of the outputs, or end-uses of woodland. Thus, the extensive semi-natural woods that characterise a large extent of Nidderdale are the product of a coppice management regime whose purpose was primarily industrial – for the production of charcoal or kiln-dried wood. Much of the dale today supports commercial plantation woodland, and similarly, many woods in Wensleydale that originated in an environment intended for leisure purposes were subsequently replanted for timber production and now take the form of commercial plantations.

Introduction

This chapter presents two elements that formed part of a doctoral thesis prepared to investigate and understand the differences in woodland character and distribution in Nidderdale and Wensleydale. The dissimilar woodland management regimes practised during the same timeframe were studied in an area of the Pennine Dales where historical tenurial frameworks were significantly different. The data were collected using documentary sources and fieldwork.

Since the original research was undertaken the writer has analysed the original data sets with the benefit of a Geographic Information System (ArcGIS) and is currently developing the research theme further by extending the geographical limitation that was originally applied. Some of the new mapping is included here.

The Grange woodlands of Fountains Abbey
In the twelfth century, large tracts of land in Wensleydale and Nidderdale were granted to monastic houses by baronial landowners. At this time, the upper Dales were virtually unpopulated following the 'Harrying of the North' inflicted by the Normans during the winter of 1069-70. Depopulated land was ideally suited to monastic agriculture and most of Nidderdale passed into the hands of the Cistercian abbeys of Fountains and Byland. Nidderdale developed into a landscape of monastic farming based upon a system of granges that were interlinked with drove roads and packhorse tracks.

Many of the granges situated in and around the margins of lower Nidderdale and particularly those near the abbey precincts held small stands of woodland that were described as 'woodland pasture'. Michelmore (1981) interprets this terminology as coppice woods in which stock were allowed to graze after the first seven years of regrowth following cutting.

References to woodland in the Fountains Abbey leases of the late-fifteenth to mid-sixteenth centuries
Large areas of coppice in Nidderdale were maintained by Fountains Abbey in order to provide the charcoal upon which its mineral smelting activities were dependent. The woodland on demesne land was directly managed by the monastery, and as such, was protected against theft, wastage and damage. When the monastery embarked upon a new estate management system, which involved the letting of some of its granges to tenant farmers, the abbey put restrictive clauses in the leases to protect growing wood and timber. The *Fountains Abbey Lease Book* (Michelmore, 1981) gives a detailed insight into the Abbey's woodland management policy in the 150 years prior to the Dissolution, not least in the repeated references in the leases to 'sprynges', a term that is interpreted as coppiced woodland (Marshall, 1788; Rackham, 1976).

The monastic leases stipulated that the grange woodlands remained under the direct control of the abbot. At its simplest, timber and underwood formed no part of any leasehold agreement, and the tenants' rights to woodland were strictly limited apart from taking fallen wood for firewood. Of the Nidderdale granges let on tenancies, 21 possessed some standing timber or underwood (Figure 1). The rights and restrictions explicit in the 21 leases are given in Table 1.

The *Bursars' Books* of 1456-1458 (Fowler, 1918) contain a wealth of detail regarding the hedging of newly-cut coppices to exclude animals for a period of seven years. In most of the tenancies, the tenants and their livestock were expressly excluded from the woodland upon pain of forfeiture of their leases, while the abbot was at liberty to use the woodland as he wished. Most leases contained a clause which allowed the abbot or convent 'to take, fell, give, sell and carry away wood or 'casualte' from their woods or elsewhere on the grange or tenement, with free entry and exit at their pleasure, without interruption from the tenants' (Michelmore, 1981).

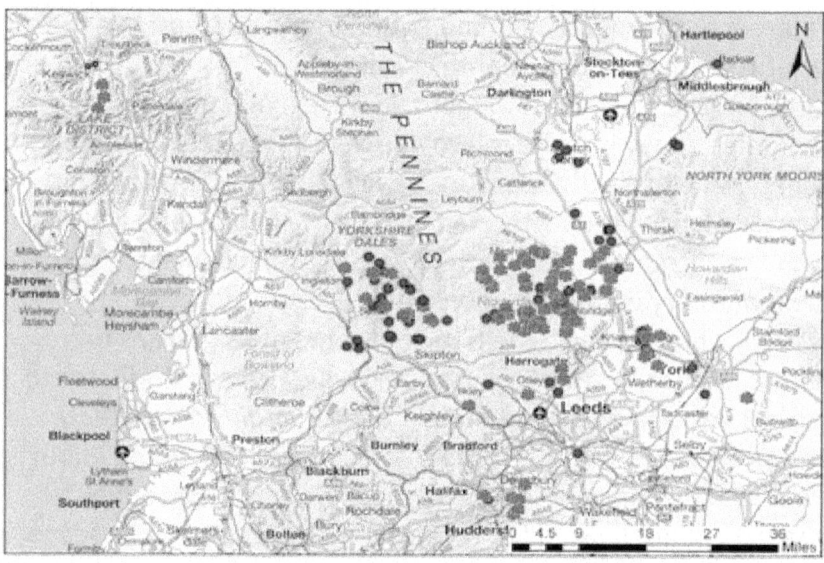

Figure 1. The Fountains Abbey granges with woodland (shown with tree symbol)

The cutting of leafy boughs ('brusynge', 'greenhews', 'watterbowes') for foddering domestic livestock was permitted in ten of the leases. At Lofthouse Grange, the tenant was bound 'not to give, fell or sell any woods growing within the bounds of the lodge', except reasonable 'brusynge' – leafy branches taken from trees for fodder (Michelmore, 1981).

Table 1: Rights and restrictions to woodland on Fountains Abbey granges let to tenants

Lease Numbers	Property	Coppice	7-yr fence time	Tenants to hedge	No cutting/ waste	Rights with Abbot	Rights to holly	Firewood	Browse
149, 279	Aldburgh	•	•	•	•	•			
156, 257	Nutwith Cote	•		•	•	•			
160, 280	Pott (Low Ash Head)				•		•	•	
216	Bewerley	•			•				•
217, 219	Dacre				•	•	•		•
212	Heyshaw				•			•	•
205, 238	Bouthwaite				•			•	•
206, 277	Lofthouse				•				•
189	Bramley	•				•			
202	Braisty Woods	•	•	•	•	•		•	•
192, 194	Brimham Grange			•	•	•		•	•
197	Brimham Lodge/Park				•				
201	Hartwith				•	•	•	•	•
198, 200	Winsley				•	•			
183	Fell Beck House	•	•	•		•			•
276	Abbey Precincts	•			•				
231	Fountains Park							•	
227, 228, 275	Haddockstones	•							
242	Cayton				•				
160	Pott			•	•		•	•	•
180	Warsill				•				

The monastic woodland at the Dissolution

Two valuation surveys of the monastic estate were undertaken by agents of Henry VIII in 1535 – four years prior to the Dissolution – and again in 1540. While transcriptions of these records have been published (Walbran, 1863), the writer has undertaken an interpretation of the data to provide a reconstruction of the mid-sixteenth century woodland.

In all but four cases, the surveys provide the area of the woods. In total, there were 802 acres (324.5ha) of woodland. Analysis of the woodland by descriptions (where they exist) and wood names, e.g. 'sprynge', provides an indication of the extent of the two types of woodland management practised by the monastery in the mid-sixteenth century. There were 571 acres (231ha) of coppice woodland and 253 acres (102.4ha) of wood pasture. This represents a ratio of 69% coppice : 31% wood-pasture. The distribution of coppice and wood pasture is shown in Figure 2.

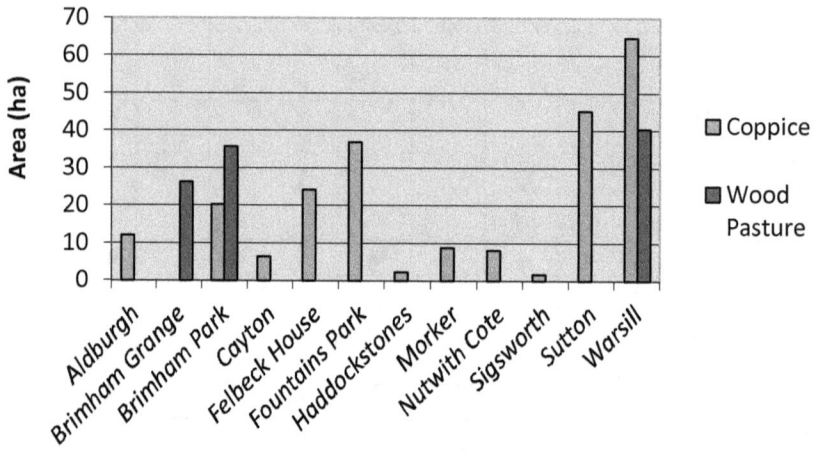

Figure 2. Managed woodland on the Fountains Abbey estate in 1540

At the time of the 1540 survey, the areas of wood-pasture had contracted markedly. Apart from an unspecified area of woodland at Pott, only three areas of wood-pasture were recorded at the granges of Warsill, Brimham and Brimham Park. The returns for Brimham Grange and Park describe that woodland as: *Cowpastore*, 30 acres, value 5s, many oaks therein; *Rise Close*, 15 acres, value 5s, full of wood; *Callfall*, 20 acres, value 5s, 15 acres of wood; *Estilwayke*, 30 acres, value 10s, most part full of great okes; *Old Parke*, 24 acres, value 20s, full of wood and carres;

Skragfold Leez, 34 acres, value 3s, 30 acres set with grete okes. The largest area of wood-pasture was *Warshall Calf Fall* at Warsill Grange to the west of Brimham which was described in the 1540 Valuation as 'coarse pasture, full of wood', covering 100 acres (40.47ha) and valued at 7s.

When the Abbey was dissolved in 1539 the greater part of the abbey's woodland was managed as coppice. Two spring woods in Brimham Park extended to 50 acres (20ha) and represented 10% of the area of coppice woodland. These two woods were *Eppett Springe* (40 acres, 12 years' growth) and *Colthuate Spryng* (10 acres, 17 years' growth), the latter possessing 'many fare tymbre okes and other treys'. Some 16% of the abbey's coppice woods, amounting to 91 acres (37ha), were situated within Fountains Park, described as: *Low Croke Wood*, 25 acres, 14 years' growth; *Mikelhaw*, 15 acres 'little underwood therein'; *Over Croke Wood*, 15 acres, 3 years' growth; *Abbot Fall Spring*, 14 acres, 14 years' growth; *Brodwod Sprynge*, 14 acres, 14 years' growth; *Wynford Wood*, 8 acres 'many fare timbre okes'.

It is apparent from the valuations that many of the monastic coppice woods were managed in large blocks rather than small coupes which were cut on short rotations. Given that, the prime function of the woodland was to provide a source of charcoal, rotations of around 15-20 years were employed. Many of the abbey's coppices were also managed to provide a source of standard trees for constructional timber.

The 1574 Valuation of former Fountains Abbey woodland

The most detailed impression of the former grange woodlands of Fountains Abbey is provided by a document purported to be a *Survey of the Woods and Trees on Certain Estates of the Late Dissolved Monastery of Fountains, taken in or about the year 1574* (Walbran, 1863). Walbran stressed the importance of this valuation, commenting that documents of this date, which give such a detailed 'picture of the sylvan aspect of this particular part of the country' are uncommon. He thought that the woodlands described in the valuation were unlikely to have been planted, and that *Aldburgh Great Wood*, the Abbey's largest block of woodland, 'no doubt sprang from the stocks which had existed at the time of the Norman Conquest'.

In an earlier valuation, taken in 1540, immediately prior to the purchase of the Fountains estate by Sir Richard Gresham, the value of the entire woodland amounted to just £380. Interestingly, the corresponding figure provided by the 1574 valuation was £1,905 13s, and this did not include the timber trees in Fountains Park which were valued at £519 6s 4d. It appears, therefore, that the earlier valuation was based upon a rough estimate rather than a detailed survey.

The main body of the valuation is concentrated upon the pricing of individual trees, in effect a 'per piece' valuation. This figure is then multiplied by the number of similar trees to calculate a total figure for a given category. The valuation differentiated between timber trees, standards and underwood, and from the style in which the assessments were presented, it is apparent that the woodland was predominantly managed as coppice-with-standards.

Standard trees
In the valuation of standard trees, which was only concerned with oaks and ashes, the surveyors employed a hierarchical pricing system, under which oak was placed into three grades and ash into one. Additionally in just two instances, the categories of 'worst oaks' and 'worst ashes' were used. These were probably dead, derelict or misshapen trees that could have been old pollards standing in areas of former wood-pasture.

Coppice-with-standards
In the 1574 valuation entry for Haddockstones Grange, the woodland is described as a wood of 30 acres 3 roods (12.45ha) in extent that had been divided into two coppice compartments of 17 years and 10-12 years in age. The valuations for the underwood placed a value upon the older compartment of 26s 8d per acre and the younger compartment of 13s 4d per acre – a

doubling in net worth over a period of about six years growth, reflecting the greater stem diameter and top height of the older trees. The standards are valued separately at 26s 8d per acre – the same areal value as the older coppice – indicating a net worth of 26.6d (a little over 2s) per tree, given an assumed stocking rate [density] of 12 timber trees per acre.

There is a marked difference in the price of the timber trees in Aldburgh Wood and Flotwood with the rest of the valuation, for here the oaks, valued at between 6s 4d and 13s 4d each were of a far greater degree of quality and maturity. The price of first grade oaks over the remainder of the valuation is in a band ranging from one to four shillings – at most less than half the price of the Flotwood trees. Similarly, first grade ashes, priced at 3s 4d each in Aldburgh Wood, elsewhere fall into a price band ranging from one shilling to two shillings and eight pence. In the sixteen fields having less than ten ash trees, it may be construed that those trees were growing in hedgerows rather than in stands of woodland.

Young trees
The relatively large numbers of young trees included in the return are thought to indicate small stands of coppice. Furthermore, the fact that discrete stands were given equal value would accord with their being even-aged and therefore attributable to a singular coppicing event. It is useful to examine the pricing structure of individual sapling trees, for this appears to be based upon the length of the coppice rotation and therefore their size. A simple interpretation of the four price bands employed: 8d, 12d, 14d and 16d shows that an incremental value of 1d per year of rotational growth per tree was applied. It follows therefore that 28% of the coppice wood was eight years old, 52% twelve years old, 10% fourteen years old and 10% sixteen years old. If a coppice rotation of 25 years was in operation, most of the woodland would have been in its second rotation following the monastery's Dissolution, or the figures may refer to restocking with maiden trees in their first cycle.

The valuation indicates that the extent of the coppiced woods was 428 acres (173ha). All the properties so valued possessed at least 10 acres (4ha) of coppice. Although Pott Grange possessed a rather disproportionate 120 acres (48.5ha) of woodland, mainly in the form of gill woods situated in remote country. The areas of coppice in 1574 are shown in Table 2.

Table 2. Areas of coppice woodland given in the 1574 valuation

Property	Area acres (ha)
Pott Grange	120 (48.6)
Aldburgh Wood	90 (36.4)
Flotwood	50 (20.2)
Bouthwaite Grange	35 (14.2)
Sigsworth Grange	30 (12.1)
Haddockstones Grange	30 (12.1)
Covill House	12 (4.8)
Thrope House	11 (4.4)
Bramley Grange	10 (4.04)
Thwaite House	10 (4.04)
Lofthouse Grange	10 (4.04)
Westholmehouse	10 (4.04)
Eastholmehouse	10 (4.04)
Total	428 (173)

Whilst restricted to thirteen properties, the descriptions of the coppice woods give an impression of their composition, area and value. As can been seen in the example of Haddockstones Grange, the compartmentalisation of woods was a feature of the coppice regime, albeit in quite large blocks of even-aged growth. The 90 acres (36ha) of underwood in Aldburgh Wood was managed in two compartments of 50 and 40 acres (20 and 16ha). At Thrope House, the eleven acres of coppice was divided into two plots of six and five acres (2.4 and 2ha). Elsewhere, the coppices appear to have been managed as large even-aged stands, as in the case of Bouthwaite: 35 acres (14.1ha) and Sigsworth: 30 acres (12.1ha).

It is possible to calculate the incremental value of coppice cycles from the given valuation figures. The base valuation for coppices with few, if any, standard trees was ten shillings per acre. This figure was applied in seven cases, where coppice growth of 20 years was concerned. Thus, it may be construed that in these cases, an increment of sixpence per acre per year of growth was applied by the surveyors to arrive at a valuation of these timber-poor coppices. A somewhat higher value of 13s 4d per acre was applied at Bramley and Lofthouse, which each possessed ten-acre (4.01ha) stands that probably included a quantity of oak standards. In the case of the higher-valued woodland, the incremental price rose from 6d to 1s 4d per acre per year of growth. This same factor can be seen to apply in the examples of Aldburgh Wood, with 50 acres of underwood at 26s 8d per acre, and 40 acres of underwood at 13s 4d per acre. By using this incremental figure, it becomes evident that the 50 acre stand was 20 years old and the 40 acre stand ten years old. Also, the same figure is applicable to the 50 acres of 17-year-old underwood in Flotwood, valued at 23s 4d per acre. An explanation for the higher valuations might result from better woodland sites affording more vigorous growth, perhaps with a higher volume of oak as underwood.

In the 1574 valuation, the granges of Thrope House and Thwaite House were recorded as each having about ten acres of coppice woods: *Thrope House Grange* – six acres of ground replenished with hazel and holly of 20 years growth, valued at 10s/acre; 16 shurb'd ashes @ 8d each. Sum of value £3 10s 8d. Also five acres of hazel, holly, alder @ 10s/acre; 16 shurb'd ashes @ 6d each. Sum of value 58s. *Thwaite House Grange* – 10 acres of hazel, alder and holly of 20 years growth, valued at 10s/acre. Also 32 shurb'd ashes @ 6d each. Sum of value £5 16s (Walbran, 1863).

Shredded trees
The category of 'shurb'd' [shrubbed] trees given in the woodland valuations for nine former granges may indicate the practice of tree shredding on the monastic estate. In a parallel drawn from the sixteenth century woodland records of the Cistercian Abbey of Cwm-hir in Mid Wales, Linnard (2000, p.63) remarks that the practice of shredding, also known as 'shrouding' or 'shrubbing', which involved the lopping-off of branches, often to a considerable height was employed for providing winter fodder for livestock.

It is evident from the 1574 returns that the price of shredded trees ranged from sixpence to one shilling each. Of particular note is the large number (300) of small shredded oaks listed at Sigsworth Grange. One can only conjecture what form this woodland took. In view of the return for Sigsworth in the 1540 valuation, which showed only a small amount of wood pasture, an interpretation offered is that these were standard trees in a young coppice wood. If the planting had taken place soon after 1540, it follows that by the time of the latter valuation the trees were approaching 40 years of age. It is possible to gain some impression of the appearance of these trees using forestry yield class curves (Rollinson 1992) which provide a calibration curve for age, yield class and height. Conservatively, assuming the oak to be in the lowest yield class (YC4), a 35 to 40 year old tree would have attained a top height of 6m. But given the knowledge that pollarding suppresses the growth of trees by removing much of the leaf-bearing branchwood, and thus reducing the capacity of a tree to photosynthesise (E. Green pers. comm.), it is probable that shredding would have a similar effect upon growth rate.

In Nidderdale, there was an almost seamless transition from the woodland management tradition of Fountains Abbey to that of one of its secular successors, the Ingilbys of Ripley Castle. Under both forms of tenure, woodland management was directed at the provision of raw materials for specific industrial end-uses. In monastic hands this was destined to support an extractive industry and in secular hands, as a revenue-generating activity. But under both systems, the inherent value placed upon woodland is clearly visible in the measures taken to ensure its conservation. For at least 500 years, stringent control of woodland resources, underwritten by legal obligations and coupled with appropriate management, ensured that such resources were not squandered. In this, the critical factor of tenure is identified as the principal influence that has provided the richly wooded landscape that is a feature of Nidderdale in the present day.

Woodland management in Wensleydale

Wensleydale is particularly important in this study of woodland management as it still retains, beneath the Parliamentary Enclosure landscape, elements of the medieval landscape in which woodland was primarily managed as an amenity. This is evident in the relics of a former landscape of parks, villages and open fields where an extensive network of former hedgerow trees provides a framework upon which a reconstruction of the medieval and post-medieval woodland can be developed.

A fundamental difference in land tenure distinguishes Wensleydale from Nidderdale and it is due to this distinctive arrangement of land-holding in Wensleydale that tenure is identified as the principal factor that determined the management of woodland there. Fundamentally, it was because the land-use was geared towards the provision of a suitable environment for the hunting of game animals such as deer and wild boar that the woodland was principally managed as wood-pasture. This had aggregations of pollarded trees and undershrubs standing in close proximity to areas of open grassland. This system of woodland management was suited to address the need for the provision of cover, grazing and a supply of harvestable small wood. Here, the pollarded trees served to provide shelter and cover for game animals as well as a source of polewood and leaf fodder, while the treeless areas supported grazing land and provided an environment where the pursuit of hunting on horseback could take place.

In the early years of the post-Conquest period, much of Upper Wensleydale was, like Upper Nidderdale, an expanse of wild and sparsely populated moorland that served as a hunting chase for the Norman lords. There were, however, in the middle and lower zones, more settlements than in Nidderdale, although at the time of Domesday Book (1086) much of this was described as 'waste'.

A landscape of parks and chases

By the fourteenth century mid-Wensleydale was a landscape of hunting with numerous deer parks created by the Lords of

Middleham around their castle at Middleham and nearby by other seigneurial families (Hartley and Ingilby 1986, p.13). Wood pasture, which favoured hunting on horseback, was a feature of deer parks.

The creation of parks followed the granting of a licence to Ralph Neville to impark his wood of Middleham in 1335 (VCH 1914, pp.253-4). To the west of Middleham lay a succession of parks extending as far as West Witton, at the foot of Penhill. Sunskew, situated to the south-east of Middleham Castle, was the largest park, covering 634.9 acres (256.95ha). West Park, situated between Middleham Low Moor and the River Ure, covered an area of 452.1 acres (182.97ha). Overall, 1087 acres (439.92ha) were set aside for hunting in immediate proximity to Middleham castle.

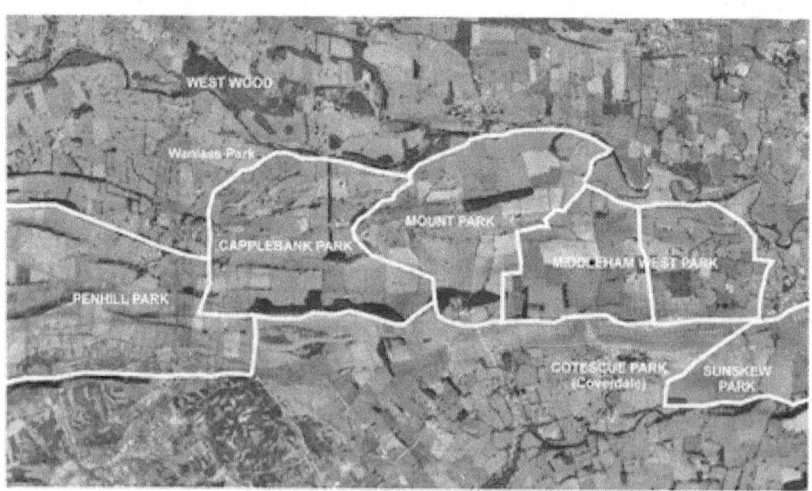

Figure 3. Hunting parks west of Middleham, mid-Wensleydale

Middleham West Park was an area set out as compartments of wood-pasture totalling 333 acres (134ha) together with 16 acres (6.4ha) of coppice which represented a substantial source of underwood and poles for firewood and fencing. The ratio of wood-pasture to coppice is calculated as 22:1. In total, the 349 acres (141ha) of wood-pasture and coppice represented 56% of the enclosed area.

The Bolton (Scrope) Estate

The Bolton estate of the Scrope family, centred upon Castle Bolton on the northern bank of the River Ure, similarly enclosed large tracts of land for hunting. West Bolton [Low] Park was one of two parks created close to the castle. A number of medieval deeds contain references to woodland owned by the Scropes.

West Wood

Two thirteenth and fourteenth century documents mention woodland in Wensley. One, dated 1285, refers to the *Wood of Wendesle* [Wensley] in an agreement setting out the formalities for its division. There is another reference to the *Wood of Wensley* in a grant of 1320 which included 'all the soil of the same wood and all lands and tenements with appurtenances in *Le Ryddings* and in *Tolouse*'. The *Wood of Wensley* is believed by the writer to be the present West Wood.

It is evident from a study of maps and estate plans that the wood has at various times had other names, including 'Redmire Wood', 'Bolton Hall Wood' and 'Lords Wood'. The pattern of the surrounding field boundaries gives an indication that the wood was in existence during the fourteenth century. Many fields on the northern margins of the wood preserve ridge and furrow features that respect the wood boundaries. A linear earthwork at the western end of the wood, aligned at right-angles to the River Ure, together with a number of veteran pollarded oaks within the modern plantation woodland, and the existence of the stumps of many more large trees, may indicate the presence of a deer park that predated the *Wood of Wensley*.

'Nanny Doune's Oak', a large oak pollard, is thought to remain from a former wood-pasture regime. With a girth of 578cm and dbh [diameter-at-breast-height] of 174cm, the age of this tree is estimated at 460 years, assuming an annual incremental growth rate of 1.27cm/yr^{-1} (Mitchell, 1966). This gives a planting date of c.AD 1540. Numerous decayed stumps of other large trees, now largely concealed in the understorey of a plantation, may be the remains of other pollards.

Figure 4: 'Nanny Doune's Oak, West Wood; a remnant of former wood-pasture

The impression that a relict wood pasture existed in West Wood in the eighteenth century is gained from Bolton Estate correspondence which mentions the presence of old pollarded trees there. In a letter dated 1 December, 1790, Thomas Maude, the agent, recommended selling more timber to improve the woods, noting that West Wood in particular had many *'rickety Trees of Elm & Ash, dead, dying & hollow which are only fit for charcoal and such inferior purposes – £60 value'* (NYCRO ZBO).

This possible survivor of a medieval deer park was incorporated into a designed landscape associated with the construction of Bolton Hall in 1678. An earthwork that follows precisely the outline of West Wood (Lord's Wood) and depicted on the Godson Map of 1737, can be identified as part of the formalised layout of *pleasaunces*, walks and carriage drives rather than a feature of medieval date.

Exploitation of the Bolton Estate woodlands
During the early eighteenth century the Bolton estate woodlands were being felled for use in the coal and lead mines, for

woodland, at that time, was perceived as a saleable resource that could be exploited to satisfy short-term financial needs. In a letter, dated 18 December, 1719, to Sir Thomas Orde the (absentee) Duke of Bolton, Mr Hammond, the estate manager, wrote: *'I am going on with the Grubing of the Thorns and Teasles in the low part of Caplebank, and the Old Trees are cutting down there for the use of the Colliery and the Lead Mines'* [NYCRO, ZBO IV 8, 172].

In 1775 problems had arisen with the river necessitating urgent repairs to the bank at a time when the estate was not in good financial health. The estate became reliant upon sales of wood to provide an income and to this end there was a wholesale onslaught upon the estate woodlands. This probably saw the destruction of most of the old pollards that stood in the former parkland wood pastures around Bolton Hall.

'The axe is often heard, but the planter is seldom seen' - John Tuke (1794)
'Of late years the passion for taking down has been much stronger than that of raising up' - William Marshall (1788)

Capplebank Park

With the construction of Bolton Hall, Capplebank Park on the opposite side of the river, became the home deer park. Subsequently, it was subdivided to create Mount Park in its eastern sector, presumably for the purposes of simplifying land management. Capplebank Park had an ovate boundary whose course can still be followed in the pattern of relict field walls. The Godson Estate Map (1737) depicts Capplebank Park as a large area of wood-pasture, with concentrations of trees interspersed by linear lawns. When Capplebank Plantation was created, the medieval deer park was lost as the woodland became the focus of new planting as an extension of the pleasure grounds. It is apparent from an estate plan of 1794 which shows the layout of the new plantation, together with the surveyors' offsets (Figure 4) that the very individual, scalloped northern boundary was an attempt to landscape the new woodland, to enhance its appearance from Bolton Hall. This relatively early plantation was quite novel in its concept, for it is as much an expression of eighteenth century landscape design as it is a feature of early forestry practice.

Bay Bolton Avenue, a formal avenue of trees, contemporaneous with the building of Bolton Hall, provided a direct link between the Hall and the Park. The avenue ascended the northern slope of Penhill, to terminate at the boundary of Capplebank Park with Middleham Moor. It is evident from the depiction of Capplebank Park on the Godson Estate Map that the formal avenue passed through three stands of wood pasture.

Figure 5. Capplebank Plantation 1794 surveyors' plan (above); 2009 view (below)

Although wood pasture was particularly widespread in Wensleydale, there were areas of coppiced woodland in the valley bottom. A number of these woods were situated adjacent to townships in which an element of the rural population was entitled to exercise the right of *firebote* (to take firewood in the form of dead wood and fallen branches). This duality of purpose in serving the needs of a hunting landscape and that for domestic firewood characterised the management of woodland in Wensleydale from the medieval period until the demise of the Lordship of Middleham in the seventeenth century.

The extractive industry in Wensleydale was on a smaller scale than that in Nidderdale during the monastic era and, in consequence, there was not the requirement to place large areas of woodland under intensive coppice management. Coppice woods on estates were, however, assiduously managed, and it is evident from documentary studies that their contribution as a source of grove timber and fuel for the mines was considerable.

The medieval landscape with its pollarded trees and hunting parks evolved into the more familiar landscape of small farms and large estates that characterise Wensleydale today. A particular feature of the contemporary landscape is the broadleaved plantation woodland that exists in the Dale to the west of Leyburn and the shelf woods that characterise the underlying geology and topography east of Aysgarth.

The advent of forestry on the Bolton Estate
In February 1795, Thomas Maude resigned from his post as Bolton Estate Steward. His replacement was John Anderson, of nearby Swinithwaite, who had previously been closely involved with the running of the estate. In the autumn of that year work began on setting out a new plantation to the north of Bolton Hall and other new plantations on Leyburn Moor and at Preston-under-Scar.

An important milestone in the development of Bolton Estate's woodland management occurred in April 1797, with the appointment of William Sadler as Agent. Sadler's influence upon the estate woodlands was profound. He reversed the tide of woodland destruction that was a feature of the previous decade and took forward and developed the major programme of new plantation establishment begun by Anderson.

In addition to raising trees from seed, young self-seeded trees were taken from established woods on the estate and planted in the Bridge Garden nursery where they were grown on in preparation for transplanting into the new plantations. Lord Bolton was clearly more disposed to taking young trees from the wild rather than buying in nursery stock.

The estate's woodlands at Downholme, on the eastern edge of Swaledale, were logistically well placed to supply most of the requirements for grove timber, but it is evident that much was also sourced from Wensleydale. From correspondence between William Sadler and Sir John Orde, it is evident that Lady Jean Bolton (the widow of Sir Thomas Orde, 1st Baron Bolton) was particularly enthusiastic for tree-planting and the creation of new woodlands. The autumn of 1808 and the spring of 1809 were particularly significant for woodland creation, during this short space of time there was a dramatic increase in tree-planting on the Bolton Estate under her influence. This resulted in the planting of 55,000 trees and the creation of 30 new plantations.

In this study of a Yorkshire estate, the remodelling of a landscape shaped by medieval hunting into one of commercial forestry characterises a significant element of the woodland history of Wensleydale over the past five centuries. Clearly, the catalyst in reversing the process of woodland depletion was the appointment of William Sadler as agent in 1795. It was due to his, and John Anderson's forward thinking that the Bolton Estate became a major influence in the rise of forestry in the north of England. In much the same way, many woodlands forming part of the Fountains Abbey estate in Nidderdale developed into commercial forestry plantations under the hand of the Ingilby family of Ripley Castle. Within these two discrete areas, indications of former woodland management regimes are evident in relict trees and field enclosure patterns.

References

Fowler, J. T. (ed.) (1918) 'Memorials of the abbey of St Mary of Fountains, III, consisting of Bursars's Books 1456-1459, and Memorandum Book of Thomas Swynton, 1446-1458'. *Publications of the Surtees Society*, **130**

Hartley, M. and Ingilby, J. (1986) *Dales Memories.* Dalesman Publishing, Clapham

Linnard, W. (2000) *Welsh Woods and Forests: a History.* Gomer Press, Llandysul

Marshall, W. (1788) *The Rural Economy of Yorkshire.* T. Cadgell, London

Michelmore, D.J.H. (ed) (1981) *The Fountains Abbey Lease Book.* Yorkshire Archaeological Society, Leeds

Mitchell, A.F. (1966) Dating the ancient oaks. *Quarterly Journal of Forestry,* **60**, 271-6

Rackham, O. (1976) *Trees and Woodlands in the British Landscape.* Dent, London

Rollinson, T. J. D. (1992) *Thinning Control.* Forestry Commission Field Book 2, HMSO, London

Tuke, G. (1794) *General View of the Agriculture of the North Riding of Yorkshire.* Board of Agriculture, London

Victoria County History, (1914) *Victoria County History of the Counties of England: Yorkshire North Riding* **3**. Constable, London

Walbran, J.R. (1863) Memorials of the Abbey of St Mary of Fountains. *Publications of the Surtees Society,* **42**

Walbran, J.R. (1878) Memorials of the Abbey of St Mary of Fountains. *Publications of the Surtees Society,* **67**

Walbran, J.R. (1918) Memorials of the Abbey of St Mary of Fountains. *Publications of the Surtees Society,* **130**

Willan, T.S. and Crossley, E.W. (eds) (1941) Three Seventeenth Century Yorkshire Surveys. *Yorkshire Archaeological Society Record Series,* **104**, 146-147

Archival sources: Estate documents

Bolton Estate archive (Ref. ZBO): North Yorkshire County Record Office, Northallerton

Ingilby Estate (Ingilby MSS): West Yorkshire Archive Service, Leeds.

William Godson's map of the Bolton Estate (1737): Bolton Hall, Wensley

Chapter 6. Bobbin Mills in the North of Scotland

Joanna R. Gilliatt
Independent Researcher

Abstract

The first bobbin mill in the UK had been set up by 1788, in the Lake District, to provide bobbins for the developing textile industries. Over the next century, bobbin making became a considerable industry in its own right, with over 100 bobbin mills in the Lake District alone. Working as a volunteer researcher for the Woodland Trust's Ancient Woodland Restoration project, with the aim of contributing towards the body of knowledge about the history and cultural significance of our ancient woodlands, my focus has been on researching bobbin mills in the north of Scotland. Many of these mills used birch from the upland birch woodlands as the raw material for their bobbin making. Evidence has been found for 88 bobbin mills (or other turning mills which made bobbins) which were established in the north of Scotland from the 1830s through to the 1930s. These mills served two main textile industries; the jute industry, which was centred on Dundee, and the cotton thread industry, centred on Paisley. The mills can be categorised into 6 groups, based on a combination of geography and the date they were established, with each group having its own set of typical characteristics. For around 120 years, bobbin making was a significant industry in the north of Scotland, yet nowadays there is little or no trace of the bobbin mills which once operated, or the impact they had, and many people are unaware that this industry ever existed. This paper seeks to explore the scale, history and characteristics of bobbin making in the north of Scotland.

Introduction

The history of bobbin mills and bobbin making is directly related to the history of textile industries. Used to wind thread or yarn around, both for storage and for use, bobbins play an essential part in textile production processes. They were required in their millions by textile industries as they developed during the nineteenth century.

The first bobbin mill had been set up in the English Lake District by 1788, and undoubtedly, the Lake District is the area of the UK most associated with bobbin mills. Around 100 mills have operated there over the years. However, bobbin mills were also found in other parts of northern England, the south of Scotland and, indeed, the north of Scotland.

Working as a volunteer researcher for the Woodland Trust's Ancient Woodland Restoration project, with the aim of contributing towards the body of knowledge about the history and cultural significance of our ancient woodlands, my focus has been on researching bobbin mills in the north of Scotland. Many of the mills used birch from the upland birch woodlands as the raw material for their bobbin making. This research has made use of primary sources, including early Ordnance Survey (OS) maps, census records (1841-1911), valuation rolls (1855-1935), business directories and newspaper archives; and secondary sources, including books and websites, as well as anecdotal evidence and personal recollections.

Using these sources, evidence has been found for 88 bobbin mills (or other turning mills which made bobbins) which were established in the north of Scotland over a period of around 100 years from the 1830s. There is evidence in primary sources for 73 of these mills and from secondary sources and personal recollections for 15 more. These mills served two main textile industries; the jute industry centred on Dundee, and the cotton thread industry centred on Paisley, though it is possible some of them also supplied other textile industries.

Although the information available is extremely patchy and many unanswered questions remain, the 88 bobbin mills can be roughly categorised into six groups. This is based on a combination of geography and the date they were established, with each group having its own set of typical characteristics.

Table 1. Typology of bobbin mills and turning mills in the north of Scotland

Bobbin Mills and Turning Mills – by geography and date established										
1830s	1840s	1850s	1860s	1870s	1880s	1890s	1900s	1910s	1920s	1930s
Perthshire: 23 mostly rural, stone-built, water powered, turning mills, which were **converted from a previous use** and supplied the jute industry										
	Aberdeenshire: 9 mostly rural, stone or **timber with stone footings**, water powered turning mills, which supplied the jute industry. .									
		Angus: 15 mostly **urban**, stone or **brick built**, steam powered, turning mills which supplied the jute industry.								
Highlands: 11 rural bobbin mills **set up by** & supplying Paisley **thread manufactures.**			**Highlands: 20** rural, timber-built steam powered bobbin mills **supplying thread mills**			**Highlands: 10** (including 3 from highland Perthshire) mostly rural, timber built, steam powered, bobbin mills **supplying jute industry**				

In order to explore the scale, history and characteristics of bobbin making in the north of Scotland, the information which is known about each of these groups is outlined below.

Turning Mills in Perthshire – established 1830s to 1880s

Processes for mechanising the spinning and weaving of jute were developed in Dundee during the 1820s & 1830s. Jute processing soon became a huge industry, with a range of different bobbins being needed for different aspects of the production process.

However, the jute was imported from India. By the mid-nineteenth century jute mills were already being set up in India, with the scale of production surpassing that in Dundee by the turn of the twentieth century. Nevertheless, the demand for bobbins continued right through to 1948, when India banned the import of bobbins from Scotland.

The earliest records of mills in Perthshire supplying bobbins to Dundee date from the 1830s. Overall, there is good primary documentary evidence for 21 bobbin mills and turning mills in Perthshire, set up between the 1830s and 1880s, with evidence for two more in secondary sources. There was a 'bobbin factory' in Perth while the remaining mills were in rural areas. The exact locations of 15 of them are known from early Ordnance Survey (OS) maps. These mills were generally set up by rivers and streams, which provided waterpower, frequently involving use of elaborate infrastructure including weirs, mill lades and sluices. Rather than being purpose-built, however, the mills typically occupied an existing stone-built mill building, such as an old corn mill, lint mill, waulkmill or oil mill.

The proprietors of the mills were usually local (often titled) landowners, while the mills were operated by tenants, who were generally local, if not to the immediate area, at least to Perthshire, Angus or Aberdeenshire. The tenants often combined running their bobbin mill with other activities, such as running a farm or sawmill, or working as a wood merchant. Some of the mills are known to have made shuttles or clothes pegs as well as bobbins. In most cases, the documentary evidence shows that the mills made bobbins for the textile industries in Dundee, though one was owned by a Lancashire cotton magnate and produced bobbins for his own thread mills in Manchester.

These mills all appear to have been fairly modest enterprises, the largest being run by a 'turner master employing 13 men and 2 boys', but little is known about how sophisticated they were or whether they produced a range of bobbins of different types, shapes and sizes, or produced one specific type of bobbin. Some are known to have used beech which was considered the best wood for making the 'roving and spinning bobbins' which were made from three separate pieces of wood (for the top, bottom and shaft respectively), and while no direct evidence has been found, they almost certainly also made 'solid spinning bobbins', which were made from a single piece of wood, usually birch (Highland, 1988).

Bobbins made at one of the Perthshire mills were transported by steamer from Perth whilst others were located close to railway stations, and it seems likely that their bobbins were transported by train. Some of the mills were sufficiently close to Dundee for the bobbins to be transported there by cart.

Though accurate dating of the mills is impossible, some of them appear to have been in operation for a very short period of time, and almost half for less than 20 years, yet others continued in operation for 75 years or more, and a few were still producing bobbins well into the twentieth century. Although the specific reasons why mills closed are not always known, there are examples of closures after a mill were damaged by fire, as a result of retirement, death or financial difficulties, in favour of other activities, such as shuttle making, farming or saw milling, and to set up another bobbin mill in alternative premises.

Turning Mills in Aberdeenshire – established 1840s to 1890s

There is good primary documentary evidence for eight of the nine bobbin mills in this group, all of them can be identified on first edition OS maps, and hence their exact locations are known. Many of these mills were water-powered and originally built for another purpose, whether as a corn mill, lint mill, barley mill or saw-mill, and later converted for use as a bobbin mill. Some were stone buildings while others were wooden buildings, with stone footings. The earliest evidence for any of these mills dates from the 1841 census records, and the last mill in the group was set up in Aberdeen in 1891.

Most of the men who operated the bobbin mills in Aberdeenshire were tenants, fairly local to the area and, as in Perthshire, quite commonly combining running a bobbin mill with other activities, such as farming, saw milling or operating as a wood merchant. The mills varied considerably in terms of their size of operation, both between mills and over time, with examples including a "wood turner employing 2 men" right through to a "wood merchant, manufacturer & farmer, employing 37 men & 5 boys". While some of the men who worked in the mills were fairly local to the area, there were also men who travelled around, working in a number of different bobbin mills over the years, presumably following work opportunities.

As in Perthshire, these mills were often known as turning mills, rather than bobbin mills and may have produced other turned goods in addition to bobbins; two are known to have made buckets at one time. The main market for the mills was the jute industry in Dundee, and in 1882 the Inchmarlo Mill in Banchory advertised that it supplied *'rove, winding, twisting and spinning bobbins; weft pirns, jenny pirns and all classes of bobbins required in the manufacture of flax, jute and wool'* (Sharp, 1882). This was clearly a sophisticated enterprise, as was the bobbin mill in Aberdeen later set up by the same family, and it may have made a wider range of bobbins than was typical.

There is very little direct information available about the type of wood used by most of the bobbin mills in this group, but photographs of the bobbin mill at Cambus O'May, on Deeside, clearly show that it used large quantities of birch wood, transported to the mill by horse and cart. This mill, like many of the others, was located quite close to a railway station and it seems likely that the bobbins it produced were transported by train.

Investigating Tree Archaeology

Figure 1. The Cambus O'May Bobbin Mill (photographs provided by Alistair Cassie)

Several of the mills in this area are known to have only been in operation for a short time, though several others continued in operation for 75 years or more. The last mills to close were the Cambus O'May mill, which was operated by three generations of the Pithie family for over 80 years and was eventually sold to the owners of the mill in Aberdeen; and the Aberdeen mill itself which closed in 1973. By then, the world had moved on and the market for wooden bobbins had ceased to exist.

In addition to the bobbin mills in Aberdeenshire, there were two other water-powered turning mills in the area which never made bobbins. Their main output for many years being herring barrel bungs and buckets respectively, both made from Scots Pine. The Finzean Turning Mills were wooden buildings with stone footings, established on the sites of existing estate saw-mills in the mid-nineteenth century, and making use of the saw mills' infrastructure for their water power. Both mills still survive in working order today, though they are no longer run as businesses, and are unable to open to the public for health and safety reasons.

Turning Mills in Angus – established 1850s to 1890s

There is good primary documentary evidence for 15 turning mills in Angus, with new mills being set up from 1850 through to 1898. While most of these mills were in urban settings, including in Dundee, Arbroath, Forfar and the smaller town of Friockheim, the exact locations of only 6 of them are known. Individual buildings in towns and cities are often not identified, even on the early OS maps.

Many of these mills were stone or brick buildings and were steam powered, and most were probably purpose built. However, in more rural locations the mills made use of existing mill buildings, including in Glamis, where a water-powered waulkmill, was converted for use as a bobbin mill.

Though some of these mills were run by tenants, and others were owned and run by partnerships or limited companies, many were family owned and run businesses. They ranged in size from those with just a few employees, up to the largest firms, with up to around 100 workers. Bobbin making was often included amongst other activities, such as general wood turning, shuttle making, saw milling, timber sales and mill furnishing.

Located in or close to Dundee, these mills made bobbins for the local textile industries, and later for export to India, though some may also have supplied other textile industries elsewhere in the UK or abroad. The mills made use of birch, beech and possibly other hardwoods, bought locally. However, by the end of the nineteenth century supplies of both birch and beech were being imported. During the twentieth century the large manufacturers, increasingly turned away from use of Scottish birch wood, preferring to import birch from Sweden and the Baltic, which was both cheaper and of higher quality (Highland, 1988).

Birch imported from Sweden by the Gateside Mill in Fife is known to have arrived in the form of bobbin blocks, that is, pieces of birch wood with a hole bored down the centre, and which had been turned on a lathe, to create the rough bobbin shape. Buying wood in this form was much more cost-effective than buying unprocessed wood, since it significantly reduced transport costs. Once seasoned, the production process was completed by turning the rough-cut bobbin using a finishing lathe, to create the finished bobbins, ready for polishing.

While most of the mills in more rural locations in Angus closed towards the end of the nineteenth century, the last closed in 1907, many of the mills in Dundee continued in operation well into the twentieth century. The largest, McGregor and Balfour only closed in 1975, by which time the production of wooden bobbins had long since ceased.

Bobbin Mills in the Highlands – established 1830s to 1850s

A process for making cotton thread was developed, early in the nineteenth century, by Patrick Clark of Paisley. Production was soon mechanised, with thread mills being set up by various members of the Clark family, who, along with the rival firm J & P Coats, came to dominate the industry. Initially the thread was sold in hanks, but by around 1820 it was being sold on wooden spools (cotton reels). The thread industry created a huge demand for both the bobbins used during the thread production process and spools to hold the finished thread.

The first bobbin mill known to have been set up to supply bobbins for the Paisley thread mills was on the island of Arran; set up by James and Patrick Clark of Paisley. The mill was probably established in the early 1830s but was abandoned by 1840 since it had exhausted the local supply of birch wood.

The earliest records of bobbin mills in the Highlands date from the 1830s, with good primary documentary evidence for six bobbin mills being established between the 1830s and 1850s. In addition, there is evidence from unverifiable sources that there were another five such mills, and the suggestion that there may have been many more (Blair, 1907).

These early bobbin mills were in quite remote, rural locations in the west Highlands and most of them were located beside, or close to, open water, enabling easy transportation of the bobbins produced, by steamer. However, while three of the mills appear on the first edition OS map, the exact location of the others is unknown.

No information is available about either the construction of most of the bobbin mills in this group or about how they were powered. However, the Highlands did not have an abundance of existing water-powered mill buildings, available to be converted into bobbin mills, and it seems likely that many of the mills were purpose-built timber buildings and powered by steam.

The defining characteristic of this group was that they were set up by thread manufacturers themselves. They leased land from the local landowner, on which to build their bobbin mills, which were then run by managers. Both the managers and most of the workers in the mills, including young teenagers, came from outside the area, especially from Renfrewshire and Lanarkshire. Evidently, the workforce was brought in by the thread manufacturers specifically to work in the mills.

These mills were set up to produce bobbins, yet it is not known whether they made the full range of different types required during the thread production process, or whether they were set up specifically to produce the wooden spools needed for storing the finished thread. In the scanty documentary evidence which exists, the wood used by these mills is always said to be birch, and the mill at Salen was reported to use 1,400 tons of birch wood annually, making 75,000 bobbins each day (Somers, 1848).

While the Inverfarigaig Bobbin Mill was in operation for over 40 years, during which it changed hands several times, the others were short-lived enterprises, often in use for a decade or less. The Salen mill closed in 1854 after a fire, but the reasons why the other mills had such a short lifespan are unclear.

Bobbin Mills in the Highlands – established 1860s to 1880s

There is no evidence of thread manufacturers themselves setting up new bobbin mills in the Highlands after the mid-1850s, and all but one of their mills had closed by the end of that decade. However, from the 1860s, independent entrepreneurs started to set up bobbin mills in the Highlands to supply the thread manufacturers with bobbins.

There is good primary documentary evidence for 13 mills set up between 1865 and 1885 (with some evidence for seven more). However, just three of the mills can be identified on early OS maps, with the exact location of the remaining mills being unknown.

The first mill in this group, the South Kinrara Bobbin Mill was set up in 1865, two years after a railway line passing through the area was opened. Indeed, many of the bobbin mills in this group were located close to railway stations, which provided a ready means of transporting the bobbins produced, and the development of the railways clearly played a major role in the expansion of bobbin making in the Highlands.

Where evidence exists, these mills are known to have been purpose-built wooden buildings, set up specifically as bobbin mills rather than as generic turning mills, and powered by steam. They were built on land leased from local landowners, and operated by tenants, who were identified in the census records as bobbin turners, bobbin makers or bobbin manufacturers, though they often operated as more general saw millers and wood merchants as well. Most of these entrepreneurs originated from elsewhere in Scotland, including from Aberdeenshire, Angus and Paisley. They had evidently come to the area specifically to take advantage of the local birch woodland, which provided the main raw material of their bobbin mills. The size of their enterprises varied considerably, with the largest employer recorded being a 'bobbin maker master employing 30 men and 2 boys', many of whom also came from outside the area.

These bobbin mills appear to have been set up specifically to supply bobbins to the Paisley (and Glasgow) thread mills, though the possibility exists that they also supplied bobbins to the jute industry or other textile industries. No evidence has been found about the type of bobbins they supplied, or how the bobbins were made, and though the South Kinrara Bobbin Mill remained in operation for 26 years, most of these mills only existed for a short period of time, often for less than a decade. The reasons why the mills closed are unclear, though in a few cases this was probably prompted by the mill being damaged or destroyed by fire. Some of the bobbin makers closed a mill in one location and opened another elsewhere. This may indicate a problematic relationship with the local landowner, or that the mill relied on the local supply of birch wood, and once this was depleted, it went out of operation.

Towards the end of the nineteenth century the demand for bobbins from the thread manufacturers dried up, since they increasingly brought their bobbin making in-house, buying Scottish birch wood for their own use and also importing higher quality birch wood from Scandinavia and North America. All the mills in this group had closed down by the early 1890s which can probably be attributed to the reduced demand for bobbins from the thread mills.

Bobbin Mills in the Highlands – established 1880s to 1930s

The defining characteristic of the bobbin mills in this final group was that they continued in operation well into the twentieth century. There is good primary documentary evidence for all 10 of the mills and five of them appeared on the second edition OS maps, though the exact location of the other five is unclear.

Most of these mills are known to have been wooden buildings and powered by steam, and they were almost certainly purpose built. Only one made use of an existing mill building, though rather than using the original water wheel, this mill was instead powered by diesel.

A few of the mills were in more built up areas (in Inverness, Forres and Pitlochry), and these were owned by the bobbin maker himself; the remaining mills were in rural settings and the owner of the mill was listed as the landowner, with the bobbin maker being a tenant. In addition to running their mill, these men also frequently worked as wood merchants and sawmillers, and both they and their workers often came from outside the immediate area.

These mills were all set up specifically to produce bobbins. Some of them initially supplying the Paisley thread mills in the late nineteenth century, but by the twentieth century producing bobbins for use in the Dundee jute mills and for export to the jute mills in India. In addition, some of the bobbin mills which operated during the twentieth century diversified into producing other wooden goods, including tent fittings, pit props, fence posts and chocks.

The main raw material used by these mills was birch wood, and evidence about how the bobbins were made is available from the recollections of past workers at several of the mills, as well as from the Cambus O'May mill in Aberdeenshire. From these recollections it is clear that only "rough-cut" bobbins were made by the rural bobbin mills in the twentieth century. Blocks of wood were sawn to size, a hole bored down the middle using a boring machine, and the rough shape of the bobbin created using a lathe. However, the mills did not go on to complete the production process. This takes place after the bobbins have been dried and involves turning them a second time to create the final shape of the bobbin, using a finishing lathe. Instead, the rough-cut bobbins were transported to the large bobbin manufacturers in Dundee, Aberdeen or Fife, for finishing and polishing, before being delivered to the jute mills in India.

The large bobbin manufacturers were evidently buying rough-cut bobbins from the rural bobbin mills, just as they were importing bobbin blocks from abroad. In the twentieth century, therefore, rural bobbin mills in the north of Scotland were supplying partially processed raw materials to the large bobbin manufacturers, rather than producing a high quality finished product directly for the textile mills.

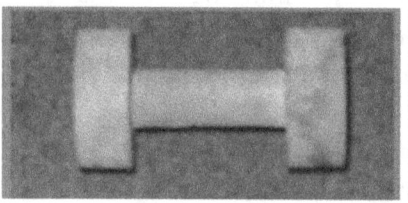 

Figure 2. Comparing a bobbin block imported from Sweden (left) and a rough-cut bobbin made at Contin Bobbin Mill (photographs A.G Highland and Alasdair Cameron)

Unfortunately, it is unclear whether this had always been the case throughout the nineteenth century, at least for some of the rural bobbin mills, or whether the earlier mills had produced finished bobbins and spools.

Some of the rural bobbin mills which operated during the twentieth century closed down after they were damaged or destroyed by fire, while others continued in operation until the early 1950s. They eventually closed largely as a result of the Indian Government's ban on the import of bobbins from Scotland in 1948 (Highland, 1988).

The impact of the north of Scotland's bobbin mills

While the bobbin making industry clearly had an enormous impact on the lives of some individuals and families, it is less clear how much of an impact it had on the communities where the mills were based, or indeed on the surrounding woodland.

The number of men and boys employed by the rural bobbin mills seems to have varied from a small handful, up to 30 or more workers. In some cases, the mills were staffed by family members, while in others there were considerable numbers of employees, including teenage apprentices. Particularly in the Highlands, many of the more specialist workers listed in the census, including wood turners and bobbin turners, came from outside the local area, (from Lanarkshire, Renfrewshire, Angus, Aberdeenshire or Perthshire), though the mills would probably also have provided employment for local sawyers and carters. Many of the mills only operated for a relatively short period of time, and some of the men who worked in them travelled around, often working at several different mills around the north of Scotland over the years. Hence, while the impact of a bobbin mill on a local community, including the impact on local employment opportunities, may have been considerable in some cases, in others it was probably minimal.

There is a lack of substantive information about the impact of bobbin mills on the local woodland in the north of Scotland, whether in the north east or in the Highlands. In the early and mid-nineteenth century the bobbin mills appear to have relied on local woodland. This continued to be the case for the rural mills, though the larger manufacturers increasingly relied on imported wood towards the end of the nineteenth century, reportedly due to its superior availability, quality and price. The limited information available suggests that rural bobbin mills might have used around 1,500 tons of birch wood each year which, with a yield of 10 tons, or around some 50 to 100 trees, per acre (Nisbet, 1912), would have involved clearing an area of 150 acres of birch trees annually. Yet there is little or no evidence of birch woodland being actively managed for bobbin making or of coppicing being used.

Contemporaneous reports do refer to the impact of bobbin making on the woodland, the beauty of Glenurquhart was reported to be '*materially impaired by the ruthless sacrifice of the greater part of its fine birch woods*' (Anderson, 1851), there was reported to be *'scarcely a birch tree of any size left standing in Rothiemurchus'* (Pedestrian, 1869) and at one time the consumption of birch wood for bobbin making was said to have threatened *"the practical deforestation of Scotland'* (Blair, 1907). Yet, in Deeside a report that *'notwithstanding the doings of the [bobbin] mill, the banks and braes still show a considerable growth of natural birch'* (Coutts, 1899), paints a much less dramatic picture. The impact the bobbin mills had on the local birch woodland evidently varied considerably and perhaps was sometimes exaggerated. Moreover, even where the impact was considerable, this would usually have been a short term effect, so long as natural regeneration was not inhibited by over-grazing.

For around 120 years there were bobbin mills scattered across the north of Scotland, making an important contribution to the Scottish textile industries by supplying them with bobbins. Indeed, bobbin making was a significant industry in its own right. Yet nowadays there is almost no trace of the bobbin mills which once operated, or the impact they had, and many people are unaware that this industry ever existed.

References

Anderson, G. & Anderson, P. (1851) *Guide to the Highlands and Islands of Scotland.* Adam and Charles Black, Edinburgh.

Blair, M. (1907) *The Paisley Thread Industry.* Alexander Gardner, Paisley.

Highland, A.G. (1988) *Gateside Mills: The Scottish Bobbin and Shuttle Trade In Its British And International Setting, 1860-1960.* unpublished PhD thesis, University of St Andrews, St Andrews.

Coutts, J. (1899) *Dictionary of Deeside.* The University Press, Aberdeen.

Nisbet, J. (1912) Utilisation of the existing woodland produce. *Transactions of the Scottish Arboricultural Society,* **Vol. XXVI**, 69-77.

'Pedestrian' (1869) The Highland Railway Line as a Sanatarium. *Inverness Courier*, Inverness.

Sharp, P. (1882) *Flax, Tow and Jute Spinning, a Handbook.* Dundee.

Somers, R. (1848), *Letters from the Highlands, or The Famine of 1847.* Simpkin Marshall and Co, London.

Wattle hurdles stacked to dry out, 1930s. Source: Ian D. Rotherham

Chapter 7. Tree Archaeology and Survey at Speech House and Brookways Ditch, the Forest of Dean, Gloucestershire

Andrew Hoaen and Helen Loney
University of Worcester

Abstract

This paper reports on a survey carried out over two seasons between 2015 and 2018 of Veteran Trees and their associated archaeology in the Forest of Dean. Funded by the Heritage Lottery Fund and supported by the Forestry Commission, the project aimed to inform and engage the local community with the historic record of trees within the Forest. Two areas were surveyed, the area around Brookways Ditch in 2015 and in 2018, the area around Speech House. In total, nearly 200 trees and around 25 archaeological monuments were surveyed. Around 80 people took part over the two survey seasons and a series of public engagements meant that the survey brought the attention of the trees to the wider public. The project used a survey day approach to ensure that tree locations were mapped as accurately as possible using differential GPS units and entered onto a GIS. The survey located elements of an older massive forest enclosure at Brookways ditch possibly part of the Great Inclosure of the seventeenth century, together with a tramroad. At Speech House, a large number of veteran hollies were surveyed. In conclusion, this approach to surveying trees using volunteers works well and has produced some interesting data which will benefit from future analysis.

Introduction

This survey was carried out by the Veteran Tree and Archaeology project, part of the Heritage Lottery Funded, Foresters' Forest, an investigation into the culture and natural history of the Forest of

Dean, Gloucestershire, in partnership with the Forestry Commission. A pilot was conducted in collaboration with Plantlife in the winter of 2015/2016, with the full project beginning in January 2018. The initial work looked at the area around Brookways Ditch (centered on SO623090), and Speech House, (centered on SO620121). The results from the survey at Brookways Ditch have been published in the Forest of Dean Local History Society's annual newsletter, Hoaen (2019). This paper will primarily discuss the preliminary findings of the first full survey season at Speech House, carried out in the winter of 2018.

The main aims of the project are to record the veteran and notable trees within defined areas of the Hundred of St. Briavels, to record any forest memorials or memorial trees and to employ a landscape archaeology approach, which attempts to bring together the record of the older trees with that of the archaeological and historical record. Equally important is the aim to connect the local people of the area with their forest history, by highlighting the survival of ancient, veteran and notable trees on the Forestry Commission estate. To this end, the project works with volunteers from the local community to record and locate trees of interest within the survey area. In addition, there are outreach efforts such as public talks, radio appearances and working with local groups such as poets and writers within the community.

Background

The pilot project at Brookways Ditch was used to develop procedures suitable for use by untrained volunteers (see methodology below). Brookways Ditch, like Speech House, is an area of waste (see map IX, Hart, 2005). It was thought that such areas would be more likely to contain unrecorded veteran and notable trees and archaeology, than the enclosed plantations. Brookways Ditch is a small steep sided valley approximately 1.5 km in length running from the village of Parkend to the former colliery site at New Fancy. Between the seventeenth and the beginning of the twentieth century the valley was part of a heavily industrialised landscape with mines and steel works, together with their attendant railways and tramroads.

The history and development of the area around Speech House is poorly understood. The Speech House itself is now a hotel but was originally built in the seventeenth century as a courthouse for administration of forest law and there is a date stone for 1676 present on the building (Hart, 2005). One question for the project is, are the present day inclosure boundaries a relatively recent feature or do they fossilise earlier boundaries?

The waste at Speech House is defined by the boundaries of several later enclosures which continue to be managed for timber extraction and their amenity value (Forestry Commission, 2006, 2008, 2014). Since 1983, part of the waste has been notified as a Site of Special Scientific Interest for its ancient woodland of oak and holly together with its rich epiphytic flora (English Nature, 1983). Archaeologically, the records in the Historic Environment Record (H.E.R.) relate to post medieval features such as gale stones, a crashed WW2 plane and other modern features. Unusually, Gloucestershire H.E.R. is one of the few H.E.Rs to record Veteran and Notable Trees within it, an example of good practice.

Tree Archaeology
The study of woods and their trees in the landscape developed as part of the environmental history movement e.g. Peterken & Game (1984), Rackham (1990), and Rotherham (2011). Archaeologists have been slow to adopt tree surveys as part of their toolbox for investigating landscapes despite calls by authors such as Bradley for the investigation of 'natural places' (2013). Despite the fact that archaeologists have tended to overlook trees as part of the historical and archaeological record (Hoaen, 2016), there is a renewed interest in the environment and approaches developed from the environmental humanities (e.g. sessions at the Landscape Archaeology conference Uppsalla in 2016). In particular, there appears to be a recent growing interest in 'tree archaeology' (ibid).

Fortunately, in terms of methodology previous work has been done by a number of writers on recording and interpreting trees in the landscape e.g. Barnes & Williamson (2011), Handley & Rotherham (2013) and English Nature (2000). It is to be hoped that recording ancient, veteran and notable trees may become a normal activity as part of wider efforts such as archaeological surveys of woodland, Historic Landscape Characterisation (England) and Historic Landuse Assessment (Scotland).

Previous work
There has been a limited amount of archaeological work carried out at Speech House and Brookways Ditch. The Forest estate was mapped by LIDAR as part of a National Monuments Programme exercise carried out in 2006 by English Heritage (Small and Stoertz, 2006). This was one of the first LIDAR based surveys of extensive woodland carried out in the UK. However, in the project study areas, few targets were identified and none ground-truthed. The survey as is standard archaeological practice did not consider the trees and vegetation as monuments or elements of the historic environment of the Forest of Dean.

The older and more notable oaks within the area were partially mapped by the Forestry Commission at the end of the twentieth century. As part of the pilot project, some of the hollies were mapped by Brian Jones and were added to the Ancient tree inventory website (2018). In addition, Ian Standing has added several trees to the H.E.R. (1986, 1987 and 2016).

There is now a proliferation of information registers for veteran and ancient trees in the Forest of Dean. The main source of baseline information for this project derives from the Forestry Commission's register of Trees of Special Interest, which is a very important resource. However, much of this data was collected in the 1980's and 1990's and has poor spatial control. The database also contains a large number of records collected through citizen science, which has poor spatial control and lacks information about species or girth. There has been a concentration on particular species with oak and other canopy trees significantly over-represented. While this register is a valuable starting point and tool, it should be used cautiously as it may not be representative of the Forest estate as a whole. To this must be added records held by Gloucester Council's H.E.R, those of the Ancient Tree Inventory, and the Wye valley AONB veteran tree survey. How these records are to be reconciled is a problem beyond the capacity of the current project.

Methodology

The survey aimed to use volunteers for data collection. Initially, it was decided not to use a 'citizen science' approach to the data collection because of the heavily wooded nature of the landscape and the issues in the pilot project with ground-truthing. The hope is however that at the end of the project a trained cohort of people will be able to contribute their findings to the Ancient Tree Inventory.

In order to maintain survey control, all data used by the project was collected during five sessions between January and May 2018, with a further session carried out with a group of local poets to provide an alternative perspective on the woodlands at Speech House. Although we had a core group of about six volunteers each survey would usually comprise a mix of backgrounds from absolute beginners to experienced naturalists. Consequently, an approach was developed from the pilot project which aimed to allow all participants to engage successfully with the survey methodology. Each group of volunteers, which ranged from around seven to fifteen, was organised into groups, within each group was an experienced individual to help any new recruits. Each group was assigned a defined area to survey.

Trees were recorded using a variation of a tree survey form based on that used by the Woodland Trust provided by Brian Jones a local veteran tree checker. Each tree was located using a handheld differential Trimble (Geo 7x); location data was subsequently reprocessed and corrected before entering into a GIS (digital mapping software). Each tree was given a unique number and a photographic record created. In order to determine whether the tree was ancient, veteran or notable characteristics derived from guides such those in English Nature (2000) and Handley & Rotherham (2013) were used. In practice, distinguishing between ancient and veteran status for the hollies was a complex task for the volunteers and so it was decided to simplify the termination, using the term veteran for both ancient and veteran hollies. Once a better understanding of the range of variation within the holly population at Speech House has been achieved then a simple metric such as girth may be utilised to record this difference.

The recording of the memorials in the Forest used a standardised memorial recording form. Each memorial and its associated tree or woodland was located using the GPS and the memorial photographed. Archaeological surface finds such as bottles and pottery from boar disturbed middens were collected and their location recorded with a note in the GPS. Similarly, the location of any "humps and bumps" of archaeological interest were noted in the GPS for subsequent recording.

Results

Brookways Ditch
Survey during the winter of 2015-16 and subsequent ground truthing demonstrated that a landscape archaeological/history approach would work in the Forest of Dean (Hoaen, in press). Using a combination of LIDAR, ground-truthing and volunteer survey the project recorded twenty veteran and notable trees within the valley of the Brookways Ditch (Table 1, Figure 1). We also recorded seven new archaeological features including a fragment of the 'Great inclosure' of the eighteenth century, and an early nineteenth century tramroad (Figure 1).

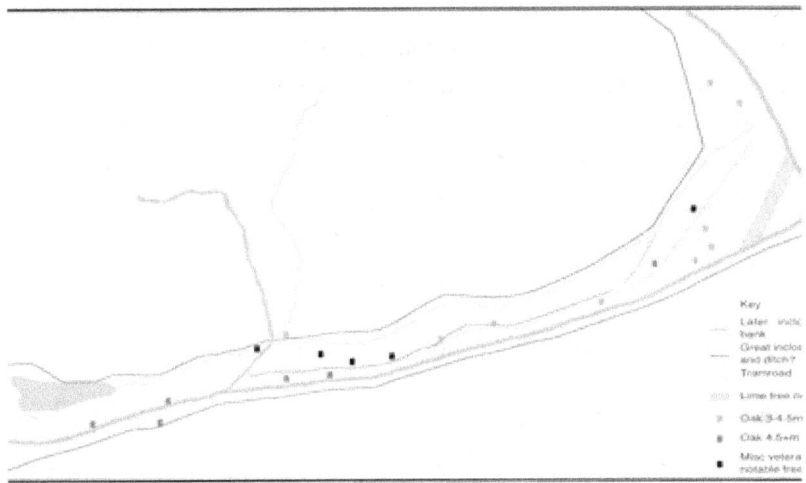

Figure 1. Veteran and Notable trees and main archaeological features at Brookways Ditch

Table 1. Summary of veteran and notable Trees at Brookways Ditch

Species	Count	Girth range	Veteran/ Ancient/ Notable/ form
Oak	14	3.07 – 5.40 m	veteran/ notable all maidens except for a single pollard
Beech	3	3.5-6 m	notable/ two maidens, one bundle with graffiti
Alder	1	4m	notable/ coppice
Holly	1	2.08 m	veteran/ coppice
Goat Willow	1	2.30 m	notable/ maiden

Speech House

The project managed to recruit nearly forty participants over the five survey days. The survey recorded a total of 136 veteran and notable trees dominated by hollies (n = 88) and oaks (n = 39) with minor species making up the remainder (Figure 2, Table 2).

The project also recorded ten memorials and their associated trees (Table 3); the archaeological features identified will be discussed in a future paper. As mentioned previously, earlier work focussed on the oaks which are concentrated in an area of 'waste' to the south and west of Speech House. This area is thought by the Forestry Commission to have a planting date of c.1745 whilst the main area of the SSSI to the north of Speech House road is thought to be later c.1812 (Williams, pers. comm.). What is noticeable is that old oaks and hollies are both defined by subsequent late nineteenth and early twentieth century inclosure boundaries. The area south of Speech House road has only partially been surveyed for hollies so the record here is preliminary; the area north of Speech House road has been surveyed completely up to the car park.

Table 2. Summary of veteran and notable trees at Speech House

Species	Count	Girth Range (m)	Veteran/Ancient/ Notable/ form
Oak	39	0.5-6.10	veteran n = 4, notable n = 35 all maidens
Holly	88	0.91-3.84	veteran n = 88, maiden n = 17, pollard n = 40, coppice n = 19
Beech	1	7.61	notable/ bundle
Hazel	1	4.60	notable/ coppice
Crab apple	2	0.70 - 1.90	veteran, notable/ maiden
Birch	1	0.75	notable/ maiden
Hawthorn	1	2.62	veteran/ maiden
Willow	1	3.80	notable/ pollard
Yew	1	4.10	notable/ maiden

South of Speech House Road

The largest of the oaks, the Verderers oak, was dedicated in a ceremony in 1991 and is thought to be c. 300 to 350 years old (Hart, 2005 p.135) with a girth of 7.03 m, dbh of 2.24 m. Prior surveys had located sixty oaks south of Speech House road with veteran or notable status. These included the Pansager oak with a girth of 3.34 m, planted in 1861, and the Philip oak with a girth of 1.90 m, planted in 1957. No hollies had previously been recorded here. The current survey did not include oaks, assuming that all the relevant specimens had been collected by earlier surveys. Sixteen hollies have been located in this area.

The project recorded three memorials commemorating the visits of royalty to the Forest in 1861 and 1957 and a separate plaque naming the 'Verderers oak'. In addition, during the pilot project a charcoal burner's platform was identified, along with a relict field system that had been truncated by the playing fields of the Forest School, and several cairns.

Figure 2. 1:2000 scale map of the veteran and notable hollies (red triangle) and oaks (green circles) at Speech House

North of Speech House Road

This is where the main work of the season's project was carried out. Seventy-two veteran and notable hollies were recorded, including the 'champion holly' for Gloucestershire at 3.90 m. Many of these hollies show repeated episodes of management in various ways followed by resurgence and regeneration to produce a range of forms. The trees have also undergone phoenix regeneration and layering after falling; some have suckered from the base of a rotten trunk to create rings or partial rings of new growth. Several of the hollies have been graffitied with a possible date of 1919 on one.

Table 3. Memorials at Speech House

Number	Grid ref (SO)	Name/date	Associated tree(s)	Material(s)
1	61945/12235	Reinclosure of Beechenhurst, Kensley Ridge and Serridge 1896	Yew grove	Cast Iron and green paint
2	61944/12235	Edward VII coronation 1902	Yew grove	Cast Iron and green paint
3	61985/12082	Prince Philip, Duke of Edinburgh 1957	Oak	Aluminium plaque on stalk
4	61980/12103	Albert Prince Consort- pansanger oak 1861	Oak	Stone on Plinth
5	61983/12089	Queen Elizabeth II 1957	Oak	Aluminium plaque on stalk
6	62011/12172	Countess of Wessex 2014	Oak	Metal plaque on Stone
7	62011/12172	HRH Earl of Wessex 2014	Oak	Metal plaque on Stone
8	620005/12168	Countess of Wessex and HRH Earl of Wessex 2014, renovation of obelix	n/a	Metal plaque on Stone
9	61692/11948	Sanzen-Baker oak 1968- since removed	Oak	Metal plaque on Stone
10	61918/11985	Verderers Oak (n.d. but erected in 1991)	Oak	Wooden Sign

Twenty notable and veteran oaks were recorded in this area the largest was 5.85 m in girth the smallest included two new notable oaks planted in memory of the visits of the Earl and Countess of Wessex in 2014 at *c.* 0.1 m. Fourteen of these oaks are located along a fragmented avenue which runs from opposite the Speech

House hotel for approximately 100 m. The variation of girth size along this avenue suggests that trees have been replaced as they have fallen.

Six memorials were recorded during the survey of the area (Table 3). Two, of particular interest, are just outside the area of waste in New Beechenhurst inclosure. One commemorates the reinclosure of 1896, the other the coronation of Edward the Seventh. Both memorials are in specially planted yew groves.

Archaeologically, in addition to the features recorded by the H.E.R., the project identified a series of shafts, midden spreads, trackways and footings associated with the industrial use of the area. One notable feature was a spring that had been landscaped to fall into a large rectangular pool, though not noted on older maps it does not appear to be a modern development.

Discussion

Whilst both sites have their own unique features, both Brookways Ditch and Speech House show the potential of areas of forest waste for locating new archaeological sites and veteran and ancient trees within the Forest estate. They share similarities in their form, the adjacent inclosure boundaries giving the entrances a funnel shape before opening up into long linear features between more formally inclosed areas. Research into the patterns of inclosure are still in their infancy in the Forest of Dean, however, there is a suggestion from the morphology of the inclosure boundaries and the survival of ancient hollies and veteran oaks, that some areas of waste such as the valley of the Brookways Ditch and Speech House may represent areas of permanent or semi-permanent wood-pasture and common land outside the inclosure system as it developed over the past 300 years or so. It may be argued, however, that we can consider that the whole of the Forest estate operated for long periods as common land and as such formally designated commons or waste were not required. However, during periods of planting it is clear that inclosures were created and maintained for periods of up to ten or fifteen years (Hart, 1966). It is reasonable therefore to assume that the broad strips of waste along major routeways represented places where commoners could continue to graze their animals during the closure of the forest. These were also areas of natural regeneration (Hart, 1966) and this may explain the survival of large veteran trees and ancient understorey trees in these areas.

Both sites demonstrate low species diversity in the survival of veteran trees. Oak dominates at Brookways Ditch with only three other species represented, holly and oak are both present in large numbers at Speech House with seven mostly notable species represented (Table 2). The low numbers of beech and absence of sweet chestnut veterans (both common trees in the Forest) at these locations suggests an element of selection either due to edaphic conditions at the site or management.

The inclosures at both Brookways Ditch and Speech House appear to represent important ecological boundaries. They define the areas of veteran trees and suggest that the surrounding pre-existing woodlands were cleared at the time of their construction and the later planting of the adjacent enclosures. The patterns of growth of the oaks are interesting because all were grown as maidens within a closed canopy presumably to supply large timbers for construction, or due to natural regeneration. The hollies in contrast are dominated by pollards (n = 40) with about equal numbers of maidens (n = 17) and coppice stools (n = 19). All the pollards and coppices have been left unmanaged for many years and have been allowed to regrow. There are now a large number of suckers growing around many of these hollies. It is probable that the Foot-and-Mouth outbreak in 2001 and the collapse of the sheep population have led to their regeneration.

The size of trees and their management, coupled with the historic records of planting, suggest that the trees and their management cover at least the past 200 to 300 years. It is hoped that future analyses will enable the identification of patterns of management, regeneration and resurgence in the holly population. There are two linear features within the oak population, one is an oak avenue by Speech House road, and the other needs further investigation. There are also two linear holly features, one is the remains of a hedge possibly enclosing an area of wood-pasture, and the other also requires more investigation.

The ten memorials (Table 3) chiefly commemorate members of the royal family and their visits to the district (n = 7). Interestingly, the oldest manages to combine memorials to a historically significant tree and two members of the royal family commemorating the planting of an oak by Prince Albert in 1861. This tree, the Pansager oak, is the offspring of a tree thought to have been planted by Queen Elizabeth the First in Pansager Park. The original oak is still alive (Chilterns AONB, 2018). The remaining memorials are to the Forest itself and the Foresters who have worked there, including a single tree dedicated as the Verderers Oak.

Conclusion and Future work

This project is still at an early phase; however, it is clear that a study of trees within a woodland has much to tell us about the use of that wood over the past 200 to 300 years and possibly longer. A study of the upstanding archaeology can tell us the structure and pattern of inclosure, a study of the trees within and without those inclosures informs us about the management and use of the Forest. The project has a further four seasons of funding and it is hoped to complete the survey of Speech House next winter, before moving on to another part of the Forest. None of this work is possible without the contribution of the local community who are willing to work in poor conditions to better understand and conserve 'their' forest.

Acknowledgements

Thanks to the Heritage Lottery Fund, The Forestry Commission and the University of Worcester, but mainly to the volunteers who make this project possible.

Bibliography

Barnes, G. and Williamson, T. (2011) *Ancient Trees in the Landscape: Norfolk's Arboreal Heritage.* Oxbow Books, Oxford.

Bradley, R. (2013) *An archaeology of natural places,* Routledge, Abingdon.

Chilterns AONB (2018) *The Pansager Oak.* https://www.chilternsaonb.org/ccbmaps/489/137/panshanger-great-oak.html

English Heritage (2006) *Gloucestershire, Forest of Dean NMP.* In: Small, F. & Stoertz, C. (eds). Research Department Report Series No. 28/2006, English Heritage, Swindon.

English Nature (1983) *Speech House Oaks,* SSSI citation, https://designatedsites.naturalengland.org.uk/PDFsForWeb/Citation/1002752.pdf.

English Nature (2000) *A Guide to Veteran Tree Management.* English Nature, London

Forestry Commission (England) (2006) *Forest of Dean Crabtree Hill Forest Design Plan.* unpublished Report.

Forestry Commission (England) (2008) *Forest of Dean Middleridge Forest Design Plan.* unpublished Report.

Forestry Commission (England) (2014) *Forest of Dean Nagshead and Russells Forest Design Plan.* unpublished Report.

Handley, C. & Rotherham, I.D. (2013) *Shadow Woods and Ghosts: A Survey Guide.* Wildtrack Publishing, Sheffield.

Hart, C.E. (2005) *The Forest of Dean: New History, 1550-1818,* Alan Sutton Publishing, Stroud.

Hoaen, A. (2019) Interim report on the Forester's Forest Veteran Tree and Archaeology Project at Brookways Ditch, near Parkend. *New Regard,* **33**.

Hoaen, A. (2016) *The Hidden Heritage of Veteran Trees and ancient woods: A pilot project in the Forest of Dean.* unpublished conference paper, https://hiddenheritage2016.wordpress.com/andrew-hoaen-hidden-heritage-of-veteran-trees-and-ancient-woods-a-pilot-project-in-the-forest-of-dean/.

Peterken, G.F. & Game, M. (1984) Historical factors affecting the number and distribution of vascular plant species in the woodlands of central Lincolnshire. *The Journal of Ecology*, **72**, 155-182.

Rackham, O. (1990) Trees and woodland in the British landscape. 2nd edition, JM Dent & Sons Ltd, London.

Rotherham, I.D. (2011) A landscape history approach to the assessment of ancient woodlands. In: Erwin B. Wallace (ed.) *Woodlands: Ecology, Management and Conservation,* 161-184, Nova Science Publishers, Inc., New York.

Standing, I.J. (1986) Ancient & notable trees in and around Dean. *New Regard,* **2**, 3-20.

Standing, I.J. (1987) Ancient & notable trees in and around Dean, part 2. *New Regard*, **3**, 25-34.

Standing, I.J. (2017) Interesting and notable trees of Dean; thirty years on. Part 1. The oaks. *New Regard,* **31**, 41-51.

Woodland Trust (2018) *Ancient Tree Inventory.* https://ati.woodlandtrust.org.uk/.

Woodland Timber Stack (IDR)

Chapter 8. Marker and Marked Trees in Anglo-Saxon England and Continuing Tradition

Della Hooke
University of Birmingham

Abstract

Trees are found in Anglo-Saxon England marking assembly points and acting as landmarks upon the boundaries of estates. It is debatable whether any of these trees were actually marked in any way but a small number seem to have been regarded as 'crucifix trees', either marked with a cross or hung with a crucifix, perhaps offering protection against evil. Tree worship was no longer tolerated in what was now a Christian country but trees acquired a new role, some as symbols of resurrection and immortality, and others seen as strengthening the healing power of 'holy' wells. Special trees continued to be decorated in medieval times, a tradition which still lingers.

Introduction

Trees were one of the commonest kinds of feature used as landmarks in describing the boundaries of estates in early medieval England. Others marked assembly points, some the meeting places of the territorial units known as hundreds, even giving their name to some of the hundreds themselves. Many other trees were actually commemorated in local place-names, many of which have endured to the present day. It is not known whether many of these trees were physically marked in any way but there are indications that at least some of them may have been, as will be shown below.

Trees at assembly points

In pre-Christian times in parts of Europe certain trees appear to have stood at tribal meeting places or marked the inauguration sites of kings. Some were indeed regarded as 'sacred'. Their role as markers of important assembly may have been deliberately echoed in the site chosen for the meeting between St Augustine and the British bishops in AD 603 which took place, according to Bede, at an oak which stood on the border between the kingdom of the Hwicce and that of the West Saxons (Bede II, 2: Sherley-Price, 1968, 100-1). The aim of the meeting was to encourage unity within the Catholic Church and also to try to determine the date of Easter; one site that has been suggested for this is a place called The Oak in Down Ampney on the Wiltshire border.

Trees frequently figured in the names of the early hundreds, the basic units of local governance, clearly referring to the place where the assembly was held. In early hundred-names, the thorn was, perhaps surprisingly, the most frequent species named (Hooke, 2010, 170, table 2) but not all were the relatively insignificant bushes usually seen today – a huge thorn-tree noted as growing from 'an enormous old stump' in a hedgerow near Down House on the brow of Horethorne Down in Horethorne, Somerset, in 1939, may itself have been a descendant of the tree that gave its name to the hundred (Anderson, 1939, 56-8). The ash was the next commonest species noted but the species is not always noted – Longtree Hundred in Gloucestershire, for instance, so-named in 1086, took its name from a tall tree which must have stood at a high point on Chavenage Down on the road leading from Tetbury to Avening, a convenient spot for the hundred court to assemble. A number of hundred tree names bear witness to particular people who must have held land or played a significant role locally: names such as Doddingtree Hundred in Worcestershire 'Dudda's tree' or Grumbald's Ash Hundred in Gloucestershire 'Grimbald's ash', but it can now rarely be known who these individuals were – their stories are lost and the trees long gone. The place-names are their only legacy.

Boundary landmarks
Larger territories began to fragment in the early medieval period as estates were granted or leased out to lesser lords (Hooke, 1998, pp. 62-83). Many of those receiving them were probably

anxious to record the transaction but it is mainly church records that survive. One method of ensuring the integrity of an estate was to record its boundaries in case future disputes should arise, a practice that increased in the later seventh century. It seems that the compilation of a written document replaced an earlier tradition of laying a sod from the land concerned upon the holy alter before witnesses (Earle, 1888, xv-xvi, 49-51). At first only a few landmarks at cardinal points along an estate boundary might be given but in time the bounds become increasingly detailed, referring to landmarks that included both natural and man-made features (Hooke, 1998, 84-102). Natural features might include streams and rivers or clearly defined topographical features such as valleys or hill spurs; man-made ones: roads, archaeological features or even settlements established close by, together with related land use. Convenient markers such as trees or stones were also often chosen. There is one record showing how such a clause could help to define a contested boundary: in AD 896 it is recorded that the bishop of Worcester claimed that he had been dispossessed of most of the woodland belonging to his estate at Woodchester, an estate close to the Cotswold escarpment in what is now Gloucestershire. He ordered his yeoman, Ecglaf, to ride the boundary of the estate with the citizens' chaplain, Wulfhun, 'and he showed him all the bounds as he read to him out of the old books, according as King Æthelbald had originally defined and granted it' (Sawyer, 1968, S 103, S 1441; Birch, 1885–99, B 164, B 574). In later times the church would organise regular perambulations of boundaries during Rogation Week before Ascension Day but these are not recorded before the medieval period; in the early medieval period such rites, regulated in England in AD 747, entailed processing around the fields to bless the growing crops (Hutton, 1996, 277-8). 'Gospel' oaks often marked the spot at which the parishioners and churchmen would pause while 'beating the bounds' on Rogation Days in order for blessings to be made and appropriate liturgies to be read out.

The landmarks noted in the two Woodchester charters quoted above were in fact four *lēah* features, probably individual areas of wood-pasture, plus one hill or barrow and a coomb; the earlier charter also adds a second coomb, named as *havoc cumb* 'hawk coombe', a *burh* or 'fort' named as *haeslburg*, and the 'Welsh way'. Often, however, single trees were used as boundary landmarks. Of these, the tree most often referred to was the thorn, *Crataegus* sp.; it is also the commonest species met in place-names (Hooke, 2010, 202, table 3). Rapidly regenerating on boundaries or at the edges of uncultivated ground, such thorn-trees are unlikely to have been outstandingly impressive specimens but in open cultivated countryside may have been selected as the most obvious feature in the immediate landscape (Figure 1). The second commonest tree recorded in both sources together was the ash, *Fraxinus excelsior*, a tree also ubiquitous throughout the English countryside. Third was the oak, especially the variety *Quercus robur*, which is usually a far more distinctive species than the other native oak *Quercus petraea*, the sessile oak, and might possess a grandeur that inevitably attracted attention (Figure 2). Few trees recorded in pre-Conquest charters nearly 1,000 years ago can be expected to survive today – the King's Yew, on the boundary of Tidenham in Gloucestershire (Figure 3), may just be the tree that gave its name to the 'yew valley' noted in a tenth-century charter (Sawyer, 1968, S 610).

Figure 1. A thorn-tree, *Crataegus monogyna*, overlooking the Vale of Evesham © Della Hooke

Figure 2. An oak-tree, *Quercus robur*, in Sutton Park near Birmingham © Della Hooke

Sometimes individual trees are more fully described, although not necessarily to aid recognition. Thus, one meets a *feger ok* 'fair, beautiful oak' and *ða hwitan biricean* 'the white birch'. On other occasions the tree singled out is described seemingly so that it might be recognised again by its form or character: such as the *coppedan ac* 'copped or ?pollarded oak', the *niþer bogenan ac* 'bent-down oak', another oak described as *ifihtan* 'ivy-covered, *ða woche sæle* and *þære wohgan apeldran*, 'the twisted or crooked sallow' and 'the twisted or crooked apple-tree', *þan langan þorne* 'the tall thorn-tree', or another thorn, *ðære ænlypigan þorn* 'the solitary thorn'. One Long Itchington (Warwickshire) boundary clause specified *þa hehan æc on wulluht grafe middum* 'the tall oak-tree in the middle of *wulluht* grove', and at Bishops Cleeve (Gloucestershire), *wata cumb, þer stondað apeltreo 7mapeltreo togædere gewæxan* 'Wat's coomb where stands the apple-tree and maple-tree grown together' (Hooke, 2010, 178-81). Sometimes trees were associated with a personal name, probably that of a local land holder – many such trees stood in prominent positions where a boundary was crossing a routeway. Figure 4 shows a typical boundary clause, that of part of the Berkshire Blewbury estate in AD 944 (for 942) (S 496; Kelly, 2000, no. 36,

148-54; Gelling 1976, 758-61). Here, on the eastern edge of the Berkshire Downs, no fewer than five thorn-trees are noted along the eastern boundary of Aston Tirrold, probably growing at the edge of cultivated land.

Figure 3. The King's Yew, Tidenham, Gloucestershire © Della Hooke

Marked trees

Several trees were indeed named in boundary clauses as 'mark or 'boundary trees' (Old English *mearc* 'mark, boundary'; and the verb *ge-mearcian* 'to mark', 'to fix the bounds or limits of a place'). These include *þone greatan mearc beam* 'the great mark/boundary tree' at East Meon etc, and a *mearc þorn* at Poolhampton, Overton, both in Hampshire (S 811; S 465, S 613), and the *mearc becean* at Bexhill in Sussex, named on the boundary of its appurtenant estate at Barnhorne as *þa ealdan mearce becan þe stent on east healfe þare rode* 'the old mark/boundary beech which stands on the east side of the clearing' (S 108; Hooke 2010, 176). Such trees were not, however, necessarily marked rather than just being known as boundary landmarks, hence as 'marking trees'. There are, however, a small number of other references to *gemearcodan* or 'marked' trees, using the past participle of the Old English verb, suggesting that the trees concerned were indeed marked in some way. Thus one encounters: *on þan merkeden ok* at Mells, Somerset; *to ðaere ge mearcodan æc æt aleburnan* at Ecchinswell, Hants, both to 'the marked oak-tree'; *on ða gemearcodan lindan* 'to the marked linden or lime tree' at Horton, Dorset; and *to ðam gemearceden stocce* 'to the marked stump' at *Loceresleage*, Hendon in Kingsbury, Middlesex (S 481; S 412; S 969; S 645).

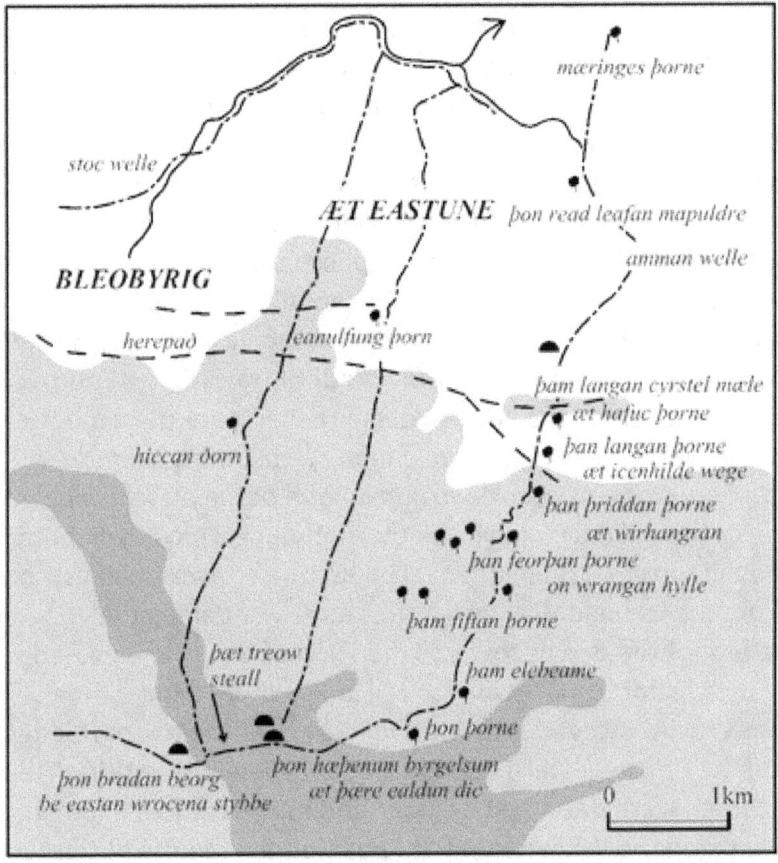

Figure 4. The boundary clause of Aston Tirrold and Aston Upthorpe, Berkshire, estates attached to Blewbury in AD 942 (from Hooke 2010, 180, figure 14) © Della Hooke

It is possible that even in these examples the verb was being used in the sense of 'to mark a boundary' but a stronger case can be made for another group of boundary trees. These were described in boundary clauses as 'cross' or 'crucifix' trees (OE *cristel-mæl*) and they must have been either marked with a cross, perhaps cut into the bark, or else they carried a Christian crucifix (one incorporating an image of Christ). References to crosses/crucifixes alone are more common and may have been actual crosses rather than marked trees, but neither are common: only sixteen are recorded in this source of evidence. One charter place-name reference, *Cristemalford* (S 466), gave rise to the parish name Christian Malford in Wiltshire and a small number of others have been noted as later recorded minor place-names, but only three of the early recordings seem to describe such features as marked or hung on trees. As Blair notes, a *cristel mælbeam* at Hawkridge in Bucklebury, Berks, recorded in charter-bounds of 956 (S 607), 'was presumably a tree, pillar, or post carved into the form of a crucifix, or with a crucifix attached to it' (Blair, 2013, 187), arguing that the term *bēam* was used for a special tree. The alleged grant to Abingdon Abbey was of an area of woodland in the north of the parish and the *christen mælbeam* may have stood beside a routeway near the north-western corner of Hawkridge Wood, possibly at a crossroads. In the Berkshire Blewbury charter noted above, one reference is *to þam langan cyrstel mœle œt hafuc þorne, þonne of hafuc þorne to þan langan þorne œt ichenilde wege* 'to the tall crucifix at hawk thorn, thence from hawk thorn to the tall thorn at Icknield Way' (S 496), the crucifix obviously not far from the Icknield Way which runs east–west along the edge/foot of the downs towards the Thames valley and passed close by a hillfort on Blewburton Hill in Blewbury (Figure 4); a second crucifix stood beside another way near the top of Hadden Hill on the north-western boundary of the Blewbury estate. A few other trees were described as 'holy' and may have fallen into a similar category. With most of the population illiterate at this time it is likely that any marks upon trees would have been simple symbols rather than letters.

Christian crosses, in general, however, seem but rarely to have been deliberately planted upon estate boundaries (Blair, 2005,

478-80) as they are relatively rare in boundary clauses and may therefore have implied some special circumstances. All such references appear in documents known to post-date the mid-tenth century (a few appear in documents claiming to be earlier but these are all known to be spurious: S 60, S 201). It may be relevant that the tenth century was a period when the Church was especially concerned to eradicate what it perceived as heathen practices, which perhaps may have been invigorated by an influx of non-Christian Danes (Bethurum, 1957, 319; Whitelock, 1965, 226). The 'crucifix trees' associated with a particular tree species in boundary clauses are also usually oaks, the oak one of the most impressive and symbolic of trees (Hooke, 2010; 2013a, 232-4).

Two of the oaks described in this way stood in Worcestershire, two beside roads leading towards Tardebigge, a high point overlooking the source of a west-flowing stream where a Christian church was to be built. One of these, a *cyrstel mæl ac* 'crucifix oak' stood on the eastern boundary of the nearby estate of Stoke Prior, and the other, again referred to as the *cristel mæl ac*, on the eastern boundary of Tardebigge itself (S 60, S 1598; Hooke, 1990, 65-9, 403-7).

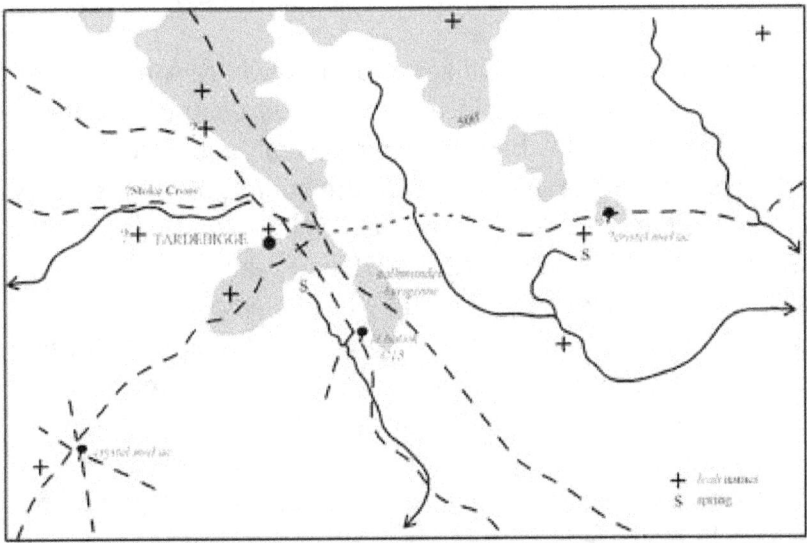

Figure 5. Routeways approaching Tardebigge church, north Worcestershire, with items noted in boundary clauses and place-names © Della Hooke

As if this was not enough, a place-name *le haliok* 'the holy oak', later Holyoake's Farm, is recorded in 1255 beside another trackway approaching from the south (Mawer & Stenton, 1927, 364) (Figure 5). The name of Tardebigge has recently been interpreted as of British derivation meaning 'height of the magpie', which in modern Welsh is *Ardd-y-Bigg* (Breeze, 2006, 75-6). Whatever significance the magpie had at this date is unknown but in later times it was regularly seen throughout north-western Europe as a bird of augury and divination, a practice especially condemned by the Church at this time. In Sweden it was even believed that sorcerers might take the form of magpies on Walpurgis Night (a traditional spring festival on 30 April or 1 May) or, throughout Scandinavia, that witches might take the form of magpies or use them as transport, its name *scadi* denoting a sense of loss or evil there and in Germany (Nozedar, 2006, 249). The writings of Wulfstan Lupus, archbishop of York and bishop of Worcester after 1002, preach directly in his *Homilies* against witchcraft and superstition: 'regard neither enchanters nor augeries, nor divinations nor witchcraft; and worship neither springs nor any woodland tree, because all idols are the delusions of the devil' ('Sermo de Baptismate', lines 165-8: Bethurum, 1957, 184). Significantly, the church at Tardebigge was later to be dedicated to St Bartholomew, 'the caster-out of devils'.

Perhaps other recorded crucifixes also stood where some heathen activity had taken place but these were not necessarily marked trees. They may have been crosses raised beside routeways such as the ones noted on the bounds of the Blewbury estate. A further crucifix stood beside a highway on the boundary of Grimley, Worcs, in 961 x 972 (S 1370 and again in a spurious charter S 201; Hooke, 1990, 115-18) where the bounds run *ondlong þæs hearpoðes to þæm criste mæle* 'along the highway to the crucifix'. This stood beside a routeway leading towards a prehistoric or Roman enclosure; the place-name here means 'Grim's Wood', Grim being a nick-name for the Teutonic god Wōden often associated with unexplained earthworks (the part-Norman church here is, interestingly, also dedicated to St Bartholomew). In both cases it is not improbable that a heathen shrine had formerly stood within the enclosures. Of all the crucifixes noted, at least half certainly stood beside routeways. Roadside shrines are, of course, common in many parts of Europe but in England one is reminded of the medieval stone crosses that marked (and still survive) on the eastern and western bounds of the Forest of Feckenham in Worcestershire; forests again often perceived as places of danger.

It is known, too, that illicit rites continued in such locations as crossroads, fords or high points in early medieval Europe (Blair, 2005, 480-1). Another 'holy oak' is recorded as a place-name Holyoaks in Stockerston, Leics, recorded as *Haliach* in 1086, in a region of Danish influence. Close by in the nearby parish of Ayston in Rutland was a grove or wood sacred to the god Þunor (Hooke, 2013a, 232). Yet another charter boundary of Chetwode & Hillesden, Bucks, began *ærest on ða halgan æc* 'first to the holy oak' (S 544). Some of these trees described as 'holy' may have been similarly marked to the 'crucifix oaks'. A landmark referred to as *ðan halgan æsce*, the 'holy ash' noted on the bounds of Taunton estates, allegedly in *c.* AD 854 and preserved in a twelfth-century document, is not, however, likely to have been a contender. This tree is alternatively described as *quondam fraxinum quem imperiti sacrum vocant* 'an ash-tree which the ignorant call holy' and may represent a genuine survival of pagan tradition (S 311; Turner, 1953; Hooke, 2010, 50; 2013a, 232).

In the early days of the conversion, attempts were made to convert pagan shrines into Christian foci of worship but attitudes were later to harden. Trees had played a significant role in pagan belief and the Christian church was increasingly anxious to discourage the practice of making votive offerings 'to trees, or to springs, or to stones, or to enclosures' (as in the Penitentials ascribed to Archbishop Theodore of York; also in Ælfric's translation of Augustine's homily 'On Augeries'), or worship at wells, trees and stones (the canons of Edgar), especially following the eleventh-century reforms of the Catholic Church (see Hooke, 2010, 31-4). However, the above examples seem to suggest that trees themselves continued to have a role to play in the early medieval period in England within a Christian context. The Church appears to have been marking certain trees in this special way, not to encourage what it saw as a devilish superstition but to protect travellers and others from evil.

Continuing tradition

Sometimes, throughout Europe, shrines dedicated to Christian saints have remained associated with trees – such as that overshadowing the shrine of St Hubertus at Sieldliska, Poland – (Figure 6), much as in the same way that 'holy' wells may also be overshadowed by a particular tree but their association with a saint, like the springs involved, has often sanctified their role. These trees are not marked in any permanent way but their association with a 'holy' well or spring is often seen to strengthen the healing powers of the spring water, again a belief often mirrored in pre-Christian cults (Ó hÓgáin, 1999, 214). The yew tree, widely planted in churchyards, may have been a symbol of resurrection and immortality but was also believed to offer protection against evil influences, and one such old tree, over seven metres in girth, spreads its branches over such a holy well in the churchyard at Hope Bagot in Shropshire. Often, however, it is the ash, long associated with healing, that is found in such an association, while ash, thorn, rowan, oak and holly may also be other trees involved in such a tradition (Hooke, 2010, 105-6).

Indeed, many such trees are today again 'marked' by the tradition of hanging upon them shreds of cloth to seek health or accompany votive offerings (Jones, 1992, 94-5), such as those shown here at Knowlton Rings, Dorset, where they hang upon two 'wishing' yews standing upon the fringes of a late Neolithic henge which became the site for a later twelfth-century Norman church, or on the trees around St Kenelm's holy well at Clent in Worcestershire, the reputed site of the murder of an Anglo-Saxon 'boy-king' (the spring is not, however, on its original site which was below the present church) (Figures 7a and b).

Figure 6. Tree beside the shrine of St Hubertus at Sieldliska, Poland © Della Hooke

Figure 7a. The 'Wishing Yews' at Knowlton Rings, Dorset © Della Hooke

Figure 7b. Trees above St Kenelm's Well, Clent, Worcestershire © Della Hooke

Symbolic 'trees' festooned with ribbons, which may have replaced an earlier practice of felling a real tree, formed part of the familiar tradition of May-Pole Dancing on village greens which goes back at least to the fourteenth century (Hutton, 1996, 233). Greenery from the surrounding woods would also be brought in, to deck streets and houses. Decorating local trees survives in a number of local traditions. At Aston-in-Clun in Shropshire the Arbor Tree is a black poplar, a replacement for an older tree, which is hung with flags on or about Oak Apple Day, 29th May. This tradition may have begun as a celebration of a local marriage as late as the eighteenth century but may draw upon older ideas of fertility rituals and trysting trees (Morton 1986, 66-70) and marriages performed beneath trees were only banned in Cromwell's time (Hooke, 2013b, 114-16).

Even if possible actual marks on trees have only rarely been significant in recognising the stories associated with these early references to trees, place-names may continue the legacy of storytelling: later place-names may provide more clues worthy of investigation, stories in their own right. One such name is Oswestry in Shropshire, recorded as *Osewaldestr'* c.1180 'Oswald's tree' or perhaps 'Oswald's cross'. This has been interpreted as the place at which King Oswald of Northumbria was killed in battle by the pagan King Penda of Mercia in 642, a battle that took place, according to Bede, at *Maserfelth* (Bede, III. 9: Sherley-Price, 1968, 156). A likeness has been seen between this name and that of Maesbury, now a hamlet two and a half miles south of Oswestry but the original centre of administration before the construction of the Norman castle of Oswestry (Gelling, 1990, 229-31). However, there can be no certainty about these identifications and the story remains only a probability. Stories attached to particular trees are another source of possible historical evidence. Cressage in Shropshire, *Christesache* in 1086, for instance, means 'Christ's oak-tree' (Gelling, 1990, 102-3), perhaps again a tree with a crucifix attached, which may have been a used as a preaching site by Christian missionaries, here perhaps the Welsh Saint Samson who travelled widely in the sixth century; the Saxon church has since been demolished. This tree has been confused by antiquarians with the stunted relic of the Lady Oak in the same parish where a young sapling has grown up within the old hollow trunk, but the original tree is not likely to have lived long enough to be even the old Lady Oak, itself unlikely to be over 800 years old (Morton, 1986, 50-4). Many had carved their initials within the shell of the old tree which finally died in the severe frosts of 1982. Another tree with a story to tell is The Abbot's Oak at Woburn in Bedfordshire which is said to be where the abbot, prior and others were hanged by Henry VIII for refusing to acknowledge his supremacy and recognise his right to marry Anne Boleyn (Wilks, 1972, 78). One final example must suffice – the Royal Oak at Boscobel in Shropshire, where the future Charles II is said to have hidden from the Cromwellian forces after his defeat at the Battle of Worcester in 1651. The original tree was plundered by souvenir hunters and was dead by 1706 but another tree growing close by carries the name today (Morton, 1986, 60-2).

Trees continued to inspire stories. In J.R.R. Tolkien's *Lord of the Rings*, for instance, trees and woods are very much a part of his imagined landscapes of Middle-earth. They appear in animate form as his Ent people such as the wise old Treebeard, over 14 feet tall with his body supported by strong, thick legs, his seven toes on each foot root-like and with his bark-like skin and his bushy, bristling beard 'almost twiggy at the roots, thin and mossy at the ends'. He describes how the Hobitts travelled past 'great ilexes of huge girth [which] stood dark and solemn in wide glades with here and there among them hoary ash-trees, and giant oaks just putting out their brown-green buds'. As Gandalf and his companions follow the road to Isengard they make their way through fearsome woods, Legolas exclaims: 'These are the strangest trees that I ever saw … and I have seen many an oak grow from acorn to ruinous age … they have voices, and in time I might come to understand their thoughts' (Tolkien, 1954, 484, 723, 570). Indeed, Tolkien may have been inspired by the trees he knew in Moseley Bog growing near his childhood home in Birmingham (Figure 8). So, trees have continued to inspire stories throughout the ages.

Conclusions

Trees continued to play a role, therefore, as 'marker trees' throughout history, still marking assembly points and important locations, serving as landmarks upon boundaries or as specimens commemorating great people and events. Although only occasionally physically marked, they offer stories in their own right.

Figure 8. An ancient oak-tree on the edge of Moseley Bog, Birmingham © Della Hooke

References

Anderson, O.S. (1939) *The English Hundred-Names, The South-Western Counties*. Lunds Universitets Årsskift 35, Lund & Leipzig.

Bethurum, D. (ed.) (1957) *The Homilies of Wulfstan*. Clarendon Press, Oxford.

Birch, W. de Gray (1885–99) *Cartularium Saxonicum*. Whiting & Co., London.

Blair, J. (2005) *The Church in Anglo-Saxon Society*. Oxford University Press, Oxford.

Blair, J. (2013) 'Holy beams: Anglo-Saxon cult sites and the place-name element *bēam*'. in Bintley, M.D.J. & Shapland, M.G. (eds) *Trees and Timber in the Anglo-Saxon World*. Oxford University Press, Oxford, 186-210.

Breeze, A. (2006) The Celts and Tardebigge. *Transactions of the Worcestershire Archaeological Society*, 3rd ser., **20**, 75–6.

Earle, J. (1888) *A Hand-Book to the Land-Charters and Other Saxonic Documents*. Clarendon Press, Oxford.

Gelling, M. (1976) *The Place-Names of Berkshire, Part III*. Cambridge University Press, Cambridge.

Gelling, M., with Foxall, H.D.G. (1990) *The Place-Names of Shropshire, Part 1*. English Place-Name Society **62/63**, English Place-Name Society, Nottingham.

Hooke, D. (1990) *Worcestershire Anglo-Saxon Charter-Bounds*. Boydell Press, Woodbridge.

Hooke, D. (1998) *The Landscape of Anglo-Saxon England*, Leicester University Press, London.

Hooke, D. (2010) *Trees in Anglo-Saxon England: Literature, Lore and Landscape*. Boydell Press, Woodbridge.

Hooke, D. (2013a) 'Christianity and the "sacred tree" ', in Bintley, M.D.J. & Shapland, M.G. (eds), *Trees and Timber in the Anglo-Saxon World*. Oxford University Press, Oxford, 228-50.

Hooke, D. (2013b) 'The British tree in myth and legend'. in Anderson, A., Craven, T., Hooke, D. *et al. Under the Greenwood, Picturing the British Tree from Constable to Kurt Jackson*. Sansom & Co. Ltd, Bristol, 105-19.

Hutton, R. (1996) *The Stations of the Sun*. Oxford University Press, Oxford.

Jones, F. (1992) *The Holy Wells of Wales*, University of Wales Press, Cardiff.

Kelly, S.E. (2000) *The Charters of Abingdon Abbey, Part 1*. Anglo-Saxon Charters VII, British Academy & Oxford University Press, Oxford.

Mawer, A. & Stenton, F.M. 1927. *The Place-Names of Worcestershire*. English Place-Name Society, **4,** Cambridge University Press, Cambridge.

Morton, A. (1986) *The Trees of Shropshire*. Airlife Publishing Ltd, Shrewsbury.

Nozedar, A. (2006) *The Secret Language of Birds*. HarperElement, London.

Ó hÓgáin, D. (1999) *The Sacred Isle. Belief and Religion in Pre-Christian Ireland*. Boydell Press, Woodbridge.

Sawyer, P.H. (19680 *Anglo-Saxon Charters. An Annotated List and Bibliography*. Royal Historical Society, London.

Sherley-Price, L. trans. (1968) *Bede. The History of the English Church*. Penguin, Harmondsworth, revised edn.

Tolkien, J.R.R. (1954). *The Lord of the Rings*. George Allen and Unwin Ltd, London.

Turner, A.G.C. (1953) 'Some Old English passages relating to the episcopal manor of Taunton'. *Proceedings of the Somerset Archaeological and Natural History Society*, **98**, 118-26.

Whitelock, D. (1965) 'Wulfstan at York', in Bessinger, J.B. & Creed, R.P (Eds) *Franciplegius, Medieval and Linguistic Studies in Honor of Francis Peabody Magoun, Jr*. New York University Press, New York, 214-31.

Wilks, J.H. (1972) *Trees of the British Isles in History and Legend*. TBS The Book service Ltd, London.

Chapter 9. Tree Species and Uses from Documentary Evidence

Della Hooke
University of Birmingham

Abstract
Most of the early written evidence of tree species present in England comes from charters and place-names which mainly indicate the distribution of species, but their usage can be deduced from this, including the recognition of wood-pasture regions characterised by certain species of trees. After the Norman Conquest, forest documents provide much more evidence for the use of particular species, confirming much that is known from archaeological sources and standing building evidence. Throughout, the oak seems to have been the most valued tree.

General woodland usage in the early medieval period
Most information for the early medieval period covers the *distribution* of tree species, either noted in place-names or as estate boundary landmarks. This in itself tells us something about usage as many species are most frequently referred to in what are known to have been regions of wood-pasture — notably the oak and ash, holly, lime and yew. That such regions were explicitly used as wood-pasture is shown by many pre-Conquest charters especially those relating to the Wealden woods of south-east England. Another example, from north-west Worcestershire, relates to a grant by Burgred of Mercia of land at Seckley in Wolverley to one Wulferd where it is noted in A.D. 866 that the woodland designated would feed 70 pigs (Sawyer, 1968: S 212; Hooke, 2010, p. 151). Although swine were the main animals driven into wooded regions for seasonal pasture the charters of south-eastern England also mention horses, cattle and sheep.

Some charters refer to the right to take wood (generally), probably covering the later rights of *estovers*, sometimes slightly more precisely as *housebote* (timber for building), *heybote* (for fencing) and *firebote* (fuel). Thus in a charter of Inkberrow, Worcestershire, Oswald, bishop of Worcester, in AD 963 leased out 'the right of cutting wood in the common copse belonging to Thorne' (S 1305), 'common' indicating rights held by the community. Rights to wood are indeed noted in numerous Anglo-Saxon charters. These may concern timber from full-grown trees or just small wood. In 785, a charter of Offa grants land at Ickham in Kent to Ealdbeorht, *minister*, and his sister but adds woodland in Andred (the Weald), Bocholt and Blean not only for swine-pasture but 'wood for felling for a building or for burning, without hindrance, and similarly wood is set aside for boiling salt ... ' (S 123). Another agreement between the abbot of Peterborough and a certain Wulfred concerns the grant of land in AD 852 at Sempringham in Sleaford, Lincs, in which the latter had to give to the monastery every year 60 fothers (wagon-loads) of wood from a certain wood, together with *tuelf foðer græfan 7sex foður gerda* , the latter translated by Robertson as '12 fothers of brush wood and 6 fothers of faggots' — clearly small wood, probably for fuel (S 1440; Robertson, 1956, No. 7, p. 13).

Domesday Book also notes the provision of wood to fuel the salt furnaces at Droitwich in Worcestershire. Thus the royal manor of Bromsgrove had up to the time of the Norman Conquest been exchanging wood as fuel for this purpose in exchange for salt: the manor receiving 300 measures of salt, for which they used to be given 300 cartloads of wood by the keepers of the wood in the time of King Edward (Thorn & Thorn, 1982, 1,1a). In the mid-sixteenth century, Leland remarked upon the need of 'coppisis of yong wood', then in short supply, for fuel for this industry but the species of trees used are not mentioned. It is likely that the wood was obtained from coppiced woodland already in the pre-Conquest period, with coppices and managed woods perhaps often referred to as 'groves' (Hooke, 2017).

Wood was also being widely used for charcoal making in the medieval period, especially oak, ash, beech, hornbeam, birch, hazel, hawthorn, and elder, of which the most important was oak, and references to charcoal or *col* are found in some pre-Conquest West Midland charters naming fords on routeways approaching Droitwich. Some place-names containing the epithet 'burnt' may also refer to this practice (Rackham, 2003, p. 143).

Sometimes, but rarely, charter grants do specify grants of actual species of tree for particular purposes — the Worcestershire Wolverley charter noted above granted in AD 866 not only wood-pasture for swine and cartloads of 'good rods', plus 'wood in plenty for fire' but 'every year one oak tree for building'.

Norman forests and medieval parks

With the afforestation of large areas under the Norman kings, the resultant forests were not only set aside for royal hunting but were also a source of revenue from the sale of timber. The king might, however, also make gifts of timber and other wood from his forests. Thus, in the thirteenth and fourteenth centuries the king made frequent gifts to magnates, local religious houses and others, of venison, timber and firewood from the forests of Chippenham and Melksham in Wiltshire. Grants of daily cartloads of fuel for small religious houses indicate what large tonnages of fuel were consumed overall (Langton & Jones, 2010, p. 39).

Often the species of tree is noted, especially when this entailed timber for building purposes. In 1236, for example, the Dean and Chapter of Salisbury were given '20 good oaks ... in Chippenham Forest, dispersed in different places, . . . to make their stalls in Salisbury Cathedral' (*Cal Close Rolls*, 1234-7, p. 279: *VCH Wiltshire*). Henry III showed especial favour to the nunnery of Lacock by making a number of **gifts of lime**, timber and firewood from Melksham and Chippenham Forests (*ibid.*, 1231-4, p. 162; 1234-7, p. 232). Unusually large oaks might be transported over enormous distances. In 1251 Henry III gave 30 oaks from the Forest of Inglewood in Cumberland to the monks of Bury St Edmund's over 250 miles way, also providing money for the transport and in the same year he presented Salisbury Cathedral with 20 oaks, gathered from different forests, to make '10 couples', *i.e.* 20 rafters (Rackham, 2003, p. 153).

In Oxfordshire, Shotover Forest was not far distant from the town of Oxford and was constantly supplying wood for both fuel and building purposes, by royal grant, during the reign of Henry III. During the first fifteen years of that monarch's reign, gifts were made of loads of dry wood for fuel to the Oxford hospitals of St. John Baptist and St. Bartholomew, to the Dominican and Franciscan friars of Oxford, to the prior of St. Frideswide's, and to the bishop of Chichester for his hearth at Oxford (*Cal Close Rolls* 1204-24, *passim*: *VCH Oxfordshire II*). Among the more interesting grants from Shotover Forest for building purposes, during this period, the following may be mentioned. In 1223, twenty tie-beams (*copulas*) were ordered to be supplied to William, chaplain of the bishop of Winchester, towards the rebuilding of the church of St. Budoc, Oxford, below the castle; it had been thrown down during the recent war for strategic purposes (*Cal Close Rolls*, **p. 559**). In the same year, the requisite timber for constructing a gaol at Oxford and for the general repairs of the castle was also obtained from Shotover (*ibid.*, **p. 540**). Ten loads of timber suitable for fencing were granted by the Crown in 1231 to Elias, chaplain to the earl of Cornwall, to enclose the churchyard of **Horsepath in Shotover**, of which place he was rector (*ibid.*, 1227-31, p. 474).

The Forest of Dean was noted for its outsize oaks; these were being intensively exploited by the thirteenth century. Many were gifted to the Gloucester Black Friars — some 61 oaks from Dean and 21 from other Forests between 1241 and 1265. Examination of the fabric shows that each tree was about 50ft in usable length and 2ft 2ins in diameter, sawn lengthwise into four or six rafters; 82 oaks of the king's gift account for about half the timber used in the original building. Although the king drew back from such benefactions in 1257, because of the destruction of so many trees, the roof of Westminster Hall, using timbers nearly 50ft long, probably used timber from Alice Holt Forest in Hampshire (Rackham, 2003, p. 153).

Much of the wood sold from the forests was for fuel, but when building timber is specified the tree species is then more often noted. Thus between 1263 and 1270 the Constable and Bailiffs of Devizes took 249 **oaks** 'for the works of the castle', and 30 dry oaks for the constable's hearth (E 32/200/14: *VCH Wiltshire IV*) from the forests of Chippenham & Melksham in Wiltshire; tallies of the number of trees felled were kept by the constable and by the foresters and verderers as a check upon unnecessary destruction of the vert (*Cal Close Rolls* 1231–4, p. 96; *ibid*. 1234–7, p. 32). Langton and Jones (2010, p. 94) note how orders for timber and timber products from Bernwood Forest on the borders of Buckinghamshire and Oxfordshire in the medieval period frequently specify timber (*fusta*) and tree trunks (*fustis*), with many orders requesting wood for rafters (*cheveronus*), braces or tie-beams (*copula*), crucks or forks (*furca*) and joists (*gista*). Between 1228 and 1316, some orders specified the location of the construction project, with orders for private building projects such as Kirtlington and Long Grendon manors, churches and monastic establishments such as St Cross Church and St John's Hospital in Oxford, for the royal manor at Brill and Kenilworth Castle, and for public works such as Aylesbury jail and Ickford Bridge (*ibid*.), those for the jail expressing a preference for oaks. Here we are seeing the oak appearing as the prime timber tree, something verified by studies of medieval buildings.

Taking the forest of Cannock in Staffordshire as an example (Figure 1), many grants of timber were made to the Church. In 1251, for instance, the king granted oaks for the stalls of the church to the canons of Penkridge (*Cal Close Rolls* 1247-51, p. 57) with a further gift recorded in the Forest pleas of 1262 of 10 more oaks in Teddesley and two oaks in Bentley Hay (E32/187). Similarly, the friars minor of Leicester were, in 1255, to have oaks for stalls and panelling in their chapel and a further 18 in **Alrewas Hay in 1262**; the prior of Coventry also in 1262, was to have 20 oaks in Cheslyn and Bentley hays; the canons of Wolverhampton six oaks in Bentley Hay; and the friars minor of Lichfield two oaks by gift of the justices 'for the king's salvation' in Alrewas Hay (E32/187). Ralph of Whittington, in 1251, was granted oaks for repairs to the bridge at Wychnor, with a further four later; and

Philip Marmion was granted six oaks for work on his castle at Tamworth in 1261 (Birrell, 1999, pp. 38-9).

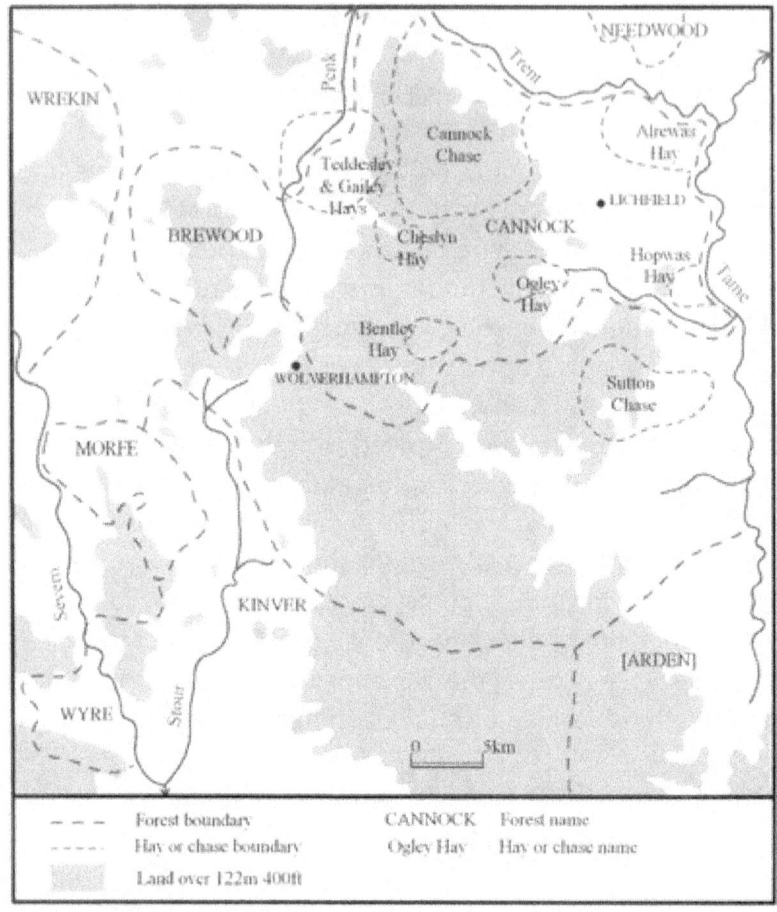

Figure 1. South Staffordshire forests: the forest of Cannock (Hooke, 2015)

But oak was not only required for building timbers. For example, dry and leafless oaks taken from Chippenham Forest provided lime for further building operations (*Cal Close Rolls*, 1247–51, p. 407). Such acquisitions of forest timber continued. The coppice of **Horsepath** in Shotover, Oxfordshire, was cleared, not for the first time, in 1592. The account of the woodward of Shotover for the sales opens with the entry of 'My Lord Norris of Ricot 1 acre of underwood 26*s*. 8*d*.' This was the usual price at that date. The colleges were again among the principal buyers. The total of the underwood sale amounted to £85 10s. 10d. Dotard (decayed) trees produced £16 12s. Twenty timber trees were sold by special warrant to the master and fellows of Balliol at 8d. each. The stems of ash realized £3 17s. 6d., and the stems of oak £22 10s. 4d. The tops of the stake trees brought in £4 9s. 10d. The charges for 'securing' the coppice by hedging and ditching amounted to £36 3s. 10d., leaving a clear profit of £115 12s. 1d. for the queen (*VCH Wiltshire IV*).

Offences against the vert, brought before forest courts, provide further evidence of the use of forest timber but here through recording illegal extraction. In the forest of Cannock even the foresters might be accused of illegally taking timber. The Forest pleas of 1271 accuse two foresters William Cardon and Benedict le Forester and one other of taking oaks both for their own use and for sale from Alrewas Hay; William even had a cart with two horses which he used to remove wood and timber from the hay to sell in Lichfield — at least a cartload a day over a period of two and a half years (E32/184: Birrell, 1999, pp. 93-94). In collusion with Hugh of Eynsham, the riding forester of the whole forest, William of Drakenage, the forester of Hopwas Hay, was also carting away timber and wood at least once every day for a year. The records show that it was mainly oak that was being removed during the period of William's tenure — by many individuals as well as by William himself — some 71 whole oaks and dozens of branches; oaks, birches, alder and underwood were taken from Gailey Hay by its forester, hidden beneath clods, moss, and thorns (*ibid.*, p. 95). Again in Alrewas Hay, under Hugh of Eynsham, three men and a woman were employed burning birch, limes and other trees, the ashes sold to dyers of cloth, thus causing 'great destruction in the hay of various trees and underwood' (*ibid.*, pp. 95-96). These are but a few examples for the story is repeated in the wood of Walsall in 1276 where over 900 oaks were taken 'at the time of the war' and an inquisition was set up to ascertain the legality of such sales (C47/11/2/7: *ibid.*, p. 107).

It will be noted how it was oak for building which predominated in all these thirteenth-century records pertaining to the forests of

Cannock and Kinver. Even more explicit are the sales of timber recorded between May and August in 1301: from the wood of Prestwood in the Forest of Kinver, 219 oaks and 60 birches, some to the Master Luke of Ely who was chancellor of Lichfield Cathedral and some to Master Elias of Napton who was archdeacon of Derby and prebendary of Eccleshalh (E101/138/28: Birrell pp. 192-3); from the Forest of Cannock, about 120 oaks from Teddesley Hay, 42 from Bentley Hay, 40 from Cheslyn Hay, 29 from Alrewas Hay and 152 from Hopwas Hay. From Chasepool Hay in the Forest of Kinver, lying to the west of the Smestow Brook, a total of 321 oaks were sold in the same year (E101/1/138/29: *ibid.*, pp.194-7).

Studies of medieval buildings confirm the role of oak for building (Figure 2). Oak was the favoured tree, especially for palaces and churches, but most rural and urban buildings were built of wood, from the smallest hovel to the more splendid public building. Building techniques became more varied over time, with the increasing use of sillbeams and a move towards the framed buildings of later periods, but post and wattle building was common.

Medieval documents also record amongst the species of trees used for building elm; and even those which produced only inferior timber such as birch in Scotland and northern England, beech, alder, aspen and black poplar (Rackham, 2003, pp. 266, 305-6, 312, 323, 341, 343).

Figure 2. Oak as a favoured timber in medieval buildings (Lower Brockhampton Hall dating from the late 14th century and Weobley 'black-and-white' village, both in Herefordshire

Although inferior as building timber, many were useful as small wood or in other ways. These include alder used in the thirteenth century to make crossbows; birch used for fences, farm implements and turner's work or later as fuel for the ironworks of the Weald; and beech used as fuel for the Wealden glass industry in the sixteenth and seventeenth centuries (*ibid.*, pp. 305-6, 312, 323).

Not all timber came from the royal forests. Parks enclosed by the king and other members of the aristocracy, often originally located around the margins of royal forests, were also sources of timber. Here, trees were often pollarded in order to produce timber grown out of the reach of browsing animals. Such a system may have been in use since pre-Conquest times for a few charters refer to 'copped' trees (OE *copped* 'polled, lopped, pollarded'), among them a 'copped oak' and at least three copped thorns. The young poles could be cut on a regular basis, usually every ten to twelve years in winter; and the leaves of the trees also gathered annually in summer as leaf fodder for domestic animals (elm and ash are the most nutritious). A tree managed in this way could live much longer than a maiden tree and many old parklands are still characterised by veteran pollards that may be hundreds of years old, some older than the recorded park which was often made in a former wood-pasture area.

Figure 3: Ancient pollard oaks in Moccas parkland, Herefordshire

Moccas Park in Herefordshire may have been carved out of the earlier medieval forest of Dorstone and its ancient pollards are distinctive (Figure 3).

Trees might also be deliberately retained or planted in hedgerows, a feature commonly shown on seventeenth-century and later estate maps; in Warwickshire. These usually included oak, ash and elm. In Britain, we no longer have 'shredded' trees a feature not uncommon on the Continent and resulting from commoners retaining the right to take the side-branches for wood or animal fodder.

Later uses for trees

As the bounds of the forests were pushed back under baronial pressure after 1301, the value of the forests as sources of timber diminished. The forests became wasted and more money was to be gained from fines for assarting and enclosure. However, the collection of wood continued.

The bark of the oak tree was used for tanning leather and again this may often have been a by-product of the building industry, stripped from building timbers. As noted above, browse-wood might be gathered from woods used as wood-pasture, including holly, and in Shotover in 1592 the presentments showed that the keepers had cut fourteen loads of oak and sallow boughs for deer-browse in the winter (Forest Survey Exch. K.R., 137/2: *VCH Oxfordshire II*). Pollard elms were often used for this purpose in Cambridgeshire; and Rackham (2003, p. 174) notes how in 1565 oak, ash, hornbeam, hawthorn, and maple were shredded for browse-wood to feed deer in the Essex parks of Newhall (Boreham) and Havering. In 1528, all the oaks and other large timber trees in Sutton Park in the West Midlands were sold by the king to Bishop Veasey but many of the trees were given as timber to the people of Sutton Coldfield for public building purposes. The townspeople were allowed to use the grazings for their cattle and horses but it is significant that the hollins were so valuable that they survive today (Figure 4), still within their enclosing wood banks. In particular, the tender outer shoots could be cut for animal feed, a practice also common in the north of England, especially during cold, hard winters.

Figure 4. The Hollins in Sutton Park, **West Midlands**

Primary Sources
PRO Public Record Office,
  Calendar Close Rolls
  Forest Survey (Exch. K.R.) **Exchequer reports**
  C47/11/2/7 Inquisition concerning waste made in Walsall Wood, 1276
  E32/187 Forest pleas of 1262
  E32/184 Forest pleas of 1271
  E101/1/138/28 and E101/1/138/29 Sales of timber from Cannock and Kinver, May - August 1301

Bibliography
Birrell, J. (ed.) (1999) *The Forests of Cannock and Kinver: Select Documents 1235-1372*, Collections for a History of Staffordshire, 4th series, **Vol. 18**, Staffordshire Record Society.

Hooke, D. (2010) *Trees in Anglo-Saxon England*. Boydell Press, Woodbridge.

Hooke, D. (2015) 'The forest landscapes of the Staffordshire hoard region: II. The later landscape'. *Staffordshire Archaeological & Historical Society Transactions*, **48**, 41-54.

Hooke, D. (2017) 'Groves in Anglo-Saxon England'. *Landscape History*, **38 (1)**, 5-23.

Langton, J., & Jones, G. (eds) (2010) *Forests and Chases of Medieval England and Wales c.1000–c.1500*. St John's College Research Centre, Oxford.

Rackham, O. (2003) *Ancient Woodland. Its History, Vegetation and Uses in England*. new edn (Castlepoint Press, Dalbeattie, Kirkcudbrightshire).

Robertson, A.J. (1956) *Anglo-Saxon Charters*. 2nd edn (Cambridge University Press, Cambridge).

Sawyer, P.H. (1968) *Anglo-Saxon Charters, an Annotated List and Bibliography* (Royal Historical Society, London).

Thorn, F., & Thorn, C. (1982) *Domesday Book,* **16**, *Worcestershire*. Phillimore, Chichester.

VCH Oxfordshire, Vol. 2, A History of the County of Oxford: Volume 2, (ed.) Page, W. (1907) Constable, **London**, 'Forestry', pp. 293-301. *British History*. Online *http://www.british-history.ac.uk/vch/oxon/vol2/pp293-301* [accessed 12 February 2018].

VCH Wiltshire, A History of the County of Wiltshire, Volume 4. Critall, E. (ed.) (1959) Oxford University Press for the Institute of Historical Research, Oxford. 'Royal forests', pp. 391-433. http://www.british-history.ac.uk/vch/wilts/vol4/pp391-433#h3-0004 [accessed 12 February 2018).

Chapter 10. Managing woodlands in the past for constructional timber: evidence from South Yorkshire and Ireland

Melvyn Jones
Sheffield Hallam University

Abstract

Using a range of historical documentary sources relating to South Yorkshire and County Wicklow in the Republic of Ireland, this chapter will reveal the sources of constructional timber used in the past. First, some examples of timber-framed buildings and other buildings using large amounts of constructional timber in South Yorkshire will be examined. This will be followed by a discussion of the management of deer parks, wooded commons and coppice-with-standards woods in South Yorkshire to supply constructional timber for local buildings, domestic and agricultural, and for industrial structures related to coal and ironstone mining and the water-powered light-metal trades. In South Yorkshire, ship timber was a minor end-product because of its location far from the coast. This was not the case in the Watson-Wentworth estate woodlands in County Wicklow in Ireland in the first half of the eighteenth century. There, besides making a major contribution to the building of the colonial landscape of churches, schools and courthouses, the woodlands were sources of constructional timber not only for agricultural buildings and industrial premises, but also for the ship building and ship repair industries in the ports of Dublin, Wicklow, Wexford and Arklow in Ireland and Whitehaven in England. Particular emphasis will be placed on the significance of sophisticated coppice-with-standards management in both South Yorkshire and County Wicklow.

Introduction

First it needs to be explained why two places such a long way apart and with no apparent connection are being discussed. The connection is woodland ownership. The Honourable Thomas Watson-Wentworth, and his descendants the Marquises of Rockingham and the earls Fitzwilliam of Wentworth Woodhouse in South Yorkshire, also had a 91,000-acre estate in Ireland, in counties Kildare and Wicklow. Here, in Ireland, they managed more than 30 coppice woods covering nearly 2,000 acres (805 hectares). They simply exported their mode of woodland management to their Irish estates.

First, some examples of timber-framed buildings and other buildings using large amounts of constructional timber in South Yorkshire will be examined. This will then be followed by examples of the uses of timber for constructional purposes from the woods belonging to the Wentworth estate in Ireland. Finally, the ways in which the woods in South Yorkshire and those in County Wicklow in Ireland, both belonging to the Wentworth estate, were managed in the past for the production of constructional timber will be discussed.

Examples of timber-framed buildings in South Yorkshire

It was not until the seventeenth century that stone and brick supplanted timber as the main building material in South Yorkshire, timber holding prime place here since the first permanent settlements were built in Neolithic times. As late as 1540, John Leland, the antiquary, on his six-year tour of England, described the town of Doncaster as 'buildid of woode'. Even castles, like the ones at Sheffield, Conisbrough and Tickhill, and parish churches were constructed of timber before they were rebuilt in stone. It is in the surviving timber-framed houses and barns that trees from the region's medieval woods can be seen. And, it is trees that we see in timber-framed buildings, for the house carpenter or housewright as he was sometimes called, did not obtain his timber in the form of ready sawn or shaped planks and beams – he often selected trees in woods and hedges that would roughly square up to the dimensions of the components required with the minimum of shaping, large trees for the beams and smaller trees for things like rafters. The timber used was mostly oak (although elm and sweet chestnut were also sometimes used) and it was sawn or shaped with an axe or adze or cleft with a mallet (called a beetle) and edge while it was still 'green' for ease of working. It should also be noted that nails were not used to hold the timbers in place because the tannic acid in the unseasoned oak would corrode them. Instead oak pegs sometimes called treenails were used; and were made in their thousands. Four interesting timber-framed buildings in South Yorkshire are described below.

Post-and-truss (or box frame), and cruck buildings are both still represented in South Yorkshire (Ryder, 1979). The roofs of post-and-truss buildings were either of the common rafter or principal rafter type. There were many variations of principal rafter roofs. In the king post type, which was almost universally used in South Yorkshire, a single vertical post rose from the tie beam; in East Anglia and the south-east the crown-post type, which had a vertical post rising from the tie beam to a collar purlin, was widely distributed. Only one crown post roof is known in South Yorkshire, in a house on Castlegate in Tickhill.

Most post-and-truss buildings have long since disappeared in South Yorkshire but there are a few outstanding examples still standing. Perhaps the earliest of these is Whiston manorial barn in Rotherham where a dendrochronological analysis suggests that the original medieval timbers used in the building were felled between 1233 and 1252 (Tyers, 2002). The barn has a simple principal rafter roof with two struts connecting the tie beam with the principal rafters. It is an aisled post-and-truss building in which extra building width was achieved by erecting the long walls beyond the principal posts to which they were connected by extensions to the roof trusses (aisle ties). The original building consisted of five bays but in the sixteenth century the building was extended by two more bays and the original timber walls were replaced by stone. Figure 1 shows the interior of the barn looking west.

Figure 1. The interior of Whiston manorial barn

Figure 2. The Hall in the Ponds, Sheffield

The Hall in the Ponds (Figure 2) is another interesting timber framed building, this time right in the centre of the city of Sheffield on Pond Street. Dendrochronological analysis shows that this timber-framed building, which survives in part as the Old

Queen's Head public house, was built of timber felled between 1503 and 1510 (University of Nottingham, Tree Ring Laboratory, 1992). The building is jettied on the south, west and east sides, has close-studded walls, a king post roof and carved heads on the exterior of the ground floor posts. An inventory of its contents in 1582 suggests it was a banqueting house in Sheffield deer park which covered 2,462 acres (nearly 1,000 hectares) (Jones, 2007)

Kirkstead Abbey Grange in Thorpe Hesley, Rotherham, is a stone building but with a very sophisticated timber roof structure. The first record of a house about to be built on the site was in 1161, when the monks of Kirkstead Abbey in Lincolnshire were leased land to mine ironstone, smelt and forge iron and to build their headquarters (Jones, 1993). The present building appears to be of late medieval date but incorporates stone and timber features from an earlier building, possibly the original one built by the monks in the twelfth century. Figure 3 shows part of the roof structure at the southern end of the building. It is a king post roof with the king posts rising from massive tie beams which rest on very thick (in places 36 inches (nearly one metre)) walls. The tie beam is 14 inches by 9 inches (35 cm x 22 cm). Rising from the end of each of the tie beams are principal rafters which are fitted into the tops of the king posts with mortise and tenon joints. In its original state the roof consisted of 212 timber components, all oak, including the shaped trunks of 183 individual trees. Treenails are used throughout the roof structure to secure joints.

Perhaps the most impressive timber-framed building in South Yorkshire is Gunthwaite Hall barn (Figure 4). This barn, which is 163 feet long and 44 feet wide, dates from the early sixteenth century. It is composed of eleven bays, covers more than 7,000 square feet and is so large it is now divided between two farms. The lower parts of the walls are of stone but the upper parts are of timber and on the outside are decorated in herringbone patterns. It has a king post roof.

Investigating Tree Archaeology

Figure 3. A king post at Kirkstead Abbey Grange

Figure 4. Interior of Gunthwaite Hall barn

Cruck buildings were common in the upland areas of Britain and parts of the Midlands but are relatively rare in eastern and south-eastern England. In South Yorkshire, there are only three records of cruck buildings in the zone to the east of Rotherham, but to the west of the town there are records of nearly 150 cruck buildings either still standing or known to have been demolished since 1900 (Ryder, 1979). In a cruck building the weight was carried on cruck blades which rise from or near the ground and meet at the apex of the roof. The blades are usually curved, having been selected from naturally bent trees. Often a bent tree was split or sawn lengthways to make two matching blades. Rackham (2006) was of the opinion that many cruck buildings were made of native black poplar which naturally often grows leaning at an angle. The structure was strengthened by tie beams connecting each pair of cruck blades. The roof of the building was stabilised by struts called windbraces. As in post and truss buildings, the original walls consisted of vertical studs rising from the sill beam to the wall plates with the gaps filled with a variety of materials as already noted or covered with horizontal oak boarding. One of the best surviving cruck buildings in South Yorkshire is the barn at Hill Top Farm, Grenoside. The barn has long been encased in stone but the cruck blades are on full view (Figure 5).

Figure 5. Interior of the cruck barn at Hill Top Farm, Grenoside

It should be noted that, whereas, in some parts of England large amounts of timber were used in the shipbuilding industry, this was never the case in South Yorkshire because of its inland location. I have only located one record of timber trees grown in South Yorkshire woods being used for ship timber. This was timber from the Duke of Leeds' estate based on Kiveton Park. Several of the managed woods still survive, for example, Anston Stones Wood, Hawks Wood and Old Spring Wood. In the accounts for the year 1701, it is recorded that 562 'straite oaken trees' were taken from these woods 'by land and by water' to his majesty's ship yard at Chatham and yielded £473 in income (Duke of Leeds' Archive at Yorkshire Archaeological Society, Leeds, DD5/35).

Managing Woodlands in South Yorkshire for Constructional Timber

The questions that naturally arise are, what were the sources of all this building timber and were the woods from which the timber came managed in specific ways to ensure that the supply was maintained? Timber for building was obtained from private and public wood-pastures and from coppice woods.

The private wood-pastures were the deer parks of which there were at least 27 in the medieval period and beyond in South Yorkshire. To use the modern term, a deer park was also usually part of the manorial 'forestry' operation. Although there are records of parks without trees, deer parks usually consisted of woodland and areas largely cleared of trees. The park livestock could graze in the more open areas and find cover in the wooded areas. The largely cleared areas, called launds or plains, consisted of grassland or heath with scattered trees. Many of the trees in the launds would have been pollarded, *i.e.* cut at least six feet from the ground leaving a massive lower trunk called a bolling above which a continuous crop of new growth sprouted out of reach of the grazing deer, sheep and cattle. In the launds, regeneration of trees was restricted because of continual grazing and new trees were only able to grow in the protection of thickets of hawthorn and holly. Some of the un-pollarded trees might reach a great age and size and were much sought after for major building projects (Figure 6).

Figure 6. A deer park laund with ancient oak tree

The woods within deer parks were managed in different ways. Some woods were 'holted', ie, they consisted of single-stemmed trees grown for their timber like a modern plantation. Most park woods were coppiced and were surrounded by a bank or wall to keep out the grazing animals during the early years of re-growth. Later in the coppice cycle the deer would have been allowed into the coppice woods.

Sheffield Park is particularly well documented, and a clear picture emerges of the woods and trees within it and the way they were used in the medieval period. This deer park, which at its greatest extent, as already noted, covered 2,462 acres (nearly 1,000 hectares) and was eight miles (13 kilometres) in circumference, came right up to the eastern edge of the town of Sheffield. Harrison, in his survey of the manor of Sheffield in 1637, named the various parts of the park including some with woodland names. These include Arbor Thorn Hirst and Stone Hirst (hyrst = a wooded hill) but they would only have been covered with scrub woods of hawthorn and holly. The cleared areas within the park are also precisely named in Harrison's survey: 'ye Lands', 'Cundit Plaine', 'Blacko Plaine' and 'Bellhouse Plaine' (Ronksley, 1908). Ye Lands is probably a corruption of laund. These launds or plains contained large aged oak trees in the seventeenth century, that would have already been very large trees two or three hundred years earlier in the late medieval period. They were described in great detail by John Evelyn in his book *Silva*, first published in 1670. Evelyn said that in 1646 there were 100 trees whose combined value was £1000. He described one oak tree in the park having a trunk thirteen feet in diameter and another which was ten yards in circumference. He also described another massive oak that, when cut down, yielded 1,400 'wairs', planks two yards long and one yard wide, and 20 cords from its branches. A cord was a pile of wood four feet high, four feet wide and eight feet long. He described another oak, that when felled and lying on its side was so massive that two men on horseback on either side of it could not see each other's hat crowns. On Conduit Plain (the Cundit Plaine of Harrison's 1637 survey), Evelyn reported that there was one oak tree whose boughs were so far spreading that he estimated (giving all his calculations) that 251 horses could stand in its shade (Evelyn, 1706 edition), 229-230).

These mighty oaks, veteran or ancient trees as they are now termed, had had a multiplicity of uses for centuries. As already noted, when felled they provided not only timber for building projects, but also charcoal (from their branches), and wood for a multiplicity of crafts and industries. They also provided the food for fattening pigs during the pannage season but also for keeping the deer population in good heart in preparation for the long winter.

Wooded commons, the public wood-pastures, were unfenced woods in which underwood and timber were harvested and in which the animals of commoners, i.e., tenants of the lord of the manor who had certain rights on the common land of a manor, were allowed to graze freely. In the manor of Sheffield as late as 1637 there were 21,000 acres of common land, much of it wooded.

Wooded commons, that is the *silva pastilis* recorded at Domesday, and their descendants, were unfenced woods in which underwood and timber were harvested and in which the animals of commoners, i.e., those who had certain rights on the common land of a manor, were allowed to graze freely. Commoners usually also had the right of the underwood and dead wood but the timber trees usually belonged to the lord of the manor. Permission had to be granted by the lord of the manor to the tenant for their rights to use the produce of the common land and woods. This was known as the right of estovers (*estoveir* is Old French for 'be necessary'. This manorial right consisted of separate rights called botes. These rights allowed tenants to take timber, underwood, dead wood and bracken from wooded commons to make and repair their hedges (hedgebote or haybote), to repair their farm equipment (ploughbote and cartbote), to take firewood (firebote) and significantly to make and repair their houses (housebote). Some wooded commons disappeared quite early but others remained until enclosure in the eighteenth and early nineteenth centuries. For example, Stannington Wood, a wooded common of 217 acres in 1637, consisted of more than a hundred small walled and hedged fields by 1890.

Wooded commons would have contained pollarded trees, unpollarded trees, many-stemmed coppice and scrub. Before the creation of enclosed coppice woods, the lord of the manor would have obtained his building timber not only from his deer park or parks, but also from his chase if he possessed one and from the wooded commons. Wooded commons were a widely distributed type of common in the central two-thirds of South Yorkshire, in great contrast to the moorland commons of the Dark Peak zone in the west and the marshland commons of the Humberhead Levels in the east. The latter did contain scrub wood on commons, but this was in the form of willow carrs and alder carrs.

Two early deeds relating to the wooded commons at Rawmarsh are also full of interest. The first, dating from 1241, refers to the vicar's rights on the common of Rawmarsh for firewood, for housebote and for hedgebote (Hall, 19154, 5). The same wooded common was included in a marriage settlement in 1557 between Lancelot Mountforthe of Kilnhurst and Margaret Wentworth of Wentworth Woodhouse. The estate described in the settlement included access to the common and woods of Rawmarsh for pasturing animals and for 'wood for their fires, hedges and houses' (Hall, 1916, 106-107).

There are graphic descriptions of several wooded commons in the late seventeenth and early eighteenth centuries. In 1650, Loxley Chase was referred as 'one Great wood called Loxley the herbage common and consisteth of great Oake timber'. About ten years earlier, another wooded common, Walkley Bank, was said to have 'a great store of rough Oake trees & some Bircke (birch) woods'. In the same year Stannington Wood, formerly part of Rivelin Chase and which covered 217 acres (88 ha) in 1637, was said to consist of 'pt of rough Timber and part of Springe wood'.

As the population grew and land was cleared for farming, wood-pastures diminished in size, timber became much scarcer and a different form of management, spring wood management i.e. coppicing, became widespread (Jones, 1988, 2009, 2012). The earliest surviving documentary record, I have seen of coppice management in South Yorkshire, is a lease written in Latin at the relatively late date of 1421. Throughout the region, the form of coppice management called coppice-with-standards, which combined the production of multi-stemmed coppice with that of single-stemmed timber trees, emerged as the most important form of woodland management from the late medieval period until at least the middle of the nineteenth century. In this kind of woodland management, in accordance with an overall plan, most of the trees were periodically (every 15 to 30 years) cut down to the ground to what is called a stool, and from the stool grew multiple stems, collectively called coppice or underwood. Some of the trees were not coppiced but were allowed to grow on to become mature single-stemmed trees, and these were the standards. It was the standards that produced timber, the coppice produced wood; hence we have timber-framed buildings but wood fires. The standards would normally grow through several coppice cycles, as the coppice rotations were known, and therefore were of various ages. Those standards that had grown through only one coppice cycle, i.e. less than 30 years old at most, were called wavers (usually written locally as 'weavers'); those that had grown through two coppice cycles and were therefore between 40 and 60 years old were called black barks; and those that had grown through three or more coppice cycles and were therefore at least 60 years old were called lordings. Together the black barks and lordings were known as reserves (Jones, 2013). A typical South Yorkshire coppice-with-standards is shown in diagrammatic form in Figure 7.

Locally, there are still woods in the landscape that are called a spring or have been in the past. For example, Low Spring at Bracken Hill, and Wilson Spring between Grenoside and Oughtibridge. In a document dating from about 1600 Greno Wood, Grenoside, was called 'Granowe Springe' and Woolley Wood was called 'Wolley Wode Spring' (Lambeth Palace Library, London, Shr PLPL/Ms698, folio1).

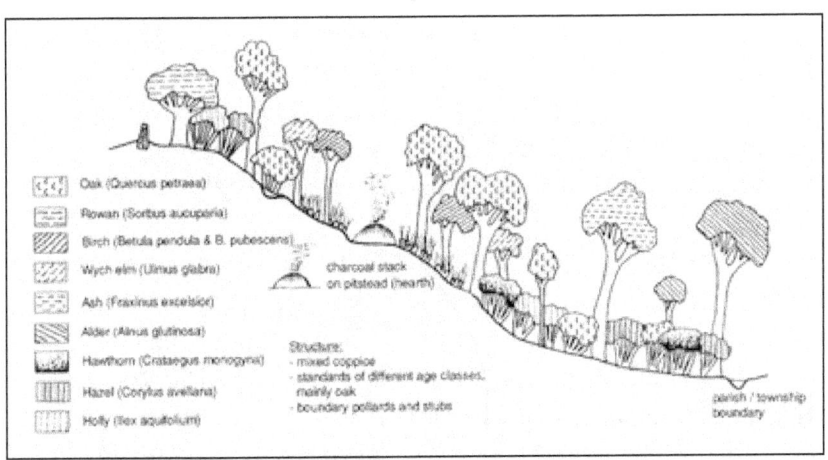

Figure 7. Cross-section through a typical coppice-with-standards wood in South Yorkshire

At the end of the coppice cycle, when all the coppice re-growth and selected trees in a small wood or a compartment within a larger wood were to be felled, the trees selected to remain standing were marked with 'raddle', a red paint. The next stage was to advertise the sale of the wood that was ready to be felled. This was done in the nineteenth century through handbills At the sale, normally held at a local inn, the woodward would write the valuation or valuations (if certain products were being sold separately) on a ticket and put it folded on the table in front of him. Within a specified time, all those bidding for the timber, underwood and other products included in the sale had to put their bids on separate tickets on the table. This was sometimes done three times, on each occasion the woodward announcing the highest bidder. Finally, the highest bidder became the purchaser provided the bid equalled or exceeded the estate valuation. It should be emphasized that timber was also sold separately from these general sales to individual buyers.

Woodland Management for Constructional Timber on the Watson-Wentworth Irish Estates in the first half of the eighteenth century

The headquarters of the estate in South Yorkshire was at Wentworth Woodhouse where, by the end of the eighteenth century, it was surrounded by an estate covering 18,000 acres. By the beginning of the eighteenth century the South Yorkshire estate contained 28 coppice-with-standard woods covering nearly 900 acres that were managed with great sophistication (Wentworth Woodhouse Muniments, WWM 1273).

The family exported their approach to woodland management to their Irish estate. These lay in six blocks, five in County Wicklow and one in County Kildare (Figure 8). This estate totalled an astonishing 91,000 acres or 37,000 hectares. By 1750, the estate contained 2,356 acres (954 hectares) of coppice and scrub woods, of which 1989 acres (805 hectares) were coppice woods proper in thirty separate woods. They varied in size from 202 to three acres. Detailed accounts of their management have survived for the period 1707 to 1749 (Wentworth Woodhouse Muniments, WWM A758-763) and a clear picture of management for underwood for a variety of local industries and for constructional timber emerges (Jones, 1986 and Jones, 2000).

During the first half of the eighteenth century, adjustments were made to the number and sizes of coppices, sometimes through planting but more usually by taking in adjacent scrub woods. Not only were existing coppices extended but completely new ones were created by enclosing good scrub woods. For example, one scrub wood called Nickson's Brow, was already a candidate in 1728 for conversion from scrub wood to coppice, a surveyor noting that 'if well reserved and fenced will make as good A Springe if not The Best in Shelelagh'. The coppices were mainly composed of oak (*Quercus petraea*) although birch was an important component of most woods. Other species included elm, hazel, holly, alder and willow.

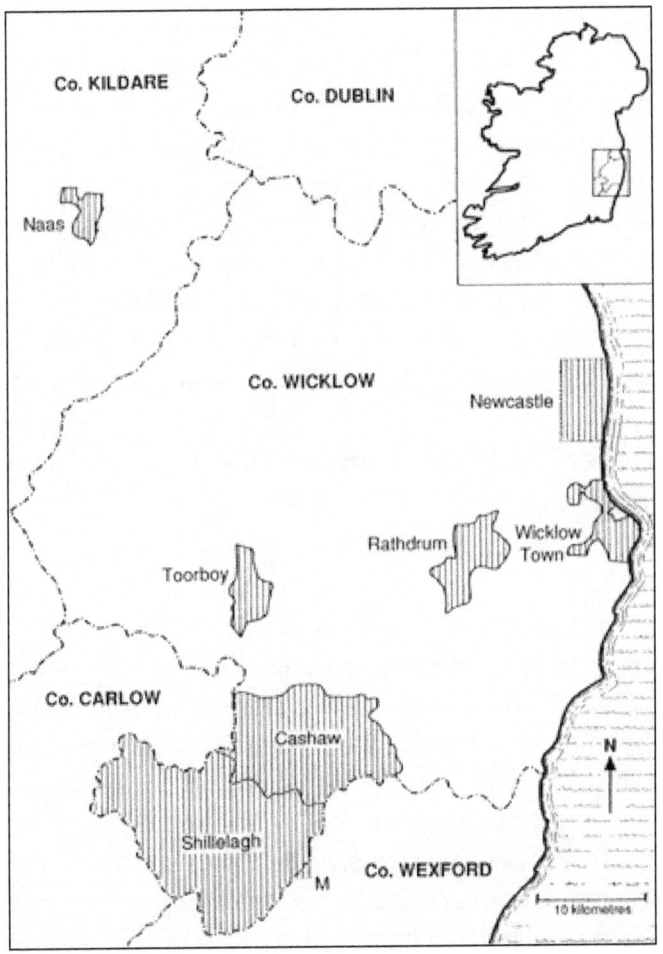

Figure 8: The location of the Watson-Wentworth properties in Ireland

The Irish coppice woods were managed as coppice-with-standards like their South Yorkshire counterparts. Between 1707 and 1749, coppice cycles varied from 16 to 33 years with a mean of 25 years. A scheme for all the woods, in 1749, assumed a 22-year cycle. The standards were overwhelmingly oak, but ash, elm and alder were also mentioned. The 1749 coppicing scheme laid down that, at each fall, 60 standards per plantation acre (37 per statute acre) should be left standing. The standards were not even-aged. The 1748 scheme stipulated that, at each fall, ten black barks (that had grown through at least two coppice cycles) and 50 wavers (that had grown through no more than one coppice cycle) should be left.

The most vital element in coppice management is protection of the coppice growth from grazing animals. The Watson-Wentworth Irish coppices were protected by ditches, i.e. ditched banks. In some places double ditches were constructed. On the banks, whitethorn hedges were planted. In some cases, there was a double hedge. Wood surveyors sent over from England sometimes recorded depredation of coppices through illegal browsing by farm animals. One surveyor, in 1728, noted that part of one coppice had been 'Eaten as Bare as A Bowling Green'!

Constructional timber from the Wentworth estate's Irish woods

Building timber was a very important product of these Irish woods in the first half of the eighteenth century. It was sold by the named piece and in undifferentiated lots. Named pieces included unworked wood described as poles and saplings and semi-finished and finished articles such as cleft spars, principals, purlins, beams, collar beams, hammer beams, rafters, laths, shingles, lintels, doorcases, clapboard and 'window stuff'. Named industrial items included helves, millshafts and timber for waterwheels. Timber was also provided for a substantial number of named building projects including Dublin Barracks for which £1,423 were received in 1708-09.(this must have been the famous Collins Barracks, now a museum, that was built between 1704 and 1710) and Dublin 'Colledge' in 1719 (the famous long room in the Old Library at Trinity College was built between 1712 and 1732).

Timber was also supplied for the construction of courthouses at Athy, Carlow and Wicklow; repairs to market houses at Blessington and Newtown Mount Kennedy; new churches at Coolkenna, Donard, Inch and Kilcullen; church repairs at Ballymore, Baltinglass, Carnew, Clonegall, Donaghmoor, Hackettstown, Hollywood, Kilcommon, Lymrick andTullow; a new gaol at Carlow; five bark mills; and a fulling mill. Timber, along with carpenters and joiners were also provided for building four 'school houses' between 1713 and 1718. Fifteen pieces of timber were also sold for making a bridge near Donard. The accounts reveal a great diversity of business with buyers great and small. Jostling with purchasers of many tons of building timber were customers like the one in 1715 who bought ten round poles for a dog-house!

Lying within a reasonable distance from the Irish Sea coast, ship timber, like general building timber, was an important product of the standard trees of the Irish woods. Ship timber was sold squared, sawn, and in the round. It was sold in the woods, at timber yards and delivered, sometimes at the estate's expense sometimes at the buyer's. It was generally sold direct to shipbuilders, whose buyers came to the estate, but some went to dealers and some was carried to Wicklow 'to be laid on the Murrow for Sale'. The Murrough is the shingle beach that stretches northwards from the town.

All types of ship timber were sold: boat boards, bowsprits, deck beans, futtocks, gunwales, keels, keelsons, knees, masts (fore masts, main masts and mizzen masts), rabbet bends (a rabbet was a notch or groove into which another timber could be inserted), rudders, ship frames, ship planks, skegs and stems, besides many 'bend trees' for unspecified uses. Scaffolding poles and bilgeways (the cradles in which the ship was built and from which it was launched) were also sold to shipbuilders, and treenails, described in the accounts as 'trunnils or 'shipp pins', were sold by the thousand.

Most of the ship timber went to Dublin and Wicklow, although a substantial proportion of that carried to Wicklow was then shipped to England. Between 1707 and 1720, twenty-one shipbuilders and ship timber dealers were mentioned by name. Of the 16 for whom a location was given, two, apparently dealers, were from within the estate itself, one was from Arklow, one was from Wexford, four were from Wicklow, four were from Dublin and five were from Whitehaven in Cumbria. There are several references in the accounts of timber for Whitehaven shipbuilders being taken by car (a two-wheeled horse-drawn haulage vehicle) to Wicklow for dispatch.

Conclusion

It is clear that, there is a strong connection between the management of deer parks, wooded commons and coppice-with-standards woods in South Yorkshire in the past and the supply of constructional timber for local buildings, domestic, agricultural and industrial. Ship timber was clearly a minor end-product because of its location far from the coast. This was not the case in the Watson-Wentworth estate woodlands in County Wicklow in Ireland in the first half of the eighteenth century. There, besides making a major contribution to the building of the colonial landscape of churches, schools and courthouses, the woodlands were major contributors of constructional timber not only for farm tenants and industrial premises but also for the ship building and ship repair industries in the ports of Dublin, Wicklow, Wexford and Arklow in Ireland and Whitehaven in England.

References

Evelyn, J (1706) *Silva or a Discourse of Trees*. Scott, Chiswell & Sawbridge, London.

Hall, T.W. (1914) *Descriptive Catalogue of the Jackson Collection*, J.W. Northend, Sheffield.

Hall, T.W. (1916)) *A Descriptive Catalogue of Miscellaneous Charters and Other Documents*. J. W. Northend Ltd, Sheffield.

Hunter, J. (1828) *South Yorkshire: the History and Topography of the Deanery of Doncaster*. **Volume 1**, J.B. Nicols and Son, London.

Jones, M. (1986) Coppice wood management in the eighteenth century: an example from County Wicklow. *Irish Forestry*, **43**, 15-31.

Jones, M. (1993) Kirkstead Abbey Grange: Part 1 – speculations on its origins. *Ivanhoe Review*, **No 4**, Spring 1993, 3-12.

Jones, M. (1997) Woodland Management on the Duke of Norfolk's Sheffield estate in the early eighteenth century. In: Jones, M. (ed.) *Aspects of Sheffield 1: Discovering Local History*. Wharncliffe Publishing Limited, Barnsley, 48-69.

Jones, M. (1998) The rise, decline and extinction of spring wood management in south-west Yorkshire. In: Watkins, C. (ed.) *European Woods and Forests: Studies in Cultural History*. CAB International, Wallingford, 55-72.

Jones, M. (2000) The absentee landlord's landscape: The Watson-Wentworth Estate in eighteenth century Ireland. *Landscapes*, **1(2)**, 33-52.

Jones, M. (2007) 'Buildid of Woode': The Lost Tradition of Timber-framed Builings. Chapter 3 in Jones, M. *South Yorkshire Yesterday: Glimpses of the Past*. Smith Settle, Skipton.

Jones, M. (2009) Sheffield's Woodland Heritage. 4th edition (first published in 1989), Wildtrack Publishing, Sheffield.

Jones, M. (2012) *Trees and Woodland in the South Yorkshire Landscape*. Whancliffe Books, Barnsley.

Jones, M. (2013) *Gapping, Raddling and Snagging, an illustrated glossary of woodland management terms*. Wildtrack Publishing, Sheffield.

Rackham, O. (2006) *Woodlands*. Collins (New Naturalist Series), London.

Ronksley, J. C. (ed.) (1908) An *exact and perfect Survey of the Manor of Sheffield by John Harrison, 1637*. Robert White and Co, Worksop.

Ryder, P. (1979) *Timber Framed Buildings in South Yorkshire*. South Yorkshire County Council, Barnsley.

Tyers, I. (2002) *Dendrochronological analysis of timbers from the Manorial Barn, Whiston, near Rotherham, Yorkshire*. ARCUS, Sheffield.

A 'Swill' or 'Spelk' basket made from thin strips of oak (spelks) woven around an ash or hazel frame. Common in parts of the old West Riding of Yorkshire. This is a newly made basket to the traditional design. Source: C. Handley (2016)

Chapter 11. Managed trees in coppice-with-standards woodland

Melvyn Jones
Sheffield Hallam University

Introduction

Until the second part of the nineteenth century ancient woods throughout Great Britain had been managed as coppices, either as simple coppice or as coppice-with-standards for many centuries. The word coppice is derived from the Old French *couper*, to cut. In coppice woods the trees were periodically (usually every seven to 30 years) cut down to near the ground to what is called a stool and from the stool 'sprang' multiple stems, called coppice or underwood (Figure 1).

Figure 1. A newly cut coppice stool in a simple coppice in Kent.

I use the word sprang advisedly, as the word spring is an alternative name for a coppice wood. The earliest record of the use of the word spring to denote a coppice wood was in an act of 1482 'for inclosing of woods in forests, chases and purlieus' by Edward IV. The rotational time gap between coppicing was known as the coppice cycle. There is no reason why a coppice stool should not supply a crop of underwood for many centuries. This form of management, therefore, conserved woods and, if properly managed and protected, became self-renewing resources and inexhaustible sources of wood and timber (Figure 2).

Figure 2. Well-grown coppice, Frith Wood, Gloucestershire.

Early records of coppice management

When coppicing began has long been shrouded in mystery. Oliver Rackham, in his ground-breaking book *Ancient Woodland: its history, vegetation and uses in England* (1980), stated that the earliest known formal account of coppicing was in the account book of Beaulieu Abbey in Hampshire written in 1269/70 (Rackham, 1980,141). But coppicing was widespread at the time of the Domesday Survey, in 1086, if the term *silva minuta* is translated as underwood referring to a coppicing tradition as opposed to *silva pastilis* (wood-pasture). If we take the results of William the Conqueror's great national survey of 1086 at face value, woodland cover had been drastically reduced by the late eleventh century and the countryside was not covered by the boundless woodland of people's imagination. Rackham calculated that the Domesday survey of 1086 covered 27 million acres of land of which 4.1 million were wooded, that is 15 per cent of the surveyed area. His figure for the West Riding of Yorkshire is 16 per cent (Rackham, 1980, 50-51). My own calculation for South Yorkshire is just under 13 per cent. By comparison, woods today, including plantations, cover just over six per cent of this region. This means that in the eleventh century, South Yorkshire, like most other parts of the country, was relatively sparsely wooded even by today's standards. And, in some counties, the traveller might have gone a considerable distance without seeing a wood. In Leicestershire, for example woodland at Domesday covered only 3.3 per cent of the county, in Devon it was 3.8 per cent, and in the East Riding of Yorkshire it was 4.4 per cent (Rackham, 1980, 50-51). At Domesday in the western half of South Yorkshire, woodland was relatively extensive with a substantial number of communities having more than 1000 acres of woodland. In contrast, in the Magnesian Limestone belt and in the Humberhead Levels further east, the picture was different. In those areas, woodland was more scattered, and amounts in individual communities were generally smaller than to the west. Additionally, the Magnesian Limestone belt, although only covering about one-eighth of the land area of the region, contained nearly a third (10 out of 33) of the places in which woodland was not recorded at all. When woods were relatively abundant and populations relatively small, they would have been able to be exploited for timber and underwood and, as common pastures for cattle, sheep and pigs, i.e., as wood-pastures. Of the 111 manors in which woodland was recorded, 102 had wood-pastures and only seven had coppices. All seven occurrences of coppice woods were in the eastern half of the region, two in the eastern part of the Coal Measures and five on the Magnesian Limestone. On the other hand, although wood-pastures were found throughout South Yorkshire, they were very extensive, and the only type of woodland found in the Millstone Grit country and throughout most of the Coal Measures. What this analysis suggests is that by the eleventh century coppice management was carried out in those parts of South Yorkshire where the population was fairly dense and settlement had been established at a very early date but that in other parts of the region wood and timber were obtained from the extensive wood-pastures.

The first known record of coppicing in other parts of Great Britain shows some variation. In Wales, for example, coppicing is shown in a manuscript dating from the early thirteenth century (Linnard, 1982, 34-35) and in Scotland there is evidence of coppicing on monastic estates in Perthshire in the late fifteenth century (Lindsay, 1980). But coppice management had been carried on for millennia even before it was recorded in the Domesday Book. Research in the Somerset Levels by Bryony and John Coles (Coles and Coles, 1986) has suggested that the record may be extended back another 4,000 years when the earliest Neolithic hurdle trackways were being made and laid down, using materials from what are believed to be managed coppices.

The coppice-with-standards woodland management system

In coppice-with-standards woodland some trees were not coppiced but allowed to grow on to become mature single-stemmed trees and these were the standards (Figure 3).

Figure 3. A diagrammatic representation of a wood managed as a coppice-with-standards. On the left is part of the wood coppiced recently and in which re-growth is limited. On the right the underwood is two or three years old and has sprung from the stools to a height of four or five feet. Among the underwood are three single-stemmed standards of various ages. The wood is bounded by a bank and ditch. The bank has a protective hedge and a pollard.

The coppice provided wood and the standard trees provided timber. The standards originated in two different ways. Most were single stemmed trees that had never been coppiced, referred to as maiden trees (Figure 4). Others were the single stems preserved and grown on after a well grown coppice stool had all but one of its poles removed. This is sometimes called stored coppice. This method also assumed importance in the nineteenth century when coppice-with-standards woods were being converted to high forest through a combination of the complete removal of coppice stools, storing of coppice and planting of new trees.

Figure 4. Part of the recently cut coppice-with-standards compartment in Felsham Hall Wood (part of Bradfield Woods), Suffolk, in the 1980s.

The standards were of various ages. The youngest timber trees, i.e. those that had only grown through one coppice cycle, were generally referred to as wavers (sometimes weavers or waivers), probably because their removal had been waived (selectively not taken place) during the cutting of the coppice. Older standard trees also had a variety of names. In an Act for the Preservation of Woods in 1543, the standards were referred to as standils and storers. Leases in Essex refer to them as staddles and storers (Rackham, 1986, 23) and in Hampshire they were variously called stadles and heirs (James, 1991, 178). In South Yorkshire, from the sixteenth century, those standards that had grown through two coppice cycles were referred to in woodland accounts and management plans as black barks and trees that had grown through more than two cycles were called lordings. Together, the black barks and lordings were known as reserves or herriors. Some standard trees, both wavers and reserves, were felled at the end of the coppice cycle along with the cutting of the coppice, but others would be felled to order, with the customer sometimes visiting a wood and selecting particular trees.

Before felling operations commenced, setting out had to take place which involved making the woodland rides passable by clearing the undergrowth (variously called swatching or brushing) and removing low growing branches. Then, the trees that were to stand or be felled had to be identified. Sometimes it was the trees that were to be felled that were identified; sometimes it was those that were to stand. Two methods of identification were used. Sometimes trees were numbered with a hooked knife called a scribe iron. Alternatively, they were marked with paint. A widely used paint was a red ochre known as raddle (not to be confused with a radle or radling which was an interwoven hurdle), reddle or ruddle that was mixed with oil. Sometimes reserves were marked with white paint and wavers marked in red. On some estates, in the late medieval and early modern period, the commencement of felling was surrounded by a certain amount of ceremony. Crews of woodmen were assembled, and jobs apportioned. Agreements often concluded with the drinking of ale and payment of 'earnest money' (a small payment to seal the bargain).

By the late Middle Ages and early modern period, coppice-with-standards management had achieved a high degree of sophistication. This is well illustrated by the agreement in the 1650s between the most powerful ironmaster in South Yorkshire, Lionel Copley. He entered into a succession of agreements with local landowners to fell and coal (i.e. to make into charcoal) their spring woods. The surviving leases illustrate contemporary coppice practice (Goodchild, 1996). For example, in 1657 Copley entered into a 10-year agreement with the 2nd Earl of Strafford of Wentworth Woodhouse to fell the underwood and selected timber trees in thirteen of the Earl's woods. Under the contract, Copley was to cut 1000 cords of wood (a pile of wood four feet wide, eight feet long and four feet high) each year for charcoal making. He was allowed to cut 'young timber trees, Lordings, Black Barks, powles, coppices and Springwoode' together with 'the Bark thereof'. The lessee was also instructed to make sure that 'all the said Springwoode [is] well and sufficiently weavered' and that the coppice was 'workmanlike cutt downe ... and the stowens [stools] thereof neare to the roote so as best preserve for future growth and next springing thereof'. He was also asked to burn the 'Ramell' in places that would be 'least prejudiciall to the weavers and Springwood which shall be left to grow'. 'Ramell' was the small brushwood (Wentworth Woodhouse Muniments, Sheffield Archives, WWM D778).

The products of coppice-with-standards woods

The timber trees, mainly oak, were for building projects. It was not until the seventeenth century that stone and brick supplanted timber as the main building material, timber holding prime place since the first permanent settlements were built in Neolithic times. Even castles and parish churches were constructed of timber before they were rebuilt in stone. The medieval house carpenter or housewright, did not obtain his timber in the form of ready sawn or shaped planks and beams – he selected trees in woods and hedges that would roughly square up to the dimensions of the components required with the minimum of shaping, large trees for the beams and smaller trees for things like rafters. The timber used was mostly oak and it was sawn or shaped with an axe or adze while it was still 'green' for ease of working. In his book, *The Woods of South-east Essex*, Oliver Rackham has shown in diagrammatic form how a crooked and tapering oak tree was converted into a crooked and tapering beam in the Prior's Chamber, Brittlewell in Essex (Rackham, 1886,42). The remains of sawpits can still be recognized through careful searching in old coppice-with-standards woods. Nails were not used to hold the timbers in place because the tannic acid in the unseasoned oak would corrode them. Instead oak pegs sometimes called treenails, were used and were made in their thousands.

There are two traditions of timber-framed building that are likely to be met with in England that used vast amounts of timber from coppice-with-standards woods: post-and-truss (or box frame) and cruck building. A post-and-truss building consisted of a series of trusses or cross-frames formed by pairs of vertical posts (principal posts) standing on large stones (stylobates) connected by tie beams. Longitudinally, the tops of the principal posts were connected by horizontal timbers called wall plates (at the top of the posts), girding beams (at mid-wall level) and sill beams (at or near floor level). For extra stability, curved timber braces were added. The walls, where not of stone or brick, were formed by vertical timbers called studs with the spaces between filled with wattle and daub, stone slates or split oak laths, all covered with plaster, or with herringbone patterns of brick. The roofs of post-and-truss buildings were either of the common rafter or principal rafter type. There were many variations of principal rafter roofs. In the king post type, which was common in the north of England, a single vertical post rose from the tie beam; in East Anglia and the south-east, the crown-post type, which had a vertical post rising from the tie beam to a collar purlin, was widely distributed. Cruck buildings were common in the upland areas of Britain and parts of the Midlands but are virtually unknown in eastern and south-eastern England. In a cruck building, the weight was carried on pairs of timbers called cruck blades which rise from or near the ground and meet at the apex of the roof. The blades are usually curved, having been selected from naturally bent trees. Often a bent tree was split or sawn lengthways to make two matching blades. The structure was strengthened by tie beams connecting each pair of cruck blades. The roof of the building was stabilised by struts called windbraces. It is assumed that most cruck blades were oak from coppice-with-standards woods but in some counties, including Worcestershire and Herefordshire some cruck blades were of black poplar, a non-woodland tree, which grows naturally in a curved shape.

Shipbuilding also consumed a large amount of timber, mostly oak, from coppice-with-standards woods. For example, in the early eighteenth century, the Watson-Wentworth family of Wentworth Woodhouse in South Yorkshire owned and managed thirty coppice-with-standards woods on their vast estate (91,000 acres) in County Wicklow in Ireland. The Irish coppice woods were managed as coppice-with-standards (Jones, 1986). Between 1707 and 1749 coppice cycles varied from 16 to 33 years with a mean of 25 years. In 1749, a scheme for all the woods assumed a 22-year coppice cycle. The standards were overwhelmingly of oak, but ash and alder were also mentioned. The 1749 coppicing scheme stipulated that at each fall, 60 standards per plantation acre (37 per statute acre) should be left standing. The standards were not even aged; the 1749 scheme stipulated that at each fall ten black barks and 50 wavers should be left in every acre of coppice wood.

Building timber was a very important product of these Irish woods in the first half of the eighteenth century. It was sold by the named piece and in undifferentiated lots. Named pieces included unworked wood described as poles and saplings and semi-finished and finished articles such as 'riberrys' (cleft spars), principals, purlins, beams, collar beams, hammer beams, rafters, laths, shingles, lintels, doorcases, clapboard and 'window stuff'. Named industrial items included helves, millshafts and timber for waterwheels. Timber was also supplied for the construction of courthouses, repairs to market halls, for new churches and church repairs, for new schools, for bark mills and, a fulling mill.

Due to their location near the Irish Sea coast, ship timber was an important product of the standard trees of these Irish woods. Ship timber was sold squared, sawn and in the round. It was sold in the woods; at timber yards and delivered; sometimes at the estate's expense sometimes at the buyer's but generally sold direct to shipbuilders whose buyers came to the estate. All types of ship timber were sold: boat boards, bowsprits, deck beans, futtocks, gunwales, keels, keelsons, knees, masts (fore masts, main masts and mizzen masts), rabbet bends (a rabbet was a notch or groove into which another timber could be inserted), rudders, ship frames, ship planks, skegs and stems, besides many 'bend trees' for unspecified uses. Scaffolding poles and bilgeways (the cradles in which the ship was built and from which it was launched) were also sold to shipbuilders, and treenails, described in the accounts as 'trunnils or 'shipp pins', were sold by the thousand. Most of the ship timber went to Dublin and Wicklow, although a substantial proportion of that which went to Wicklow was then shipped to England. Between 1707 and 1720 twenty-one shipbuilders and ship timber dealers were mentioned by name. Of the 16 for whom a location was given, two, apparently dealers, were from within the estate itself, one was from Arklow, one from Wexford, four from Wicklow, four from Dublin and five were from Whitehaven in Cumbria.

The oldest recorded and most important use of coppice poles and branchwood from the standard trees was for charcoal making (Figure 5). Although the market for charcoal for iron smelting gradually disappeared in the eighteenth century with the spread of the use of coke, charcoal continued to be important for making blister steel in cementation furnaces well into the twentieth century. Coppice woods are dotted with charcoal-making sites – level areas, with considerable design variation, about fifteen feet ($c.5$ m) in diameter called charcoal hearths or pitsteads. In steep-sided woods they were cut out of the hillside. Another important fuel made from coppice wood between $c.1575-1750$ was whitecoal which was used in a mixture with charcoal in lead smelting. Whitecoal was small slivers of wood, dried in a kiln until all the moisture was driven out. The remains of whitecoal kilns survive in woods in north Derbyshire, South Yorkshire, the Yorkshire Dales and in Wales. They are in the form of depressions varying considerably in size usually on slightly sloping ground with a spout at the down-slope end. They were originally covered by stone lintels on which the wood was placed for drying.

Investigating Tree Archaeology

Figure 5. A drawing based on an old, faded photograph found in an attic. Charcoal makers are shown beside their hut on the edge of a South Yorkshire coppice-with-standards wood in the late nineteenth century. Note the hut for the dog. The standard trees not to be felled have been marked with paint. Courtesy of Avril Bramhall.

Coppice-with-standards woods also provided the raw materials for a bewildering variety of crafts and industries. Stout oak poles made good pit props or 'puncheons'; tall underwood poles were used as hop poles, for scaffolding and for ladders; oak bark was used for making the liquor used by tanners in the leather industry; hazel rods were woven into hurdles; oak, hazel and willow were used in basket making; alder, which was easy to work and waterproof, made excellent clog soles; ash and hazel made springy brush and tool handles. Oak, beech, ash and elm were used to make cottage furniture including of course the famous Windsor chairs. Holly was grown in special woods called holly hags or hollins and the trees were coppiced and pollarded to provide 'leaf fodder' for sheep, cattle and deer in winter. And, brushwood was made into besom brooms and bundled together to make faggots for heating bread ovens or for protecting riverbanks.

For all these reasons, sites of the seasonal dwelling places of charcoal makers, whitecoal makers, chair bodgers and other woodland craftsmen can also be found in former coppice woods. This is besides the living archaeology of neglected coppice stools and standard trees, and archaeological features like charcoal hearths and whitecoal kilns.

Protecting coppice woods

The boundaries of ancient woodlands converted into coppice woods tend to be zig-zagged with well marked peninsulas and bays like a rocky coast as if giant bites had been taken from them. This unevenness is the result of the unplanned, piecemeal clearing process, which in the medieval period was known as assarting and resulted in the creation of small irregular fields (Jones 1989; Jones 2012a). The shapes of the woods are sometimes most peculiar as if a giant pastry cutter had been at work with the woods representing the left-over pastry. Despite their peculiar shapes, it was of the utmost importance to carefully protect coppice woods from grazing animals in their early years of growth after felling. This was not only to protect young coppice growth but also the next generation of standard trees. For this reason, they were looked after by a woodward who had general responsibility for safeguarding the coppice growth across an estate, aided by individual coppice keepers who all kept a vigilant eye open for trespassers, thieves and unsupervised livestock from neighbouring farmland.

The proceedings of local manorial courts and woodwards' accounts are full of instances of waiting for and catching offenders (human and animal), of accusations of trespass and theft, of appearances in court, of fines, and of payment to woodwards' helpers for tracking down suspects and repossessing stolen timber, wood and bark (Jones, 1987; Jones, 1997). The illegal felling and carrying away of timber were the most widely reported offences. For example, in 1564, William Dungworth was fined twelve pence for felling and carrying away wood from the Earl of Shrewsbury's Wincobank Wood in Sheffield and in the same year, Thomas Beaumont was similarly fined for felling and taking away two loads of wood from 'le Firth of Rivelinge', the earl's private forest that contained valuable coppice woods and holly hags. From time to time there were eruptions of widespread theft and these led to concerted action. Towards the end of the second decade of the eighteenth century (1718) the level of thefts from the Duke of Norfolk's woods in South Yorkshire was such that the Duke's woodward was granted a warrant by the justices of the peace instructing local constables to 'make diligent search ... in the most suspitious houses' and to bring suspects before the magistrates. The inclusion of such strong instructions to the constables as 'All Excuses & Delays Sett apart' and 'Faile not at your perills' reflect the seriousness of the situation. Whether or not falls had taken place generally in particular woods, there were also particularly sensitive times of the year. In late summer and autumn, when berries and nuts were ripe, and in winter when firewood and food supplies were low, thefts and trespass by poachers were particularly common. The practice of collecting hazel nuts in local woods caused widespread damage to wood boundaries and the underwood and often prompted the posting of warning notices around estate and woodland boundaries (Figure 6).

When the coppice was well grown owners' and/or tenants' animals were allowed access to the coppice woods to graze on payment of a fee. For example, in the eighteenth century, in the coppices belonging to the Crown in Rockingham Forest, Northamptonshire, deer were admitted into coppices after four years of re-growth and cattle after seven years (Peterken, 1976, 130). The practice was known as herbage or agistment. Detailed agistment records have survived for the 300-acre Ecclesall Woods in Sheffield for the period 1709 to 1714. The animals grazed during that period were horses, mares, foals, cows, calves, heifers and stirks. The lengths of time that they were grazed in the woods varied between a full gist (four months), half a gist (two months) or for just a few weeks. But, when animals got into the woods during the early stages of coppice growth they were rounded up, put in the village pound and the owners fined. For example, in 1718, Enoch Moor of Charlton Brook Farm was fined one shilling when nine of his sheep were pounded out of Greno Wood at Grenoside near Sheffield, and in 1720, two men were paid three shillings and sixpence for their trouble in 'pounding 5 sheep belonging to Mr Watts that was trespassing in the neighbouring Little Hall Wood'. Public announcements were sometimes made at the end of a coppice cycle when young growth was just beginning to re-grow. The vicar of Ecclesfield was paid twopence in 1718 by the Duke of Norfolk's woodward for giving notice to tenants and freeholders, presumably at a Sunday service, 'to take care that their cattle do no longer Continue to Graise in Greno Wood for spoyling ye young sprouts'.

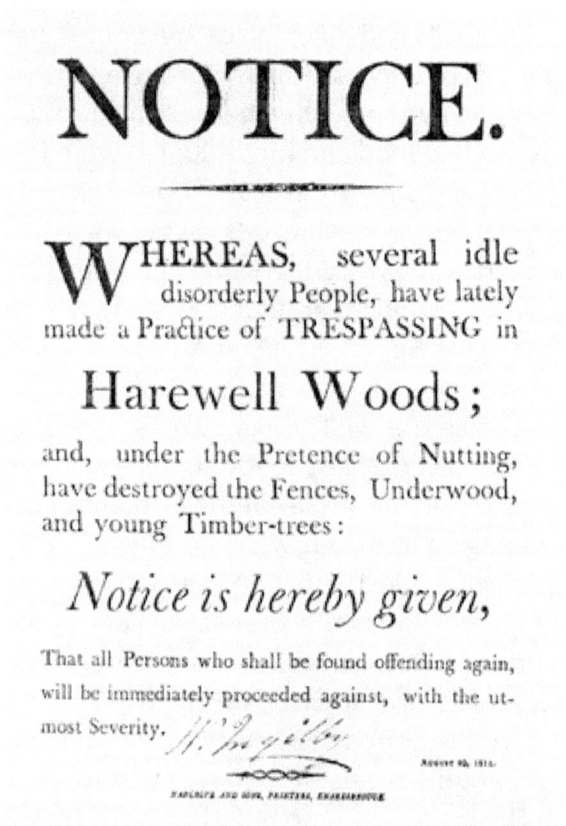

NOTICE.

WHEREAS, several idle disorderly People, have lately made a Practice of TRESPASSING in

Harewell Woods;

and, under the Pretence of Nutting, have destroyed the Fences, Underwood, and young Timber-trees:

Notice is hereby given,

That all Persons who shall be found offending again, will be immediately proceeded against, with the utmost Severity.

Figure 6. Nutters poster for Harewell Woods on the Ripley Hall (Ingleby) estate, Nidderdale, North Yorkshire, 1811.

Good fences therefore, in the form of ditched banks surmounted by stone walls, hedges or paling fences, free-standing, on banks or revetted into banks, were absolutely essential around coppice woods. Indeed, the verb 'to encoppice' means to protect the underwood and young standard trees prior to rotational felling in a <u>fenced</u> wood. The Watson-Wentworth Irish coppices, referred to above, were protected by ditches, i.e. ditched banks. In some places double ditches were constructed. On the banks, whitethorn hedges were planted. In some cases, there was a double hedge. But even then, if the hedges were destroyed by bad weather or by human negligence it could be disastrous for young coppice growth. One woodland surveyor, in 1728, reporting on the state of the Watson-Wentworth Irish coppices noted that part of one coppice had been 'Eaten as Bare as A Bowling Green' (WWM A769 in Sheffield Archives).

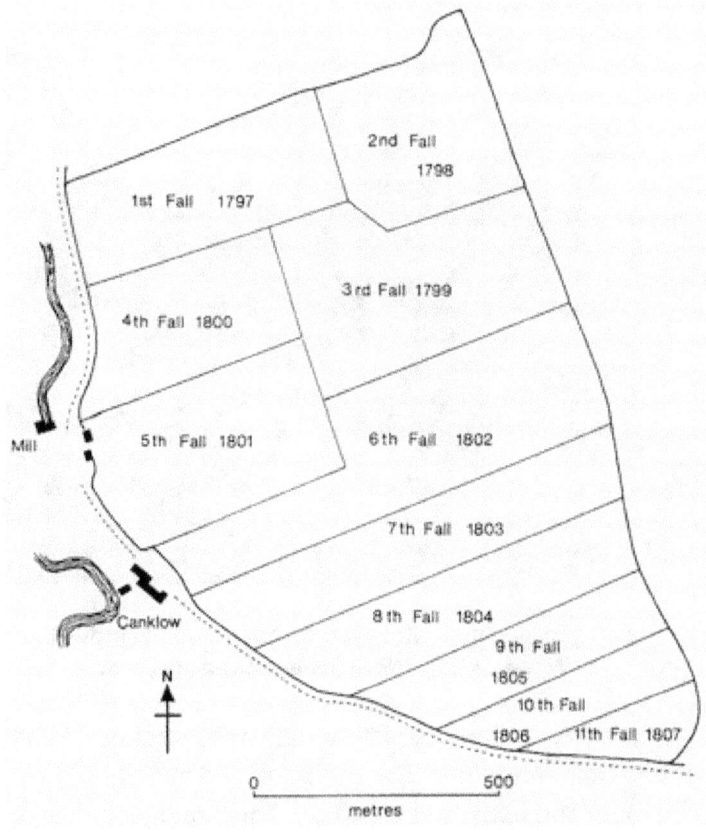

Figure 7. The 243-acre Canklow Wood, in South Yorkshire in 1807 showing the boundaries of its eleven compartments and the dates of last 'falls'.

Boundary features may not only surround old coppice woods. In the case of large woods that were compartmented and sometimes leased to different individuals at different times, there will be internal boundary features (Figure 7). Ecclesall Woods in Sheffield, a 300-acre continuous stretch of woodland, in the mid-seventeenth century, was divided into twenty separate woods, each with its own woodland name and with the coppice growth varying from two years to sixteen years To eliminate boundary disputes and to prevent animals that were being agisted in the well-grown coppices straying into newly cut ones, compartment fences, which appear from surviving fragments to have consisted of banks and walls, would have been essential. Compartments had a number of regional names: cants, coupes, falls, fells, and haggs, for example.

Figure 8. The broad woodbank with external ditch made to protect Felsham Hall Wood, Suffolk. Note the woodbank pollard.

Wood banks surrounding coppice woods have ditches on the <u>outside</u>. The higher and broader the bank and the deeper the ditch, the older the bank is likely to be. Thick hedges or wooden post and rail fences surmounted these banks and where trees grew on them, they were often pollarded so that animals grazing along the woodland edge could not feed on the new shoots (Figure 8). These woodbank pollards, if they still survive, are usually by far the oldest trees still growing in a former ancient coppice wood.

Figure 9. Woodland boundary bank with external ditch and beyond that a stone boundary wall surrounding Greno Wood at Grenoside, South Yorkshire

Walls took the place of banks and ditches where good wall stone outcropped. What is interesting is that in two of the most widely read modern works on the history and archaeology of woods by Oliver Rackham (Rackham, 1976, 1980) which were based on research in eastern and southern England, wood-banks are dealt with at length but walls are dismissed in a sentence. But the truth is that in the north and west of Britain, in 'stone wall country', both walls and banks were used to protect coppice woods. And, the walls protecting woods in these regions, as noted above, come in a variety of forms: a wall on its own, a wall on a bank, a wall revetted into a bank and even a wall on the outside of a wood-bank and external ditch (Figure 9). Walls are not uniform features. The oldest walls were made from orthostats, boulders removed from the land as clearances were made. Whole walls or the lower parts of walls made with orthostats may still be found surrounding woodlands and these are likely to be of medieval date at the very latest. After the Middle Ages, double-skinned drystone walls with rows of topping stones became general. One word of warning must be given about trying to date stone walls:

through human and animal interference and through demolition to remove wood and timber, an enormous amount of patching (called 'gapping' in some areas) has taken place over the centuries, and so many walls are made of a combination of the work of the original waller and patches made at various times since its erection.

Figure 10 shows a small selection of coppice wood boundaries found in South Yorkshire and north Derbyshire. The wood is on the left in each case. The first five boundaries are all mainly or wholly banks. The Rollestone Wood bank has a shallow external ditch but there is no evidence of a wall topping the bank; there may once have been a laid hedge. The Low Spring bank still has the footings of an old wall that ran along the top of the bank. The Tinsley Park bank is doubly interesting. It is very broad and has no external ditch. Tinsley Park was once a deer park later converted into a compartmented coppice wood. This particular stretch of the woodland boundary was also not only a park boundary and then a coppice wood boundary, but also formed a parish boundary. The Holmesfield Park boundary in north Derbyshire is the most remarkable one. The bank is well above head height when the observer is standing in the ditch outside the wood and even so for double protection a wall was built on top. The ditch is deep and wide and functioned as a pack horse route to bring lead ore from the White Peak to the South Yorkshire water-powered ore-hearths. The second Holmesfield Wood diagram has an internal ditch, betraying the origins of the wood as a deer park, with the ditch positioned to keep the deer in the park. The last two diagrams show stone wall boundaries of coal measure sandstone. Free-standing walls like the first one shown at Smithy Wood were quite common, but often they were revetted into natural or man-made boundary banks as shown in the second diagram also at Smithy Wood. One curious ecological note can be added. The grass, wood melick (*Melica uniflora*) has a 'circumboscal' distribution, i.e. it tends to occur along woodland boundaries, often occurring on medieval woodbanks, indeed Oliver Rackham refers to it as the 'woodbank grass' (Rackham, 1980).

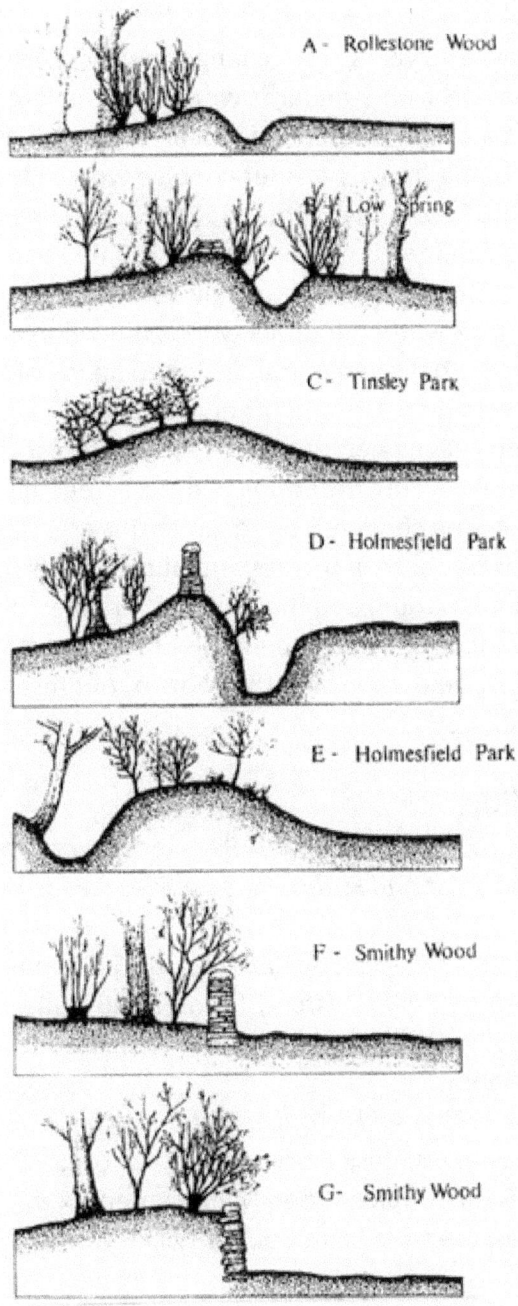

Figure 10. Examples of coppice wood boundaries in South Yorkshire and north Derbyshire

Conclusion

During the last 150 years great changes have occurred to surviving coppice-with-standards woods. By the late 1980s, it was estimated that of the million and a quarter acres of broadleaved ancient woodland (mostly former coppice woods) that had survived until 1945, 30 per cent (375,000 acres) had been converted to coniferous plantation and 100,000 acres had been cleared altogether. But encouragingly, increasing numbers of surviving coppice-with-standards woods are being managed as such, and those that are, are mostly in the hands of local authorities, wildlife trusts and other conservation bodies. Many coppice woods have been converted to high forest through a combination of singling the coppice, natural regeneration and planting (including conifers). But despite this great loss, many gems still survive, both in private and public ownership. They need to be understood, and their history, archaeology and ecology recorded using a combination of documentary and field evidence. They take us back to the roots of our history and are irreplaceable.

Select Bibliography

Atherden, M.A. and Butlin, R.A. (1998) (eds) *Woodland in the Landscape: Past and Future Perspectives*, Leeds University Press.

Coles, B and Coles J (1986) *Sweet Track to Glastonbury: The Somerset Levels in Prehistory*, Thames and Hudson, London.

Edlin, H.L. (1974) *Woodland Crafts in Britain.* Country Book Club, Newton Abbot.

James, N.D.J. (1991) *An Historical Dictionary of Forestry and Woodland Terms.* Basil Blackwell Ltd, Oxford.

Jones, M. (1986) Coppice Wood Management in the Eighteenth century: an example from County Wicklow. *Irish Forestry*, **43**, 1, 15-32.

Jones, M. (1998) *The rise, decline and extinction of spring wood management in south-west Yorkshire*. In: C. Watkins (ed.) *European Woods and Forests: Studies in Cultural History.* CAB International, Wallingford, pp. 55-71.

Jones, M. (2009) *Sheffield's Woodland Heritage*. 4rd Edition, Wildtrack Publishing, Sheffield.

Jones, M. (2013) *Gapping, Raddling and Snagging: an illustrated glossary of terms associated with woodland management in South Yorkshire, 1086- c.1900*. Wildtrack Publishing, Sheffield.

Lindsay, J.M. (1980) *The Commercial use of woodland and coppice management*. In: M.I. Perry and T.R. Slater (eds) *The Making of the Scottish Countryside, Croom Helm*, London.

Linnard, W. (1982) *Welsh Woods and Forest: History and Utilization*. National Museum of Wales, Cardiff.

Marren, P. (1990) *Woodland Heritage*. David & Charles, Newton Abbot.

Muir, R. (2007) *Be Your Own Landscape Detective*. Chapter 1 'Trees and Woods'. Sutton Publishing, Stroud.

Peterken, G.F. (1976) Long-term changes in the woodlands of Rockinghan Forest and other areas. *The Journal of Ecology*, **64**, 1, 123-146.

Peterken, G. (1981) *Woodland Conservation and Management*. Chapman & Hall, London.

Rackham, O. (1976) *Trees and Woodland in the British Landscape*. J. M. Dent & Sons Ltd, London.

Rackham, O. (1980, revised edition, 2003) *Ancient Woodland: its history, vegetation and uses in England*. Edward Arnold, London (1980), Castlepoint Press, Colvend, Dalbeatties (2003).

Rackham, O. (1986) *The Woods of South-East Essex*. Rochford District Council, Rochford.

Rackham, O. (2007*) Woodlands*. (100th volume in the New Naturalist Series), Collins, London.

Rotherham, I. D., Jones, M., Smith, L. and Handley, C. (eds) (2008) *The Woodland Heritage Manual: A Guide to Investigating Wooded Landscapes*. Wildtrack Publishing, Sheffield.

Watkins, C. (1990) *Woodland Management and Conservation*. David & Charles, Newton Abbot.

A traditional Besom Maker or Broom Squire, 1930s (IDR)

Chapter 12. From tree-rings to timber trade: Dendrochronological evidence for woodland history in Scotland

Coralie M. Mills
Independent Consultant

Tree-ring evidence from Scotland's medieval buildings

An accumulating body of tree-ring evidence for Scotland over the last thousand years (Figure 1) allows some general observations to be made regarding the timber supply and woodland history. The medieval tree-ring record indicates that native oak was the principal source of structural timber in Scottish buildings before about AD 1450, often very long-lived oak which started life in the tenth and eleventh centuries (Baillie 1977; Crone & Mills 2002; Crone & Mills 2012; Mills & Crone 2012). At first sight this seems like an impressive resource to have on hand, but it may really signify a lack of sustainable forestry practices and difficulties in regeneration, meaning that younger timber was not available. The contributing factors were complex, very probably including intense grazing pressures, widespread bark-stripping, difficulty of timber transportation, social disruption from waves of war and disease, and worsening climate.

The Scottish parliament passed legislation in the fifteenth and early sixteenth centuries placing penalties on bark peeling and theft of green wood, and requiring land owners to plant trees, as a response to the perceived poor condition of the country's woodland resources 'considering that the wood of Scotland is utterly destroyed' (Smout et al., 2005, 38). We do sometimes see planting dates from this period in our oldest surviving oak woods, for example at Dalkeith (Mills, 2015), Cadzow and Lochwood (Baillie, 1977). However, the evidence from timbers in late medieval buildings rather suggests that, on the whole, these Acts were too little and too late. After 1450 until about 1600, the majority of tree-ring dated and dendro-provenanced oak in Scotland was imported, with structural timber coming from

Scandinavia and fine boards from the Eastern Baltic (Crone & Mills, 2012).

The post-medieval and early modern periods

In the late medieval and early post-medieval periods, there are only a handful of identified buildings with native Scottish oak, and the timber quality in them is often poor. Importation continues in the seventeenth and eighteenth centuries, but is almost wholly of pine, initially from Scandinavia but after the mid-eighteenth century, more usually from the eastern Baltic. This is despite increasingly frequent documented attempts to exploit the native Caledonian pine woods (Stewart, 2003; Smout et al., 2005).

The huge political and social upheavals of seventeenth and especially eighteenth century Scotland brought great changes to the ways in which woodlands were managed and used, especially in the Highlands, where much of the surviving native woodland lay. The increased drive by landowners for profit often eclipsed local traditional rights of use. Formerly open grazed woodlands were often enclosed and many contracts were sold to timber merchants and other adventurers to fell tracts of Highland pinewoods (Stewart, 2003). However, many such contracts failed well before their end date due to difficulties in extracting sufficient good quality timber of sufficient size, and particularly in transporting it profitably to markets (Smout et al., 2005).

The Napoleonic Wars, between 1793 and 1815, disrupted foreign imports, and led to price rises for domestic products and an escalation in the commercial exploitation of Scottish woodlands, especially in coppiced oak for bark and charcoal and native pine for timber. By the mid to late nineteenth century, cheap imports again eclipsed the domestic woodland products, and both oak coppicing and native pine exploitation were largely abandoned in Scotland. Many surviving native woods were converted to forestry plantation in the nineteenth and twentieth centuries, often for commercial conifer production, and only recently have we begun to unpick that through PAWS (Plantation on Ancient Woodland Site) restoration schemes.

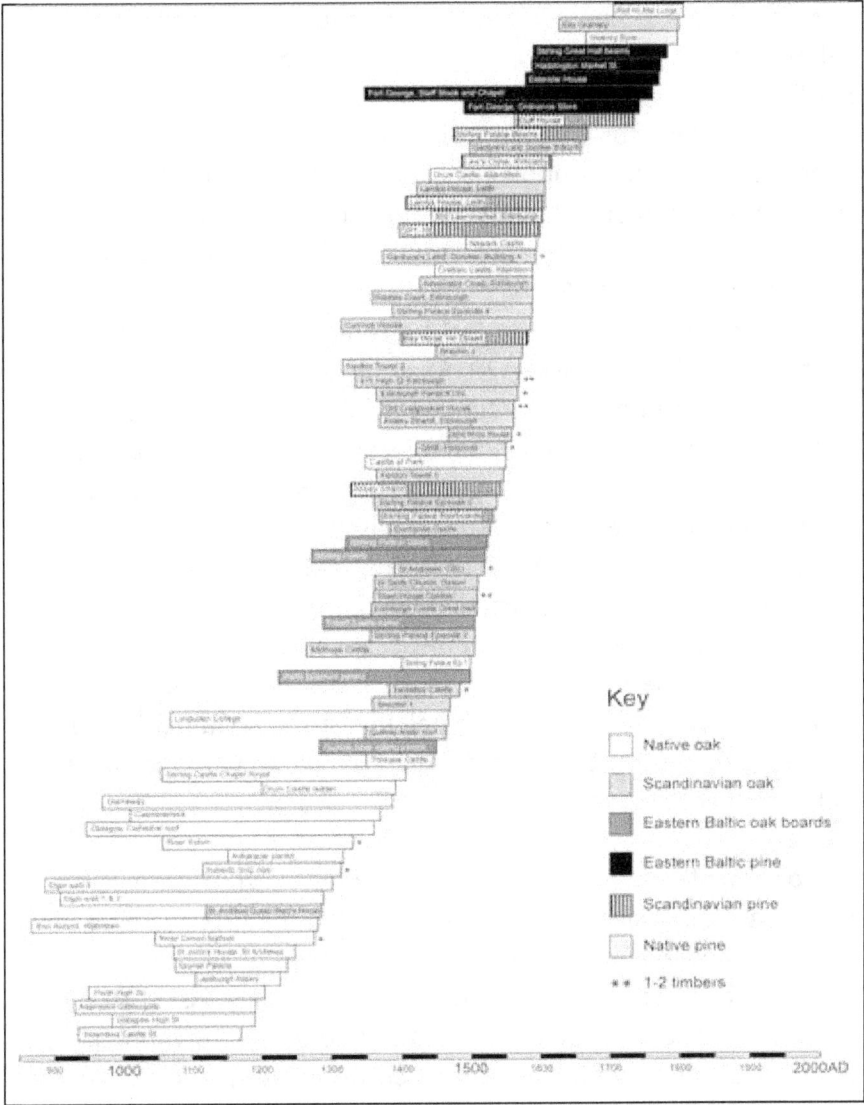

Figure 1. Overview of dendro-dated oak and pine sites in Scotland (before the addition of the SCOT2K native pine buildings); see Crone & Mills 2012; Mills & Crone 2012

Redressing bias in the oak data

The overall picture of oak woodland history and timber trade from the dendrochronological evidence is rather skewed in favour of imports because, firstly, the majority of historic buildings investigated are on the east coast where importation was most pronounced, and secondly, it has been much easier to recognise and date imported oak timber through the extensive network of reference chronologies in Europe for the medieval and post-medieval periods. There are far fewer native Scottish oak chronologies for comparison, and the record is patchy both geographically and chronologically. This is being addressed through research programmes to build native Scottish oak chronologies and investigate historic buildings in regional gaps, such as the recent NOAP (Native Oak and Pine) project for North East Scotland (Crone & Mills, 2011; Crone & Mills, 2012; Mills & Crone, 2012; Crone & Mills, 2015) and the new South East Scotland Oak Dendro (SESOD) project (Mills, 2017). SESOD is using as a basis the long oak chronology recently built from deadwood samples of the Old Oaks at Dalkeith Park, the oldest of which originate in the sixteenth century (Mills, 2015). The dendrochronological research at Dalkeith also identified phases of planting and coppicing, charting development of the wooded park from the late medieval period onwards. The SESOD project aims to extend the native south east Scottish oak record back in time by locating and analysing native oak in historic buildings in the region from 1700 and earlier, so that an overlap with the Dalkeith oaks chronology is established.

The dating of an oak-built townhouse in Jedburgh (Figure 2), well inland in the Scottish Borders, has provided the first example of the post-medieval use of significant quantities of local oak in south east Scotland (Macfadyan *et al.*, 2013; Mills, 2013). In the absence of local oak reference data, the Jedburgh townhouse was dated, with some difficulty, against chronologies from the far north of England. However, the subsequent chronology building work at Dalkeith and in the new SESOD project should make future identification and dating of south east Scottish native oak much more straightforward. Interestingly, the oak used in the Jedburgh townhouse was all from one source and quite young, with the chronology produced spanning 1581 to 1667. The origin date is interesting as it may reflect the commercial exploitation of former ecclesiastical assets. The timbers come from stems which at the earliest started to grow in about the 1570s, just after the Reformation. This is at a time when, elsewhere in Scotland, there is evidence of entrepreneurial land-owners investing in new oak plantations and other industrial developments on former church lands, for example at Balgownie in West Fife where a commercial oak coppice was established in the late-sixteenth century on former agricultural land belonging to Culross Abbey (Quelch & Mills, 2016). Could something similar be the case at Jedburgh too? Some of the stems have fused multiple centres, hinting at a possible origin in coppice woodland, although early grazing damage is another possible cause, and clearly at around 60 to 90 years old, this material was allowed to grow on beyond a normal coppice cycle.

Figure 2. Seventeenth century native oak joists in the Jedburgh Townhouse
(Photograph: C. Mills)

Native pine developments

Until recently, the position for pine was much the same as oak, with little native Scottish pine tree-ring chronology coverage compared to the network of pine reference chronologies from Scandinavia and other timber exporting regions of Northern Europe and the Baltic Sea area. However, over the last few years, the ability to identify and date native Scottish pine has been made much more possible by SCOT2K and other elements of the Scottish Pine Project (Mills, 2008; Wilson *et al.*, 2011). The project has built a robust network of native Scottish pine wood chronologies alongside targeted work on Highland pine buildings. The main driver for the work has been climate research (Rydval *et al.*, 2017) but the native pine chronologies produced are equally important for dating and provenancing historic timbers. Furthermore, the application of a new dating methodology, which uses 'Blue Intensity' as a proxy for latewood density (Wilson *et al.*, 2017), has facilitated the dendro-dating of the first tranche of twenty Scottish native pine historic buildings, most of them in the Highlands close to the native pine woods, but occasionally further afield (Mills *et al.*, 2017). In fact our earliest native pine identified so far is from a fifteenth-century construction phase in St John's House (Figure 3), a townhouse in St Andrews, Fife. This is a long distance from the native pinewoods, and no doubt in receipt of Highland timber transported by river and sea. The timber used there was incredibly slow grown, with up to 300 rings and quite small scantling, and it must reflect cutting of an ancient 'hill pine' wood, such timber being traditionally valued as extra-resinous and rot resistant (Bob Powell pers comm). The pine chronology from St John's House matches reference data from the Northern Cairngorms better than any other reference data at home or abroad. Currently, only this native pine region's record extends back far enough in time to fully overlap with St John's House and so we are keeping an open mind to the slight possibility that it could be a very early example of imported Scandinavian material. Further development of the native pine chronology network will allow more certainty as to its provenance.

Ancient pine in woods and lochs

The network of native pine chronologies against which the various Scottish buildings have been dated were created using a combination of living tree and sub-fossil material from lochs (Wilson *et al.*, 2011; Rydval *et al.*, 2017). In the course of this work, we have identified some very ancient individual living pine trees, the oldest two so far encountered being at Glen Loyne in Lochaber and Glen Derry at Mar Lodge in the Cairngorms, both hailing from the mid-fifteenth century, yet small enough in girth for one person to put their arms around them. The old trees are not necessarily the big trees, and the oldest pine examples tend to be small, oddly shaped and inaccessible trees which escaped the felling axe historically.

Figure 3. (L) St John's House, St Andrews; (R) Slow-grown fifteenth century pine, Sample SJH02 (Photographs: C. Mills)

Tree-ring studies in native woods: Loch Katrine case study

This chapter has so far concentrated largely on the evidence from timbers in old buildings. However, our understanding of woodland history in Scotland is also being expanded by investigations of a range of surviving historic Scottish woods, using a combination of tree-form, tree-ring and documentary evidence. The most comprehensive of these studies has been at South Loch Katrine in the Trossachs where a diverse range of wooded cover survives, including upland wood-pastures, old farm trees and commercial coppices, and where Gaelic place-name evidence is also informative (Mills et al., 2009; Mills, 2011). Documentary evidence revealed that this area was part of the Hunting Forest of Menteith with strict controls on grazing and other uses exercised through the traditions of Forest Law well into the post-medieval period. However, by 1740, the remaining ancient oak woodland in the study area was being evaluated for sale, and we believe was mostly 'charcoaled out' by the late eighteenth century. This is reflected in the field evidence of widespread charcoal platforms well beyond the current extent of oak. Oak bark would have been another extremely valuable product obtained from these woods.

Many native deciduous tree species are present at Loch Katrine but most of the tree-ring work was focussed on the ring porous species, oak and ash, which were most amenable in terms of ageing and cross-matching from ring patterns. Two remarkably different forms of oak were investigated, the tall slender maidens and multiple stems of an old oak coppice-with-standards wood and the squat stubby gnarled 'scroggy' oaks of adjacent wood-pasture (Figure 4). The oldest of the maiden oaks in the coppice originated in about 1800, while the ages of coppiced stems showed that the wood had last been cut-over in the early 1870s. The tell-tale remains of old buildings and fields under the woodland show that much of the oak coppice was established over the remains of pre-improvement farming.

Based on their visual characteristics, we expected the 'scroggy' wood pasture oaks to be much older than the coppice wood, but the dendro results showed them to be a little younger, with origin dates in the early- to mid-nineteenth century. Their formation processes were complex, with multiple centres often detected. We interpreted the evidence as indicating that the stubby 'scrogg' oaks had originated as cut coppice in peripheral parts of the oak wood which had not continued to be protected by enclosure and had consequently become fused under grazing pressure. The settlement in this remote area had changed during the late-eighteenth century from a number of small mixed farming tounships (groups of several farming families), with cattle farming their most important economic activity, to a single large sheep farm retaining the old Gaelic name of one of the tounships, Glasahoile. Meanwhile, the area under oak coppice had contracted into an enclosed core at Glasahoile as the nineteenth century wore on. Performance of woodland duties did continue however, even into the sheep farming period, with tenants continuing to be required to provide water carriages of bark from the coppice wood.

Investigating Tree Archaeology

Figure 4. South Loch Katrine, Trossachs; (L) squat 'scrogg' oak, Glasahoile, and (Middle) overgrown oak coppice, Glasahoile, both of nineteenth century origin; (R) Late seventeenth century ash of pollard form, Murlagan. (Photographs: C. Mills)

The oldest ash trees so far aged in Scotland are from this same area of South Loch Katrine (Figure 4, (R) right). They were scattered around the lower parts of a scree slope under the Bealach nam Bo pass on the lower slopes of Ben Venue, close to the archaeological remains of a pre-improvement era farmstead at a place known as Murlagan. This Gaelic farm name is known from eighteenth century and earlier estate rental books and in the deep memory of a retired local shepherd who still called it 'Mulligan's Park'. Some of the ash trees at Murlagan had a pollard form, including a particularly large specimen with a girth of 3.9m, which proved to originate in the late-seventeenth century. Its tree-ring pattern had a cyclical element through much of the eighteenth century, which could have been formed by pollarding at roughly ten to twelve year intervals, and coinciding with the final occupation period of Murlagan farm which probably went out of use in the late-eighteenth century. A younger cohort of ash trees represented a period of ash regeneration in the very late-eighteenth century which could have occurred between the abandonment of Murlagan and the advent of improvement-era intensive sheep farming. Another ash tree, a few hundred metres further away from the old farm, on a steep slope above the loch, also originated in the late-seventeenth century but showed no evidence of having been managed and was only 1.5m in girth. Again, the tree ring evidence shows that the old trees are not always the big trees, and often it is the slow growing, puny trees in difficult growing sites which live the longest.

Developing the dendrochronology of ash
The ash chronology developed at Loch Katrine spans 1728 to 2008 and is part of a wider body of native ash wood chronology development in Scotland. This work has also investigated Rassal Ashwood National Nature Reserve in Wester Ross, producing a chronology spanning 1789 to 2009 (Mills, 2010a; Cooper, 2011) and storm-thrown ash trees on Dundonnell Estate, the oldest of which spans 1734 to 2008 (Mills, 2010b). With a little more developmental work on Scottish ash chronologies, it should become possible to date the ash crucks in old cottages such as Sunnybrae Cottage, Pitlochry (Crone, 2001) and Moirlanich Cottage near Killin (Mills & Crone, 1996). The threat of *Chalara* disease and the losses due to an increasingly stormy climate perhaps add further incentive to obtain data from the remarkable historic ash trees of Scotland as opportunity arises.

Alder dendrochronology
The only other Scottish native species which has seen a significant amount of dendrochronological research is alder because of its frequency in prehistoric crannogs (Crone, 2014). Alder is an important element of Scotland's native tree cover and is especially prevalent in old wood-pastures as well as wet places. As a diffuse porous species, its ring patterns are more difficult to see, and some limited work on alder wood-pasture trees at Loch Katrine (Mills *et al.*, 2009) has shown just how complex their formation processes can be too, with coalescing secondary basal shoots and hollow, rotten, fused or fragmented multiple stems being common. Coring is rather inadequate in the face of such complexities, and forensic style dissection of whole fallen alder trees would probably be needed to get to grips with the histories preserved within wood-pasture alders.

Heart of Scotland Dendro Project
Finally, another project in development is the Heart of Scotland Dendro Project (Mills, forthcoming) which aims to tackle the development of native oak, pine and ash chronologies in the centrally positioned county of Perthshire which bridges the Highlands and the Lowlands. This should enable tree-ring connections to be made between the various existing data sets from the north and south of Scotland and provide new means of dating the rich architectural heritage of that county and beyond. Ongoing work by Anne Crone on alder from the Loch Tay crannogs will complement this project.

Conclusion
Thus, through projects like NOAP, SCOT2K and SESOD the balance is being redressed in terms of broadening native tree-ring data coverage in Scotland, and the continuing role of native timber in the late- and post-medieval periods is becoming increasingly recognised. The story emerging from the timber in Scottish buildings is being augmented by investigations of historic woods, with particular emphasis on relating tree-forms and tree-ring evidence to historic maps and other documentary evidence. Together, the evidence from our native woods and old buildings can provide a closely dated history of the management and use of our Scottish native woods.

Acknowledgements
This brief chapter draws together observations on the growing body of tree-ring work in Scotland created with several colleagues, particularly Anne Crone of AOC Archaeology and Rob Wilson of University of St Andrews, to whom I am very grateful. The founding dendro work by Mike Baillie and David Brown on Scottish oak in the 1970s and 80s continues to be an important resource for our tree-ring research in Scotland. Archaeo-dendro colleagues across the British Isles and Europe have been hugely helpful, especially in helping us to identify imported timber. In Scottish woodland heritage studies, enormous thanks go to Peter Quelch who has been so generous in sharing his knowledge in our collaborations. I am also greatly indebted to the work of Scottish

woodland historians, including John Gilbert, John Harrison, Chris Smout, Mairi Stewart and Fiona Watson. Encouragement from many quarters, including Chris Badenoch, Colin Edwards, Cathy Tyers and the NWDG, regarding the value of native species dendro research in Scotland, has been much appreciated. SCOT2K was funded by NERC (Grant: NE/K003097/1) while principal supporters of other projects mentioned include Historic Environment Scotland, Forestry Commission Scotland, Forest Research, The National Trust for Scotland, Scottish Borders Council and the Loch Lomond and Trossachs National Park Authority. Thanks go also to the many owners and managers of individual properties and woods who allowed this work to take place.

References

Baillie, M.G.L. (1977) 'An oak chronology for South Central Scotland'. *Tree-Ring Bulletin*, **37**, 33-44.

Cooper, T. (2011) 'Rassal Ashwood NNR: Exploring the cultural dimension'. In: C M Mills (ed.) *Woods as working and cultural landscapes, past and present*. Scottish Woodland History Conference: Notes XV (2010), 29-34.

Crone, B.A. (2001) *Analysis of the roof timbers from Sunnybrae Cottage*. Unpublished report for Historic Scotland.

Crone, A. (2014) 'Dendrochronological studies of alder (*Alnus glutinosa*) on Scottish crannogs', *J Wetland Archaeol.*, **14**, 22-33.

Crone, A. & Mills, C.M. (2002) 'Seeing the wood **and** the trees; dendrochronological studies in Scotland'. *Antiquity*, **76**, 788-94.

Crone, A. & Mills, C. (2011) 'The Native Oak and Pine Project – some observations on timber and woodworking in Scottish buildings circa AD 1600 – 1800'. *Vernacular Building*, **34**, 19-42.

Crone, A. & Mills C.M. (2012) 'Timber in Scottish buildings, 1450-1800: a dendrochronological perspective'. *Proc. Soc. Antiq. Scot.*, **142**, 329-369.

Crone, A. & Mills, C. (2015) 'List 279: Dendrochronologically dated buildings from Scotland: the native oak and pine project'. pp 125-8, In: Alcock, N. & Tyers, C. (2015) 'Tree-Ring Date Lists

2015'. *Vernacular Architecture*, **46**,1, 89-128, DOI: 10.1080/03055477.2015.1123415.

Macfadyan, K., Addyman, T. & Mills, C. (2013) 'High Street, Jedburgh: Standing building recording and watching brief'. *Discovery and Excavation in Scotland 2013*, 166-7.

Mills, C.M. (2008) 'Historic pine and dendrochronology in Scotland'. *Scottish Woodland History Discussion Group: Notes XIII*, 9-14.

Mills, C.M. (2010a) *A dendrochronological analysis at Rassal Ashwood NNR, Wester Ross*. Report for Forest Research and Scottish Natural Heritage.

Mills, C.M. (2010b) *Dendrochronological analysis of ash disks from Dundonnell*. Report for Dundonnell Estate.

Mills, C.M. (2011) *Old oak coppices, South Loch Katrine: their dendrochronology and history*. Report for FCS (Cowal and Trossachs District) & Loch Lomond & Trossachs National Park Authority.

Mills, C.M. (2013) *Dendrochronology of oak timbers in Groups A and B at 31 High Street, Jedburgh*. Report for Scottish Borders Council.

Mills, C.M. (2015) *Technical report on chronology development from the Dalkieth Old Oaks*. Report for the Buccleuch Estates and Historic Scotland.

Mills, C.M. (2017) *SESOD: South East Scotland Oak Dendrochronology Project Design*. Proposal to HES, Forestry Commission and other project partners.

Mills, C.M. (forthcoming) 'Big Tree-Ring Country? Dendrochronology and its potential in Perthshire'. In: *Scottish Woodland History Discussion Group: Notes XXII*.

Mills, C.M. & Crone, B.A. (1996) *Dendrochronology of timbers from Moirlanich Longhouse, Killin, Perthshire*. Report for the National Trust for Scotland.

Mills, C.M. & Crone, A. (2012) 'Dendrochronological evidence for Scotland's native timber resources over the last 1000 years'. *Scottish Forestry*, **66**, 18-33.

Mills, C.M., Crone, A., Wood, C. & Wilson, R. (2017) 'Dendrochronologically dated pine buildings from Scotland:

The SCOT2K native pine dendrochronology project'. *Vernacular Architecture*, **48**, 23-43.

Mills, C.M., Quelch, P. & Stewart, M. (2009) *The evidence of tree forms, tree-rings and documented history around Bealach nam Bo, Loch Katrine.* Report for Forestry Commission Scotland.

Quelch, P. & Mills, C.M. (2016) 'Planting phases in Balgownie Wood: Evidence from Historic Woodland Survey'. In: Mills, C.M. (ed.) *Plantations in Scotland.* Scottish Woodland History Conference 2013: Notes XVII, pp 9-17.

Rydval, M., Loader, N.J., Gunnarson, B.E., Druckenbrod, D.L., Linderholm, H.W., Moreton, S.G., Wood, C.V. and Wilson, R. (2017) 'Reconstructing 800 Years of Summer Temperatures in Scotland from Tree Rings'. *Climate Dynamics*, 1-24. DOI 10.1007/s00382-016-3478-8.

Smout, T.C., MacDonald, A.R. & Watson, F. (2005) *A history of the native woodlands of Scotland, 1500 – 1920.* EUP, Edinburgh.

Stewart, M. (2003) 'Using the woods, 1600-1850 (1) The community resource (2) Managing for profit'. In: Smout, T. C. (ed.) *People and woods in Scotland.*.EUP, Edinburgh, 82-127:

Wilson, R., Loader,N., Rydval, M., Paton, H., Frith, A., Mills, C., Crone, A., Edwards, C., Larsson, L. and Gunnarson, B. (2011) 'Reconstructing Holocene Climate from Tree Rings – The Potential for a Long Chronology from the Scottish Highlands. *The Holocene* **22**, No.1, 3-11.

Wilson, R., Wilson, D., Rydval, M., Crone, A., Büntgen, U., Clark, S., Ehmer, J., Forbes, E., Fuentes, M., Gunnarson, B.E., Linderholm, H.W., Nicolussi, K., Wood, C. and Mills, C. (2017) 'Facilitating tree-ring dating of historic conifer timbers using Blue Intensity'. *Journal of Archaeological Science*, **78**, 99-111.

Chapter 13. Reading the past lives of working trees

Helen Read[1] & Ted E. Green[2]
[1]City of London Corporation, [2]Independent Consultant & Founder President of the Ancient Tree Forum

Introduction
The term 'working tree' was coined by Ted Green and is a very useful expression that encompasses trees that are, or were, pruned by man for his use. This could be what was initially cut from the tree, for example, wood, leaves, or the end-product when the tree was finally felled, such as timbers for ship building.

Another phrase that Ted has coined is 'cutting to the form of the tree'. This expression is a great one because it implies a degree of *ad hoc* management, using the shape of the tree to determine where and how it is cut. Formulaic management was probably not common in most traditional tree management systems. When cutting for leaves or small-scale wood, the exact shape of the tree after cutting would generally have been less important than the product. While it is clear that there were fashions, local trends and regional techniques, there must have always been trees that were cut slightly differently to the norm for the area. Non-conforming trees may sometimes have been removed but most often they were probably tolerated, giving rise to trees that could be out of character to those nearby. Trees must also have died and cutting sometimes must have precipitated this. Sometimes, these trees were removed, and new ones planted, at other times, they must have been left where the work to remove them was more than would have been gained by leaving them.

The tree shapes discussed here are those that have been produced largely as a result of traditional tree management rather than modern pruning techniques, and examples have been taken from across Europe as well as the UK. Sometimes these trees may have become incorporated into urban landscapes so that some street trees may be 'read' in similar ways. Techniques for the regular management of street trees have often been borrowed from those of traditional tree management, although, they can be different and may be more akin to horticultural techniques such as pleaching. Living trees were also used in horticultural systems as, for example, a woody frame for crops to climb up (Ferrini, 2007) and these may also have had different shapes to those discussed below. Also, trees were managed differently for fruit or nut production, where pruning aims to maximise the fruit crop while ensuring it can ripen and then be harvested easily, and these techniques produced very differently shaped trees.

Guiding principles

Open grown trees vs closed canopy woodland – the natural development of a crown

Before considering the impacts of pruning on tree shape, it is important to first consider the shapes that trees naturally take. Different tree species can have very different canopy shapes, the comparison between silver birch and oak illustrates this clearly. However, two trees of the same species can have contrasting canopy shapes. One which has developed in fully open conditions where the sunlight has been plentiful all around the crown that can expand fully in all directions; and the other has grown up in the middle of a wood so that the light reaches the top of the crown but the lower branches have not developed, or have died back as they became shaded. The former tree will have large horizontal branches low on the trunk and potentially reaching down to the ground, whereas the latter will have all the leaf bearing branches high on the trunk. Trees on the edge of woodland, or as part of a small group of trees, will have one side shaped like a woodland tree and one as an open grown tree. These different characteristics enables us to spot trees that were once standing in open conditions, but which are now hidden within relatively young woodland. Their larger, lower and predominantly horizontal branches are still present but are dead or dying from lack of light.

Other aspects of tree form

There is considerable variation both between and within species in how a tree responds to cutting. Willow, for example, generally responds well to cutting and has a good capacity for producing epicormic shoots. Beech in contrast produces far fewer (Lonsdale, 2013). Our ancestors clearly understood this and varied their cutting technique accordingly. However, even in a species that does not pollard or coppice easily, some are more responsive than others. It is noticeable in populations of trees cut extensively in the past that there is a high proportion of individuals with a tendency to produce epicormic growth. Good examples of these are the oak pollards at Ashtead Common, beech at Low Scrubs in the Chilterns (Figure 1) and some of the beech pollards in Epping Forest and Burnham Beeches.

Figure 1. Whiskery previously 'worked' beech trees at Low Scrubs in the Chilterns

The impact of pruning

The pruning of trees alters the shape of the crown, either by removing branches entirely or pruning them in ways that alter their growth patterns.

The diameter of a branch is related to its age and, while assigning exact age will depend on the growing conditions of the tree, relative diameter can be helpful in assessing relative age of different branches on the same tree or different trees in the same location. However, it is always worth bearing in mind that it is perfectly possible for a smaller diameter branch to be older than a larger diameter one and a small branch can be very old.

When trees have been cut back repeatedly to approximately the same point a swelling usually develops. This is a consequence of the starch being stored in the area in the winters immediately after cutting and a build-up of occluded tissue that has grown each time following the cuts. The relative size of the swelling can give an indication of how many times the tree has been pruned back to roughly the same point.

Tools used
The traditional management of trees was mostly carried out using a bladed tool like a billhook or an axe; hand saws seem not generally to have been used in tree work until more recent times; of course, chain saws are a modern invention. Cutting

Figure 2. Branch of a pollard ash tree in the Austrian Alps cut the previous year

with a bladed tool can be done very accurately when wielded by a competent user but it is generally not possible to cut below the point of origin of the branch. Pruning would aim to maximise the length of branch cut off, but inevitably small stubs would generally be left. Making a second cut to 'tidy up' the tree would almost certainly not be made as this is in effect a waste of effort (but something that is very easy when using a chain saw). Consequently, each cut would be slightly higher than the previous one and the subsequent growth would make a swelling which would gradually get larger. Figure 2 shows an ash pollard under a regular cutting cycle cut in Austria; notice the long stubs and generally 'untidy' appearance.

Different types of tree form

Coppice
Cutting a tree repeatedly just above ground level seems to have been a very common technique in the UK and other European countries, for producing small scale wood products (Figure 3). The produce included flexible rods from species like hazel for making hurdles, thatching spars, house walls (wattle); small diameter wood as firewood or for wood products like beanpoles, chair legs, tool handles; wood for making charcoal; or bark for tanning leather.

Figure 3. Coppice lime stool in Lincolnshire

One cut of a tree at ground level may produce what appears to be a multi-stemmed tree but multiple cutting usually results in a clear 'stool' or swelling from which the branches arise. Over decades of cutting, this swollen base can become quite large and stand a metre or more above the ground in species such as oak. In tree species that regularly sucker, so that new branches arise from the roots rather than on or near the cut surface, the stool may be more like a ring of branches that gets progressively wider over the years. Very old, large, above ground stools may eventually decay to also leave a ring of apparently young trees and it has been suggested that some of these very large rings could be extremely old and the result of centuries of cutting. Hazel naturally grows with a multi-stemmed habit and it can be very difficult to distinguish this from coppiced hazel.

In the early nineteenth century in the UK, there was a period when some coppice woodlands were converted to 'high forest' with the aim of producing a timber crop (timber being the produce of whole tree felling, such as planks whereas wood is small diameter stems (Rackham, 1976)). This process of 'singling' was the removal of all the branches from the stool except one and was frequently done in oak coppices. The past coppice history of management can still be seen in the swollen base of the tree. Even if this is not especially evident now, the base of the trunk usually has a clear curve. Because coppicing was usually carried out on a block of trees, a high proportion of the trees of a particular size class generally have swollen or curved bases in an area (even if not all of them).

Coppicing of trees to form hedges
Hedging techniques are variable across the UK and there are many local variations resulting in different tree shapes (TCV, 2019). This article is not the place to discuss these techniques. However, one legacy of past hedgerow management regularly encountered within, or on the edges of woodlands, or in open areas, is a line of trees which may be a remnant wood bank with trees. Trees that stand on the top of the bank often have horizontal stems and twisted branches towards the base. They were previously coppiced to form a stock proof barrier and could have extended great distances along the banks which divided

areas of different ownership or management. Sometimes, these have grown out so that tall trees arise from strange shaped bases. The trees may also have suffered from lack of light and died right back, sometimes they are clearly like large but elongate coppice stools. Lack of management of the trees on the banks frequently results in the banks being badly damaged when the top-heavy trees fall.

Pollards
Pollarded trees were managed in a similar way to coppice but the cutting point was well above ground. This allowed some other form of land management to be carried out between the trees. This frequently involved the grazing of livestock but could also be some other form of cultivation. In the past, it was thought that pollarding required the removal of all the branches of a tree, but with certain tree species, in certain locations, it seems that this was not always the case and sometimes selective removal of the branches was carried out. It was usual however, that a large proportion of branches were removed, not just the odd one or two. As with coppice, a single cut results in a tree with multiple branches arising from, or close to, the cut point and can appear like the natural branching pattern. Multiple cuts, however, cause the trunk to swell at and above the cut point so that an obvious pollard bolling is produced. As with coppicing this can be a relatively small size or, if cutting has been done many times, a little higher or wider each time, this can produce a larger structure. In addition, trees pollarded for specific purposes gained a clear shape, either because the pruning intended to produce that shape or because it inadvertently resulted in one.

The distinction between a pollard and a coppice stool is not clear cut and there is some overlap. Cutting coppice at ground level maximises the amount of wood produced but is hard work. Cutting at the normal pollard height allows grazing but is difficult to do because the cut must be done 'up in the air' requiring the tree to be climbed, perhaps using a short ladder or the back of a cart. Therefore, the most convenient height to cut is about waist level. 'Pollards', this size, were frequently cut for willow wands in areas that were too swampy to graze and where the cutting was done in short rotations. The small diameter branches were used for basket making and other wickerwork products as well as helping to bind the soils alongside rivers. Some willows were pollarded at the 'conventional' height i.e. above that which livestock could reach, where they occur in livestock grazed meadows close to rivers or in wet or low-lying landscapes such as in Somerset, the Netherlands or Flanders.

Other examples of trees cut as low pollards include the oaks at Low Scrubs in the Chilterns. It seems the wood here was used as firewood (or leaves for fodder) but the land under the trees was not managed intensively so that the trees could be short and squat rather than have taller main stems.

In Epping forest there are examples of trees that appear to have been coppiced (or are perhaps suckers) and then pollarded (Figure 4). The resulting structures have been called coppards (Dagley, 2017).

Figure 4. Coppard beech in Epping Forest, Essex

The differences in pollarding techniques and the uses of the tree products appear to have been much more varied than that of coppice. Depending on the methods used, the trees can have very distinct appearances and we do not always know the reasons behind these.

Pollard types
The most typical pollard is that of a stem with a single swollen bolling at the top, from which arises multiple rod-like branches forming a lollipop shaped canopy (Figure 5). The cutting cycle consists of the branches being cut back to the bolling repeatedly, once they reach a rough pre-determined size or length.

Figure 5. Ash (*Fraxinus angustifolia*) at Madarcos, Madrid Province, Spain

Aside from willows, most trees were cut either for their leaves or for their wood. Leaf hay is a valuable source of fodder for domestic livestock in hot dry summers or in places where grass hay is unreliable, or the winters so long that extra feed is needed. The branches were generally cut from the pollard when the leaves were still on the trees and either fed directly or dried and stored for winter use. In Scandinavia, trees could also be cut in the winter for the stock to eat the twigs if the winter was particularly hard. Because the leaves are usually the reason for cutting, the trees were cut on a short cycle of every two to six years to maximise the proportion of leaves to wood (see Slotte, 2000 for more details) (Figure 6). Cutting every year could only be done in extreme circumstances or when the youngest new branches were left on the tree each time (as in Austria, see Figure 2). Maximising the leaf crop could also be done by cutting the side branches on a tree rather than the simple beheading. If the tree produced many side branches, this increased leaf production.

Figure 6. Wooded meadow with pollards cut for fodder at Halstad in Sweden

Pollarding for a different type of leaf crop is carried out on mulberry trees where the leaves were used in the summer months for feeding to silkworms for the production of silk (Figure 7). Common in silk producing areas like Central Asia these trees can also be found in Italy and Hungary, the branches were cut very frequently, probably every year or two.

Pollarding a tree for the wood product requires the cutting cycle to be longer, so that the balance of leaves to wood is tipped in favour of the quantity of wood and thus cycles were generally eight to twelve years but could be longer, especially as the trees became older. The wood removed could be relatively small diameter, such as that cut from the hornbeam trees of Epping Forest to form faggots of firewood for the bread ovens of London, or large diameter for roof beams as cut from black poplars in the Spanish region of Teruel (de Jaime & Herrero, 2007) (Figure 8).

Most wood was probably used as some form of firewood, either domestic or for more industrial uses and some was probably made into charcoal. The simplest way of producing small scale wood is cutting back to the bolling each time. Tree shapes, however, sometimes lead to a different approach – cutting to the form of the tree – so that, for example, two almost separate pollard bollings might result or one on top of another (Figure 9).

Figure 7. Lapsed mulberry pollard, formerly cut to feed silkworm caterpillars in Hungary

Figure 8. Black Poplar pollards in Teruel Province, Spain cut in the past for roof timbers

Investigating Tree Archaeology

Figure 9. Oak pollards cut with two bollings, La Hiruela, Madrid Province, Spain

Natural pollards are the result of wind, snow or ice damage, or grey squirrel damage. These trees generally have only had the tops removed once and, while they may have a group of branches arising from the same height on the trunk, they will not have a clear knobbly bolling indicating repeated cutting.

However, it can sometimes be difficult to distinguish between old gnarly trees that have had the tops blown out in a storm event and old lapsed pollards. For example, the oaks at Sherwood Forest where the past management and impact of natural events on the trees is still a topic of debate. This is compounded by both variation in pollarding style and resulting shapes of the trees. Tree species that do not tend to respond well to pollarding (for example birch and beech) tend to be cut in a more open, candelabra style, probably as longer stubs were left at the time of each cut to ensure leaves were retained and the tree survived the cut. However, cutting to the form of the tree and understanding their likely response can also lead to other shapes of pollard, for example the flat topped rather square shaped trees as seen north of Vitoria in Spain (Figure 10). Some of these latter do resemble the trees at Sherwood.

A slightly different form of natural pollards is that formed by browsing of goats directly in the trees. This can be seen in parts of Greece and North Africa.

Figure 10. Oak pollard (perhaps previously shredded too), Araia, Alava, Spain

The shape of the tree also depended on the product required. In the Basque area of southern France and northern Spain, two styles of pollard could be found side by side. One, the classic pollard shape with a compact bolling at the top of the trunk, and the other, with wide spreading horizontal branches and uprights coming off these at almost a 90° angle (Figure 11). The former type was solely for small diameter wood for charcoal making; the latter shaped to produce specific pieces of wood for ship building with the pruning off-cuts used for charcoal (Aragón, 2009). Ship building wood in other countries, e.g. Denmark, was obtained from open grown or 'compass trees' which had natural growing horizontal branches (see examples in the Fiskeri-og-Søfartsmuseet in Esbjerg, Denmark)).

Production of specific shaped pieces of wood through tree pruning and methods such as tying branches down to encourage horizonal growth was clearly widespread in Spain and Italy. How common this method really was in the UK, other than for fruit trees, is not clear.

Figure 11. Pollard cut to form shaped timbers for ship building, Oquino, Spain

Lapsed pollards
A pollard that has been left uncut so that the branches become large in diameter can be referred to as a 'lapsed pollard'. In the south of England regular cutting of pollards largely ceased well over 100 years ago, and sometimes nearer 200 years. These trees also frequently became surrounded by secondary woodland which encourages the branches on the pollards to grow very tall. The trees acquired a distinct shape and grandeur which attracted the attention of admirers in the Victorian and later eras. A consequence of this legacy is that their current management is now challenging. In some places, these trees are now in a regular

management regime again, although because of the age and fragility of the trees, this is now quite different to their past management. The reduction of height and weight can be referred to as restorative work on the lapsed pollards. 'Repollarding' is an ambiguous term that is best avoided, as it implies cutting back to the bolling, which is not recommended for these trees (Read, 2013). The length of time that a pollard has been uncut (i.e. out of its cutting cycle) to the point that it requires restoration is a source of debate.

Shredded trees

Instead of cutting the top off a young tree for its produce, thus creating a pollard, the other option is to cut the side branches. This was done largely for leaves but sometimes for small diameter firewood. One example is in Britany, northern France, where shredded trees can still be seen very widely in the landscape (Figures 12 & 12a). The advantage over pollarding is that many more leaves can be cut each time; the disadvantage is that the trees grow much taller and therefore cutting becomes more difficult or dangerous. Combining the two methods (pollarding to create multiple branches and then shredding each branch) probably yields the most leaves.

Figure 12 & 12a. Shredded oak trees in Brittany, France (L); Close up of shredded oak, Brittany, France (R)

Shredding was a method formerly used in the UK but it is now difficult to spot long-lapsed shredded trees in the landscape. It is therefor hard to know how common the practice was. Old photographs, for example of picking belladonna in Liston, show shredded trees in the background of the picture.
 http://www.foxearth.org.uk/ListonPictures/Page.html (accessed 16/9/2019).

Some pictures of trees over time (e.g. Lonsdale, 2013, page 31) represent the few visual records we have. Perhaps we are just not good at recognising them when they are lapsed.

Fruit tree pruning
Detailed descriptions of the methods of fruit pruning and their consequences for the tree shape are beyond the scope of this article and best explored by reading older fruit production manuals. In summary, trees produce more abundant fruit from horizontal branches so pruning favoured these, however the tree's response is usually to produce large numbers of upright shoots (water shoots) as a result. This legacy can be seen on fruit trees that were once regularly pruned but have been abandoned. A framework of older, largely horizontal branches can be distinguished and then there is a mass of younger stems filling the gaps between them. The other main aim of fruit tree pruning is to produce a tree shape that has open structure so that light can reach the ripening fruit which can be easily picked, and the

framework branches generally still show remnants of this pattern. Different countries, regions and time periods have favoured different ways of doing this.

Pruning of cobnuts for nut production was done very differently. These plants look like hazel nut bushes and are regularly mistaken for them. One pruning method selected a small number of upright stems that were cut around waist height with the outward facing branches retained, producing an open structure (Figure 13). Another method selected a single trunk, from which smaller stems arose, like a miniature pollard. Once abandoned the plants produce many new stems from the base which swamp the previously pruned ones.

Figure 13. Pruned cob nut in a plat, Oldbury, Kent

Other pruned trees

Trees are pruned for many other reasons. In urban areas, they may be pleached to create an aesthetic shape and to create shade. Methods for stimulating the production of acorns or nuts may, for example, create trees that resemble open pollards and, in other countries these techniques have been refined over centuries.

Conifers are generally less likely to be pruned as their response to removal of branches tends to be less inducive to the production of new branches. There are however some notable exceptions. In the Alps, the side branches of fir trees were removed for use as bedding for livestock; confusingly this has been referred to as pollarding. Continued removal of branches caused the trees to grow very slowly. In the East Anglian Brecks, lines of Scots Pine were cut as hedges for wind breaks and have subsequently grown out into the characteristic twisted shapes of the pine lines.

Reading the context of the tree

A great deal can be learnt about the past history from the shape of the tree, but the land around it can also be helpful. Trees that have been pollarded must have existed in relatively open conditions and not in dense woodland; this is also true of open grown trees. Coppice may have originated in a coupe that was all cut at a similar time, but linear 'coppice' found on wood banks may have delineated areas that in the past were subject to different woodland management techniques (and / or had different owners). In the UK, most of our pollards stood within wood-pastures, where the land around the trees was grazed. In Scandinavia, there are also wooded meadows where the land underneath was cut for hay (Emanuelsson, 2009). These different uses result in different plant species and structure. A hay-cut generally does not favour the development of scrub, except in areas like stone piles, which cannot be cut. Wood-pasture tends to have a greater proportion of prickly shrubs and if abandoned, the shrubs can either become very rare if they are light-demanding species (such as rose or hawthorn) or very abundant (such as holly) if they are shade tolerant.

An idea of the length of time since the tree was regularly managed can be attempted by looking at the age of the surrounding scrub as well as looking at the rings of the trunks or branches of any trees that have fallen. In addition, if the abandonment has been relatively short, looking at the length between the terminal bud scars on the old trees may help, if it is possible to distinguish them (Lonsdale, 2013, page 84). Shoots grow more when they have more light and growing conditions are good; they grow significantly less well in shade. It may be possible to determine when the growth started to decline and hence when the shade becomes too dense for light demanding plants to grow well.

Hedges are good places to find both coppice (where trees have been cut to form the hedge) and pollards (trees left in the hedges and cut, usually for wood). A broken line of coppiced or pollarded trees seen in a field is usually an indication of a past hedge which divided the field (Figure 14).

Figure 14. Line of trees, formerly a hedge, Redgrave, Suffolk

Two close hedges or lines of trees running parallel often indicate an old trackway, which, if very long-established may be sunken between the lines of trees which are often on banks. The shape of the trees and the bank can still be seen even though these may now be hidden in woodland (Figure 15).

Conclusions

Looking at the shapes of trees to attempt to infer their past management and that of the land around them is fun but is best carried out in association with other sources of information. This could be from documentary sources, but these are not always easy to find. Talking to local people is invaluable, especially in other countries where the lapse of traditional management may be shorter than in the UK.

Figure 15. Old track to a monastery with young ash pollards cut for fodder, Leitza, Navarra, Spain

It is interesting to ponder on the way that the current era will be viewed by people attempting to read the trees of the future. Present day tree management includes production of wood chip for boilers and agroforestry; methods that may both stem from a basic understanding of past tree management methods but also have been adapted to new uses. Art and rural crafts have also had an impact on some of our trees producing very special shapes. However, many of our trees today are in urban or suburban areas where they have been pruned to reduce the size that is too big for its surroundings. This is usually done by tree surgeons working in the crowns to thin or reduce them. In addition, there is a trend to cut previous street tree pollards at increasingly higher levels, creating pollards on top of pollards. All these methods will create interesting shapes for people in the future to try to interpret!

Acknowledgements
Ted Green has been a great promoter of the art of reading the past history of trees from their current shape and this article is very much inspired by the time spent travelling and looking at trees with him. Discussions with other Ancient Tree Forum

members have also contributed to the information in this article, especially Jill Butler and Vikki Bengtsson.

References

Aragón, Á. (2009) Los robles trasmochos guiados o ipinabarros: una apuesta sostenible de futuro para una téchnica forestal olvidada. *Cuad. Soc. Esp. Cienc. For.*, **30**, 137-142.

Dagley, J. (2017) 20 years on Epping Forest, seeing the trees for the wood. *Arb. Magazine.* **179**, 66-71

De Jaime, C. & Herrero, F. (2007) *El Chopo cabercero en el sur de Aragón, la identidad de un paisaje.* Centro de Estudios del Jiloca.

Emanuelsson, U. (2009) *The rural landscapes of Europe.* The Swedish Research Council Formas, Forskningsrådet.

Ferrini, F. (2007) L'étêtage et ses effets sur la physiologie de l'arbe: regard sur la gestion des arbres adultes et sénescents en Italie. In: *Les Trognes en Europe. Maison Botanique.* 71-79. Maison Botanique, Boursay, France.

Lonsdale, D. (2013) *Ancient and other veteran trees: further guidance on management.* The Tree Council, London.

Rackham, O. (1976) *Trees and woodland in the British Landscape.* J. M. Dent & Sons, London.

Read, H., Dagley, J., Elosegui, J.M., Sicilia, A. and Wheater, C.P. (2013) Restoration of lapsed pollards: Evaluation of techniques and guidance for future work. *Arboricultural Journal.* **35**(2): 74-90.

Slotte, H. (2000) *Lovtakt I Sverige och pa Aland.* Agraria, 236. Acta Universitatis Agriculturae Sueciae.

TCV, *Hedging a Practical Handbook* (online edition) https://www.conservationhandbooks.com/hedging/the-hedgerow-landscape/characteristic-regional-hedges/ (accessed 16/9/2019)

Bark Peelers at work in the 1930s in the West Midlands, England. Courtesy: Ian D. Rotherham

Chapter 14. Hidden Woodland Heritage in South-east Wales

Nicola Strange
Independent Researcher, Woodlands Roots
woodlandroots@hotmail.com ; www.woodlandroots.co.uk

Abstract
The archaeological value of abandoned managed trees is highlighted through the study of Deri Fach woodland, south-east Wales, demonstrating that woodlands are as deserving of survey and analysis as 'traditional' archaeological sites. Deri Fach's stools and pollards are the remains of a working landscape, which encompassed local industries, lifeways and identities. The nature and duration of woodland management is associated with the charcoal iron industry, oak-bark tanning and sheep farming. Variant forms of wood-pasture were practiced throughout Deri Fach, including a previously unrecorded system of 'coppice with stub-pollards'.

Introduction

Woodland archaeology and survey
Recent decades have seen a widening recognition of woodland archaeology and the development of guidance for fieldworkers (Rackham, 1990; Bannister et al., 2005; Bannister, 2007; Rotherham et al., 2008; Glaves et al., 2009; Rotherham, 2013). However, the archaeological value of pollards and coppice stools is often overlooked in surveys and reports (Cannell, 2005; Castle & Mileto, 2005). The heritage value of managed trees can therefore be lacking from academic discourse and public awareness, with trees failing to receive appropriate analysis or preservation statuses.

Project aim
Large, unrecorded sessile oak (*Quercus petraea*) pollards were observed by chance within Deri Fach, alerting the author to the

potential of unrecognised woodland heritage. The project aimed to record and analyse the features of Deri Fach, including pollards and stools, to consider past human-woodland relationships and highlight the heritage value of managed trees.

The study area
Location
Deri Fach woodland is in south-east Wales within the Brecon Beacons National Park, approximately 3 km north-west of Abergavenny (SO2761016986) (Figure 1). The old county boundary between Monmouthshire and Brecknockshire, approximately 2 km west of the wood, now separates Gwent and Powys (Ordnance survey 2017c). The wood is a Site of Special Scientific Interest and a Special Area of Conservation due to its ancient woodland and forms part of a National Trust-owned common (Mitchell, 2008).

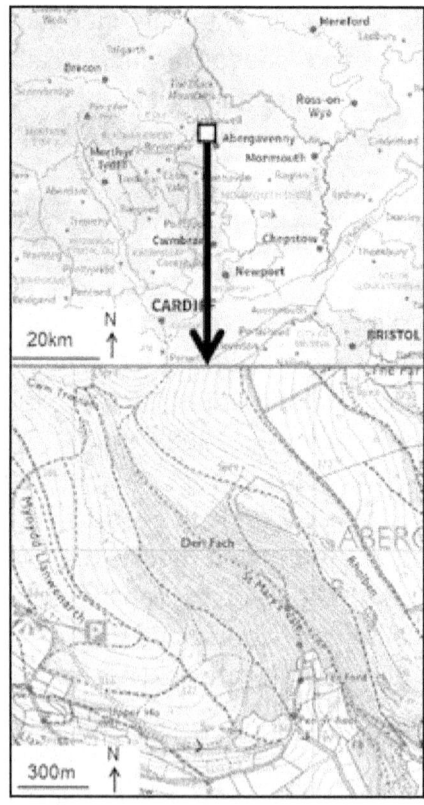

Figure 1: Location of Deri Fach wood. Source: Ordnance survey 2017a and 2017b

Deri Fach nestles in St. Mary's Vale on the south side of the Sugar Loaf Mountain at elevations of 180 to 350 m above sea-level. The valley drops towards the south-east as the Nant (stream) Iago flows towards the River Usk. The wood covers approximately 90 ha (220 acres) and is bordered to the west, north and east by bracken (*Pteridium aquilinum*) dominated moorland. The southern edge borders pastoral fields leading to Abergavenny. The valley consists of Devonian mudstones and sandstones underlying freely draining, loamy soil (British Geological Society, 2008; UK Soil Observatory, 2013).

Archaeological and historical contexts

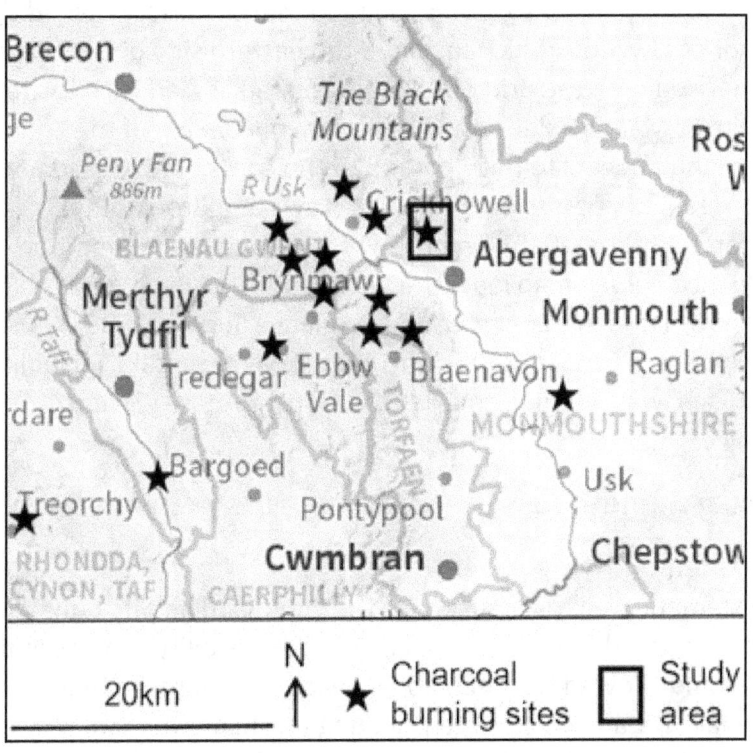

Figure 2: Charcoal burning sites near the study area. Sources: RCAHMW, 2017a-d; Base-map Ordnance Survey, 2017a

Lithics, burial mounds and a defended enclosure highlight prehistoric activity close to Deri Fach (Cofiadurcahcymru, 1998; Laws & Brooks, 2006; Wiggins, 2006). Nearby Roman remains include burials and find-spots associated with the first to third century Roman fort of Gobannium, located under present-day Abergavenny (Cofiadurcahcymru, 1998; Pearson, 2002; Crawford, 2010; Portable Antiquities Scheme, 2017). The remains of a two hectare Medieval deer park are found east of Deri Fach, with the park pale lying within 50 m of the study area. Numerous charcoal platforms have been recorded in south-east Wales, including 50 within Deri Fach woods (figure 2) (Rippin, 2013; RCAHMW, 2017a-d).

The history of Deri Fach is likely to be connected to Abergavenny castle and St Mary's priory, both founded in Abergavenny in the late eleventh century (Phillips, 2000; Crawford, 2010; Burton & Stöber, 2015). Bradney (1906) claimed that the priory owned the manor of Llwyndu, which included the eastern side of Deri Fach. A connection with the priory is also suggested as Deri Fach is sited within 'St Mary's Vale'. Post-dissolution, ownership of the woodland appears to have passed to the Lords of Abergavenny, who retained possession until 1918 (Laws and Brooks, 2005; Burton & Stöber, 2015). The tithe records and the first edition Ordnance Survey map label the woodland 'Deri Bach' or 'Fach', meaning 'Little' or 'Lesser Oaks' (Ordnance Survey, 1886; Wade, 1909; Laws & Brooks, 2006). The Sugar Loaf mountain, including Deri Fach, was gifted to the National Trust in 1935 (Gwent Archives, 1950).

Research methods

Field methods
A systematic walk-over survey of the woodland and its boundaries was completed in early spring 2017. Good visibility in most of the woodland allowed transects to be spaced at approximately 100 m intervals. Data were collected relating to the nature and distribution of archaeological features, including earthworks and managed trees. The GPS location of features was recorded by smart-phone software, with a margin of error of 6-8 m (Embleton 2016). Ancient woodland indicator (AWI) species were recorded in a 10 m radius around features and at 'transect stops'- every 100 m along each transect.

Analytical procedures

Data was uploaded onto Quantum Geographic Information System (QGIS) software, facilitating a visual appraisal of potential relationships between features.

Classification of stools, stub-pollards (stubs) and pollards were made according to the height of the knuckle (the top of the permanent stool or trunk):

	Stool	Stub	Pollard
Knuckle height	<0.50 m	0.50-1.49 m	>1.50 m

Tree and shoot age estimates have been based on available advice and data (appendix 1). Growth rates provide a broad estimate to tree ages and have been supported by morphological indicators of age, including hollowing and epiphyte growth (Castle & Mileto, 2005).

Survey results

Managed trees

Figure 3: Beech pollard (feature no.153) Note the fluted bolling, indicative of veteran age. Source: author

Figure 4: Oak stub (feature no. 88) Note the hollowed bolling, indicating veteran age. Source: author

Figure 5: Oak stool (feature no. 91): The stool presented hollowing, dead wood in canopy and on floor, and hard ferns (*Blechnum spicante*) growing on branches. Source: author

Table 1: Estimated ages of managed trees. See appendices 2 and 3 for full details.

Tree type	Number recorded	Diameter range (cm)	Estimated age range (years)	Estimated date of start of growth
Oak stools	42	80-197 DAB	267-657	1361-1751
Oak stubs	106	60-198 DBH	218-721	1297-1800
Oak pollards	23	40-158 DBH	146-575	1443-1872
Beech stubs	5	100-158 DBH	229-455	1563-1789
Beech pollards	16	100-172 DBH	209-544	1474-1809

DBH - diameter at breast height of 1.5 m or narrowest point near to 1.5 m below knuckle (top of the permanent trunk); DAB- diameter at base

Investigating Tree Archaeology

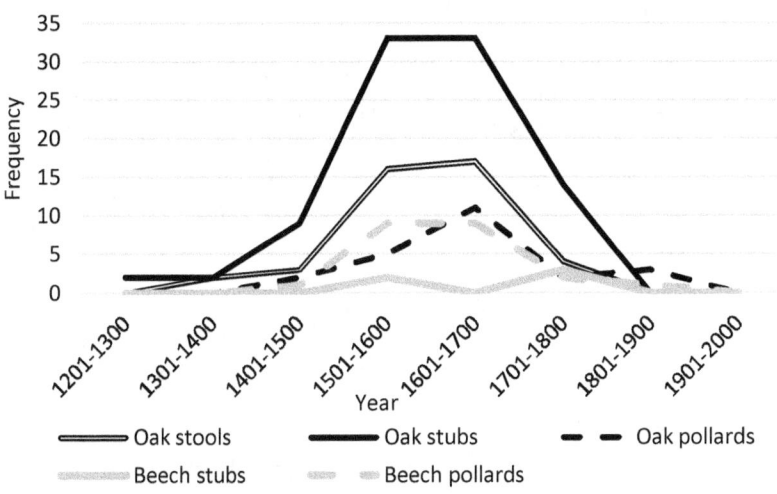

Figure 6: Estimated date of start of growth of managed trees

The survey logged the location and morphology of 192 managed beech (*Fagus sylvatica*) and oak (*Quercus petraea*) (Figures 3 to 5; Appendices 2 and 3). Girth measurements suggest that cropping was initiated on most of the trees during the fifteenth to eighteenth centuries (table 1 and figure 6). Veteran or ancient status of the trees is also indicated by the frequent occurrence of qualifying arboreal characteristics (appendix 2). Pollarding and coppicing are likely to have been initiated when trees were less than 50 years old and to have continued regularly until abandonment (Lennon, 2009). Shoot diameters suggest management was neglected through the nineteenth century until final abandonment around the mid-twentieth century (Table 2). In the first half of the twentieth century, thirteen oak stubs appear to have been singled into timber trees (Figure 7). Multi-stemmed alder (*Alnus glutinosa*) recorded near the Nant Iago stream has been omitted from the discussion, as it cannot be established if the alder coppiced naturally or through human intervention.

Table 2. Estimated ages of shoots of managed trees

Shoot type	Diameter range (cm)	Estimated age range of shoots (years)	Estimated date of last cutting
Oak stools' shoots	35-100	120-222	1796-1898
Oak stubs' shoots	30-100	115-222	1796-1903
Oak pollards' shoots	25-100	65-176	1842-1953
Beech stubs' shoots	20-80	30-134	1884-1988
Beech pollards' shoots	50-100	63-161	1857-1955

Figure 7: Singled oak stub. Source: author

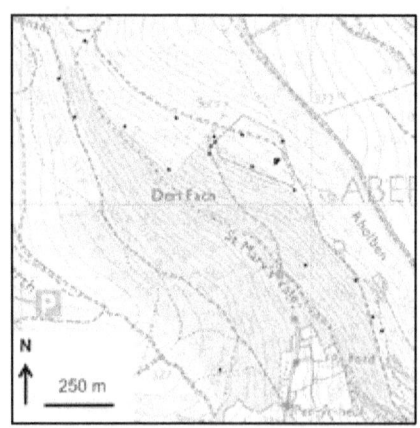 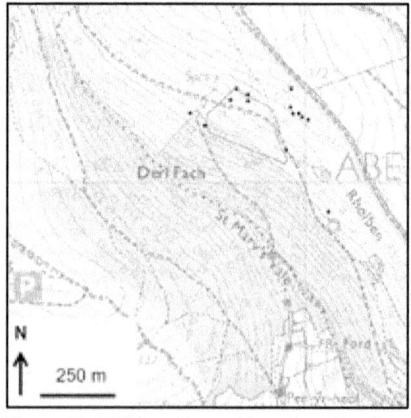

Figure 8: GPS locations of oak pollards. Source: Ordnance Survey 2017b

Figure 9: GPS location of beech pollards. Source: Ordnance Survey 2017b

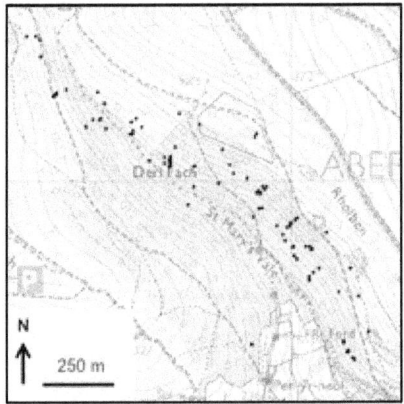
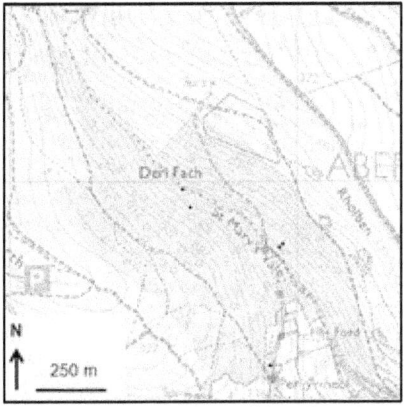

Figure 10: GPS location of oak stubs.
Source: Ordnance Survey 2017b

Figure 11: GPS locations of beech stubs.
Source: Ordnance Survey 2017b

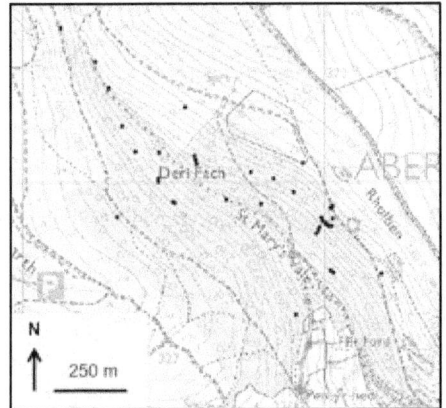

Figure 12: GPS location of oak coppice stools. Source:
Ordnance Survey 2017b

Most of the oak and beech pollards were located along or outside of the eastern woodland edge (figures 8 and 9). Beech and oak stubs and oak stools were generally situated in the south-east and lower altitude north-west sections of the woodland (Figures 10 to 12). Sessile oak (*Quercus petraea*) standards with a diameter of 80-120 cm DBH (diameter at breast height of 1.5 m) were observed on the lower, eastern slopes of the woodland (Figure 13). The oaks to the north were found to have low, large branches due to probable growth in open woodland or non-woodland conditions (Figure 14). The large oaks to the south lacked low, spreading branches due to growth in competitive, closed woodland conditions (Figure 15). The south-west section of the woodland was dominated by sessile oak of a uniform character and size, appearing to be the results of planting in the late-nineteenth to early-twentieth century (Figure 16).

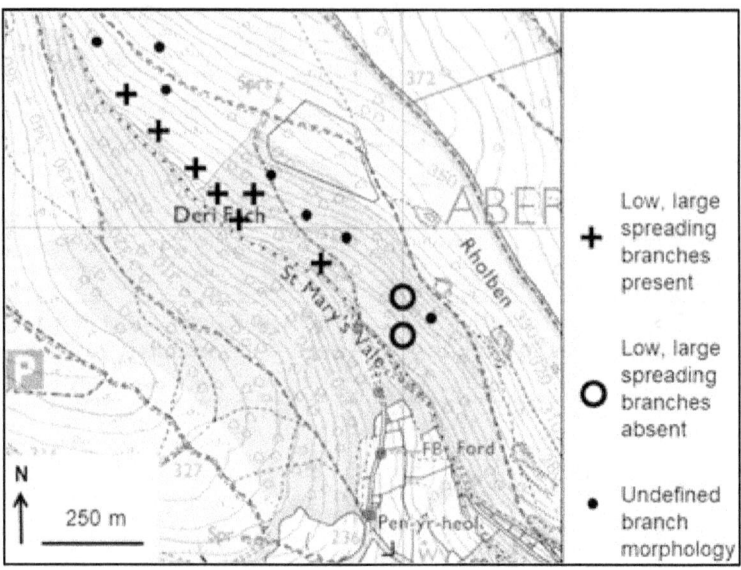

Figure 13: Location of 80-120 cm DBH oak standards. Source: Ordnance Survey 2017b

Figure 14: Oak standard with low branches. Source: author

Figure 15: Oak standard without low branches. Source: author

Investigating Tree Archaeology

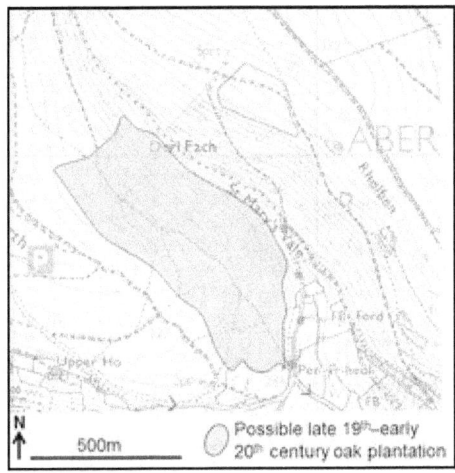

Figure 16: nineteenth to twentieth century sessile oak plantation. Source: Ordnance survey 2017b

Herb and ground layer

The presence of bilberry (*Vaccinium mytillus*) indicates a history of moorland or open woodland conditions in the west and north sections of Deri Fach for at least 2000 years (Figures 17 and 18) (Ritchie, 1955; Rotherham *et al.*, 2008; McKernan & Goldberg, 2011; Hotchkiss, 2016). The distribution of other AWIs suggests the lower reaches and western edge of Deri Fach have been wooded under a closed canopy for at least 400 years (Figures 18 and 19).

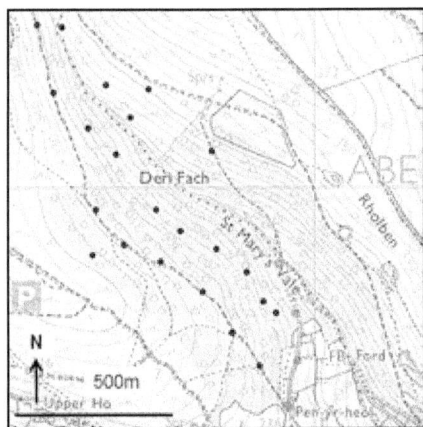 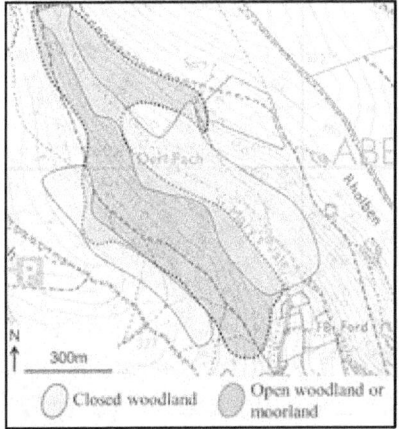

Figure 17: Transect stops with bilberry (*Vaccinium mytillus*) present. Source: Ordnance Survey 2017b

Figure 18: Proposed distribution of closed and open woodland or moorland based on ancient woodland indicators. Source: Ordnance Survey 2017b

Investigating Tree Archaeology

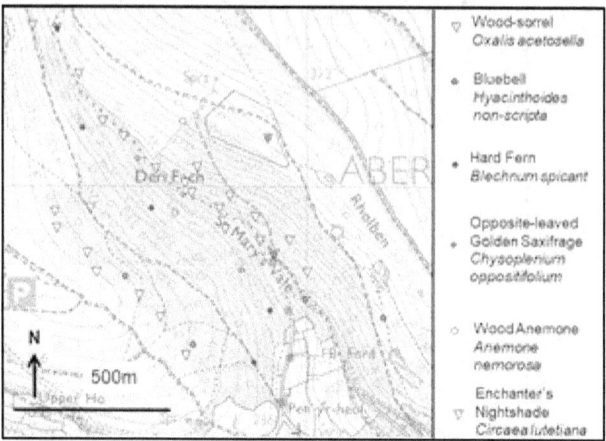

Figure 19: Transect stops with Welsh ancient woodland indicators present.
Source: Ordnance Survey 2017b

Earthworks

Platforms

Sixty-five platforms were logged, measuring 4.5 to 10 m in length and 4 to 7 m in width (Appendix 2). Most of the platforms recorded were oval, with their longer side parallel to the valley contours (Figure 20). Platform morphology, in conjunction with black soil and charcoal remnants, indicates that the platforms are likely to have functioned as charcoal burning hearths. Platforms were loosely grouped in sections of the woodland according to their size (Figures 21 to 23). A smaller range of flora was recorded on platforms under 6.9 m in length, suggesting these platforms were abandoned more recently than the larger platforms (Figure 24).

 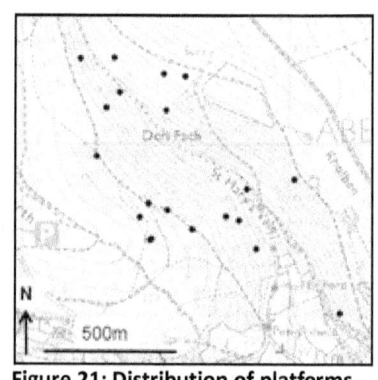

Figure 20: Platform (feature no. 042) viewed from the south. Note the dark soil on the left edge of the platform. Source: author

Figure 21: Distribution of platforms under 6.9 m in length (long side). Ordnance Survey 2017b

Investigating Tree Archaeology

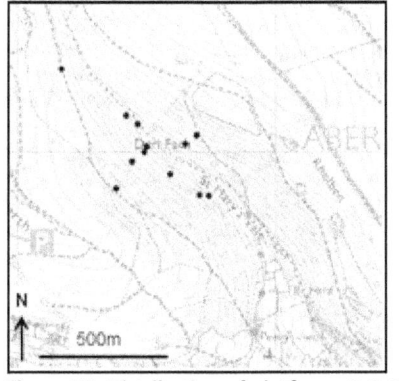

Figure 22: Distribution of platforms 7.0-7.9 m in length (long side). Ordnance Survey 2017b

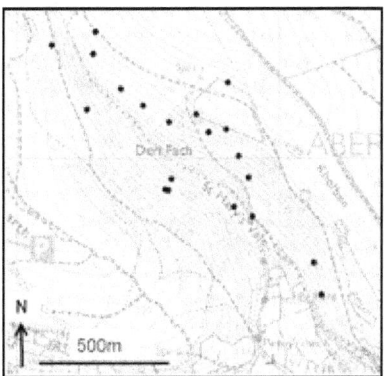

Figure 23: Distribution of platforms over 8 m in length (long side). Ordnance Survey 2017b

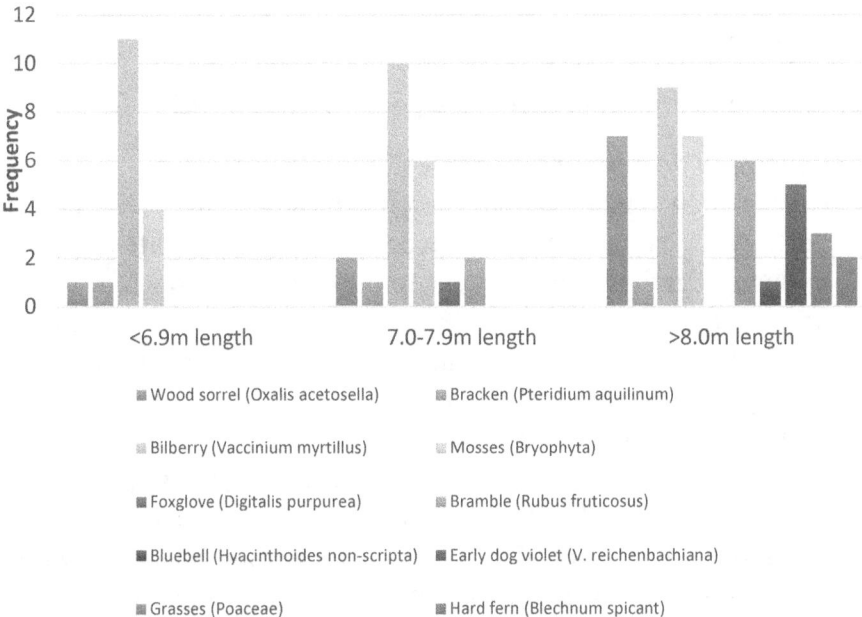

Figure 24: Presence of flora on platforms- frequency according to length of platform

Pits and mounds

Elongated pits and accompanying mounds, recorded in ten locations, appear to be the remains of saw-pits, infilled soon after use or by natural processes (Figures 25 to 26 and appendix 2). Saw-pits were covered by a limited range of flora, suggesting that they were used more recently than the charcoal platforms.

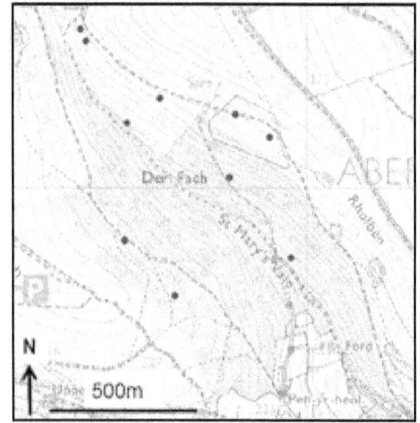

Figure 25: GPS locations of saw-pits.
Source: Ordnance Survey 2017b

Figure 26: Saw-pits, Feature no. 70.
Source: author

Discussion

Woodland and landscape management at Deri Fach

Coppice-with-stubs and standards
Oak and beech stubs within the south-east and lower altitude north-west sections of Deri Fach do not appear to relate to any boundary features and are likely to have been fashioned to accommodate grazing sheep (Rotherham *et al.*, 2008). Oak stools amongst the stubs indicate that a previously unrecognised management system of 'coppice-with-stubs' was utilised at Deri Fach through the fifteenth to nineteenth centuries. This appears to be a variant of 'coppice-with-pollards' management (Peterken, 1993). Saw-pits and closed woodland oak standards may represent the remains of a timber-growing tradition in the south-east of the woodland. Sections of Deri Fach may therefore have been managed as coppice-with-stubs and standards (figure 27). Ground flora indicative of ancient closed woodland is compatible with this interpretation (figure 28). Underwood harvesting appears to have been abandoned though the nineteenth century, while changes in management towards high forest are indicated by the twentieth century singling of stubs into timber trees. Archival research complements the survey results, with widespread references to coppicing and pollarding in south-east Wales during the twelfth to eighteenth centuries (Figure 29) (Linnard, 1982). The use of timber in the region is less well

documented; although timber was exported to England in the eighteenth century for naval use, and used locally as pit-props from the 1850s (Figure 30) (Linnard, 1982; Rackham, 2006). Additionally, timber was milled and traded in Abergavenny until at least the late-nineteenth century (Ordnance Survey, 1881; Kelly, 1895).

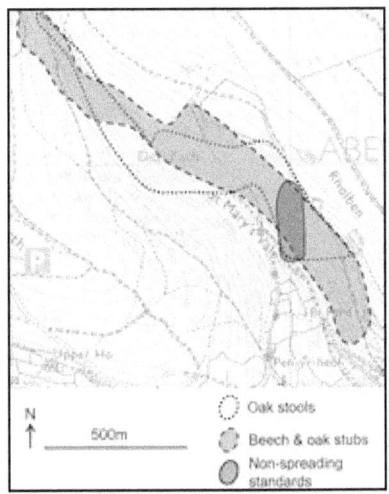

Figure 27: Distribution of oak stools, beech and oak stubs and non-spreading oak standards. Source: Ordnance Survey 2017b

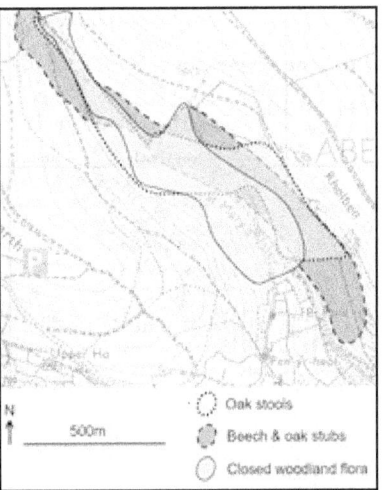

Figure 28: Distribution of oak stools, beech and oak stubs and closed woodland flora. Source: Ordnance Survey 2017b

Figure 29: 13th century illustration of a coppiced tree from a manuscript of the Welsh Laws. Source: Linnard 1982

Figure 30: Pit-wood extraction at Tongwynlais, 1920s, 50 km south-west of Deri Fach. Source: Linnard 1982

Wood-pasture

The initiation of stub pollarding within the south-east and lower altitude north-west sections of the woodland through the period of the fifteenth to the eighteenth centuries indicates the ongoing pasturing of sheep. The spacing of trees, alongside AWIs within these sections suggests wood-pasturing took place under a closed canopy (Figure 31). There may have been an additional area of closed canopy wood-pasture on the south-west edge of the woodland, although the absence of pre-plantation trees prevents further discussion.

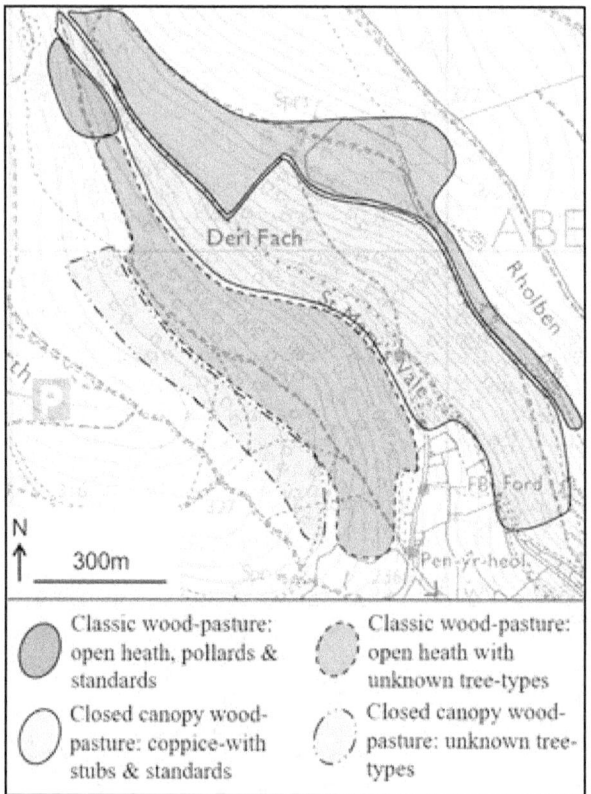

Figure 31: Woodland management systems at Deri Fach. Source: Ordnance Survey 2017b

Open woodland flora, oak pollards and spreading oak standards within the north-east and higher altitude north-west sections of the woodland are likely to be the remains of a classic, upland wood-pasturing tradition, dominated by heath and widely-spaced trees (Figure 31) (Peterken, 1993; Rackham, 2006). Heath-dominated wood-pasture is also indicated on the eastern edge of Deri Fach, in the form of oak and beech pollards. The presence of bilberry suggests the lower altitude south-west section may also have been managed as classic, open wood-pasture, although disturbance associated with the plantation again thwarts discussion.

Figure 32: Twenty-first century sheep pasturing within Deri Fach. Source: author

The wood-pastures at Deri Fach may have formed part of the medieval Moelyfan or Moel hunting Forest, accessed by commoners for pasture and estover (Bradney, 1906; Wade, 1909; Langton, 2009). Wood-pasturing under the Sugarloaf Common laws continued through the twentieth century to the present-day (Figure 32) (Commons Registration Act, 1965). A local farmer recalled the annual return of hundreds of pasturing sheep from the Sugar Loaf in the 1960s, as "like milk flowing down the lane".

In summary, the survey results indicate that large proportions of Deri Fach were likely to have been managed as wood-pasture for at least 500 years (Figure 31). In addition, from at least the fifteenth century the south-east and lower altitude north-west sections were managed as coppice-with-stubs and perhaps standards. Coppice, easier to cut than stubs yet prone to grazing, may have been introduced when grazing pressures were subordinate to non-agricultural woodland industries, such as bark and charcoal production (Warren *et al.*, 2012).

Industries associated with Deri Fach woodland management

Charcoal burning and the iron industry

The southern group of smaller platforms correlates geographically with the nineteenth to twentieth century oak plantation (Figure 33). These platforms may have utilised wood cleared from this area to allow planting or relate to an earlier period of charcoal burning.

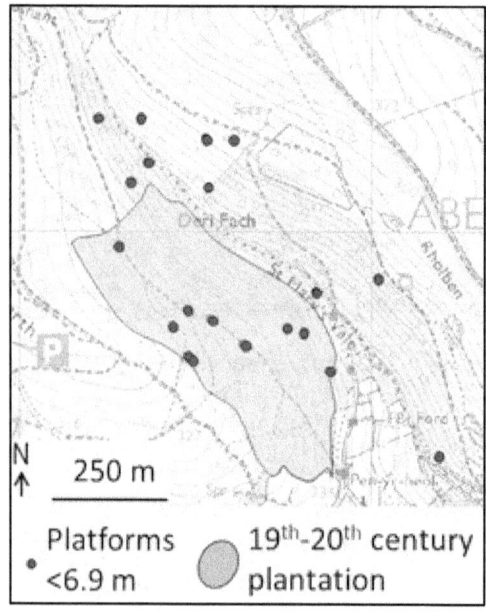

Figure 33: Distribution of small platforms and plantation. Source: Ordnance Survey 2017b

Moderate to large platforms are predominantly located within the coppice-with-stubs sections of the woodland (Figures 34 and 35). Oak and beech underwood, favoured for charcoal production, is likely to have been burnt on these platforms (Linnard, 1982; Gale, 2003; Stout, MacDonald & Watson, 2007; Warren et al., 2012; Rippin, 2013). Based on tree and shoots girths, the estimated duration of harvesting from the stools and stubs places charcoal burning in the fifteenth to nineteenth centuries. Charcoal was produced in south-east Wales for domestic and industrial use from at least the early medieval period, however the well-preserved nature of the platforms at Deri Fach suggests they were used more recently (Williams, 1738; Trueman, 1921; Poggi, 1928; Edlin, 1973; Linnard, 1982; Gale, 2003; Rotherham *et al.*, 2008). An association seems likely with the seventeenth to eighteenth century upsurge in the use of charcoal in iron production (Wheatley, 1913; Linnard, 1982; Harris, 1988; Gale, 2003; Rippin, 2013). Numerous furnaces and forges are known to have operated close to the study area, with at least four works lying at a distance appropriate for the transport of charcoal from Deri Fach (Figure 36 and Table 3) (Hammersley, 1973; Harris, 1988; Rippin, 2013).

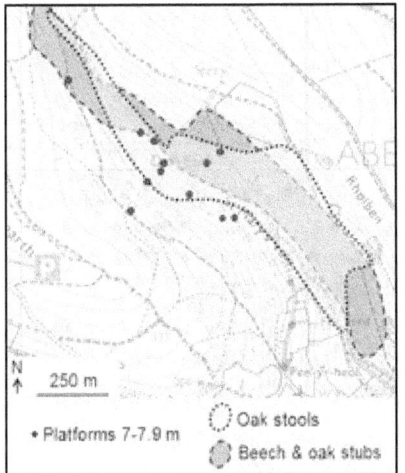 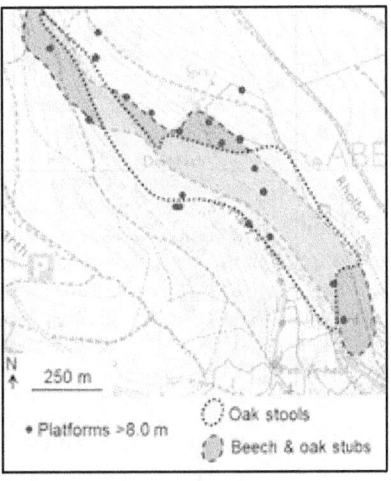

Figure 34: Distribution of moderately-sized platforms, stools and stubs. Source: Ordnance survey 2017b

Figure 35: Distribution of large platforms, stools and stubs. Source: Ordnance survey 2017b

While local forges and iron processing works required notable volumes of charcoal, the seventeenth to eighteenth century blast furnace at Llanelly is likely to have made the greatest demands. Llanelly is reported to have had a yearly output of 410 tons of iron. Based on a minimum rotation of 16 years, this required charcoal derived from at least 752 ha of coppice (Linnard, 1982; Riden, 1987; Warren *et al.*, 2012). There are 700 ha of known ancient woodland sites within 6 km of the furnace, including 90 ha Deri Fach (Natural Resources Wales, 2011). It therefore is highly likely that Deri Fach charcoal was utilised at Llanelly.

In summary, arboreal and archival evidence suggests high levels of charcoal production at Deri Fach during the seventeenth and eighteenth centuries. Analysis of excavated charcoal may allow definitive dating, which alongside further archival and archaeological research relating to local iron working, may push charcoal production into earlier centuries.

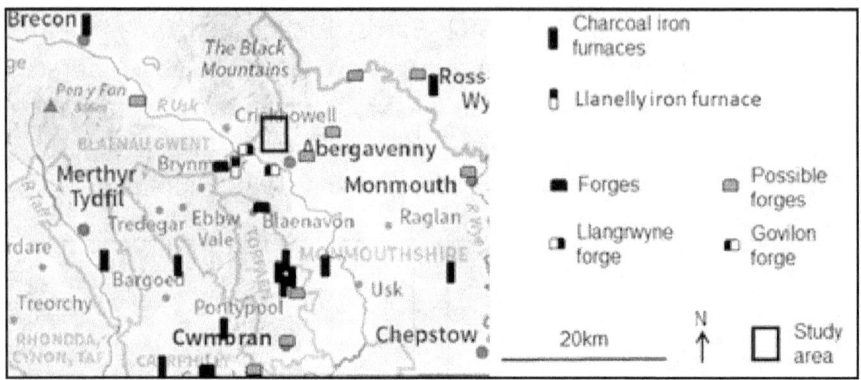

Figure 36: Location of blast furnaces and forges. 'Possible' forges are identified by dwelling names e.g. 'The Old Forge'. Forge date of use and fuel used is unknown. Sources: Linnard, 1982; Riden, 1987; Rippin, 2013; Jenkins, 2016; Base-map: Ordnance Survey 2017a

The tanning industry

The duration of oak underwood harvesting at Deri Fach appears to correlate with the elevated use of oak bark within the tanning industry (Table 3). The slopes of the Sugar Loaf Mountain have been associated with tanneries in Abergavenny, where the industry was important through the sixteenth to the eighteenth centuries, with some operations continuing into the nineteenth century (Steel, 1847; Bradney, 1906; Crawford, 2010; Fyfe, 2012; Morgan, 2012). Brecknockshire and Monmouthshire oak bark was heavily used in other Welsh, Irish and English tanneries during the 'boom' in oak bark trading from the mid-eighteenth to mid-nineteenth centuries, with over 4000 tons of bark shipped annually from Chepstow during the 1790s (Poggi, 1928; Jenkins, 1970; Linnard, 1982; Rackham, 1990; Harris, Harris & James, 2003; Stout, MacDonald & Watson, 2007). The nineteenth century abandonment of stools and stubs may be associated with the subsequent collapse of the oak bark trade (Harris, Harris & James, 2003).

Table 3: Woodland management, charcoal and bark use

Shaded areas indicate the estimated durations of harvesting and uses of charcoal and oak bark. Harvesting durations are based on estimated tree ages and approximate date of last cutting. The darker shading indicates when the demand (or anticipation of demand) for harvested material was greatest.

Period	Woodland management			Charcoal iron industry (distance from Deri Fach by road)				Oak bark tanning industry	
	Oak coppicing	Oak stub pollarding & pollarding	Beech stub pollarding & pollarding	Llanelly forge & charcoal iron furnace (8.5 km)	Llangrwyne forge (6 km)	Govilon forge / Wildon Wire Works (5 km)	Abergavenny blacksmiths & foundries (4 km)	Abergavenny tanning industry	Peak of exports
2000-1951									
1950-1901	░	░							
1900-1851	░	░				░	Likely to be older		
1850-1801	░	▓	░	▓	Possibly older	░	Likely to be older	░	▓
1800-1751	▓	▓	▓	▓	Possibly older	░	░	▓	▓
1750-1701	▓	▓	░	▓		░	░	░	
1700-1651	░	░	░	▓		░	░	░	
1650-1601	░	░	░	▓				░	
1600-1551	░	░	░					░	
1550-1501	▓	░						░	
1500-1451	▓	░						░	
1450-1401	▓							░	
1400-1351	▓	░							
1350-1301	░	░							
1300-1251									

Sources: Ordnance Survey, 1881; Pigot, 1842; Steel, 1847; Kelly, 1895, Bradney, 1906; Poggi, 1928; Riden, 1987; Rackham, 1990; Harris, Harris & James, 2003; Stout, MacDonald & Watson, 2007; Crawford, 2010; Hankinson, Britnell & Silvester, 2012; Rippin, 2013; Govilon Heritage, 2017; Glamorgan-Gwent Archaeological Trust, 2017a-b; RCAHMW, 2017e-f

Deri Fach: embodiment of a working landscape

The managed trees, platforms and saw-pits at Deri Fach are the remains of at least 500 years of human-woodland interactions. As the owners of the woodland, the monks of St Mary's priory and the Lords of Abergavenny are likely to have entered Deri Fach to hunt or for pleasure, and to have employed managers to direct further activities (Gwent archives, 1950; Linnard, 1982; Stout, MacDonald & Watson, 2007). Seasonal workers and local people entered the woodland as employees, commoners or trespassers (Commons Registration Act, 1965; Linnard, 1982; Rackham, 1990; Harris, Harris & James, 2003). Activities within Deri Fach were likely to have been performed in methods and customs particular to the locality and social group. Young people learnt local or family techniques while cutting stubs, removing bark or using woodland products with elders. Harvesting, crafting and the use of products therefore formed elements of personal and community identities. Specific locations and trees within the woodland would have been saturated with memories of harvesting and crafting. These memories and identities are embedded within the trees, as each cut influenced the tree's form, such that the trees themselves can be seen as embodiments of past human identities and relationships with the woodland. Many activities within Deri Fach were vital components of a wider working and economic landscape. Harvesting and charcoal burning were essential to iron production at Llanelly and the subsequent use of iron further afield. The harvesting of bark, likewise, reached out of the woodland to tanneries and the production and consumption of leather items in Britain, Europe and beyond. The remnants of human activity within Deri Fach are, therefore, also the embodiment of this wider working landscape.

Conclusions

Survey and analysis of the trees and earthworks within Deri Fach reveal a management history reaching back at least 500 years and connecting with local and national socio-economic activity. The duration of underwood harvesting correlates with the use of charcoal within the local iron industry and bark within the tanning industry. The creation of stub pollards indicates sheep pasturing within the lower-altitude woodland, while heath-dominated wood-pasturing occurred at higher altitudes. The wealth of information available through the study of managed trees highlights the importance of their inclusion within routine archaeological field surveys.

Bibliography

Bannister, N. (2007) *The cultural heritage of woodlands in the South East*. South East AONBs Woodlands Programme, Kent

Bannister, N., Bartlett, D., Jennings, T., and Cherry, C. (2005) *Exploring your woodlands history: A guide for community groups and woodland owners*. Canterbury Woodlands Research Group, Kent.

Bradney, G. (1906) *A History of Monmouthshire, part II, the Hundred of Abergavenny*, Mitchell Hughes and Clarke, London.

Burton, J. and Stöber, K. (2015) *Abbeys and Priories*, University of Wales Press, London.

Cannell, J. (2005) *The Archaeology of Woodland Exploitation in the Greater Exmoor Area in the Historic Period*. British Archaeological Reports, British Series, **398**, Oxford.

Castle, G. and Mileto, R. (2005) *Development of a veteran tree site assessment protocol*. Nature Research Reports Number 628, English Nature, Peterborough.

Crawford, J. (2010) *King Henry VIII School, Abergavenny: Archaeological desk-based assessment*. Report 2010/049. Glamorgan-Gwent Archaeological Trust, Swansea.

Edlin, H. (1973) *Woodland Crafts in Britain*. David and Charles Ltd, Newton Abbott.

Fyfe, F. (2012) *Brecon Beacons National Park Landscape Character Assessment: Landscape Character Area 12: Skirrid and Sugar Loaf*. Brecon Beacons National Park Authority, Brecon.

Gale, R. (2003) Wood-based industrial fuels and their environmental impact in lowland Britain. In: Murphy, P. and Wiltshire, P. (eds) The environmental archaeology of industry. *Symposia of the Association for Environmental Archaeology*, **20**, 30–47.

Hammersley, G. (1973) The Charcoal Iron Industry and Its Fuel, 1540-1750. *The Economic History Review*, **26**, 4, 593-613.

Hankinson, R., Britnell, W. and Silvester, R. (2012) *Medieval and Early Post-Medieval Industry in East and North-East Wales: The Scheduling Enhancement Programme.* CPAT Report No 1144, The Clwyd-Powys Archaeological Trust, Welshpool.

Harris, E., Harris, J. and James, N. (2003) *Oak, A British History*, Windgather Press Ltd, Macclesfield.

Harris, J. (1988) *The British Iron Industry 1700-1850.* Macmillan, London.

Hotchkiss, A. (2016) *Guide to Ancient Woodland Indicator Plants*, FSC Publications, Telford.

Jenkins, J. (1970) Rural Industry in Brecknock. In: Davies, D. (ed.) *Brycheiniog*, **Vol. XIV**, 1-41. The Brecknock Society, Newport.

Jenkins, P. (2016) *The industrial archaeology and history of Rural Monmouthshire.* http://industrialgwent.co.uk/f21-rural/index.htm. Last accessed 01/07/2017.

Kelly, F. (1895) *Kelly's Directory of Monmouthshire and South Wales 1895.* Kelly and Co., London.

Laws, K. and Brooks, I. (2005) *Parc Lodge Farm, Abergavenny, Archaeological Survey.* EAS Client Report 2005/16 for the National Trust.

Laws, K. and Brooks, I. (2006) *The Sugar Loaf, Abergavenny, Archaeological Survey.* EAS Client Report 2006/1 for the National Trust.

Lennon, B. (2009) Estimating the age of groups of trees in historic landscapes, *Arboricultural Journal*, **32**, 3, 167-188.

Linnard, W. (1982) *Welsh woods and forests: history and utilisation.* National Museum of Wales, Cardiff.

McKernan, P. and Goldberg, E. (2011) *A review of the revision of the Ancient Woodland Inventory in the South East.* Natural England Research Report NERR042, Natural England, Peterborough.

Mitchell, D. (2008) *Core Management Plan for Sugar Loaf Woodlands SAC/SSSI.* Countryside Council for Wales, Cardiff.

Morgan, I. (2012) *Abergavenny Through Time.* Amberley, Stroud.

Pearson, A. (2002) Roman roads and *vici* in Southeast Wales. *GGAT Report No. 2002/061*, Glamorgan-Gwent Archaeological Trust Ltd, Swansea.

Peterken, G. (1993) *Woodland Conservation and Management.* Chapman and Hall, London.

Phillips, N. (2000) Abergavenny Castle 1087-1535. *Gwent Local History: The Journal of Gwent Local History Council*, **88**, 17-31.

Pigot, J. (1842) *Directory of Monmouthshire.* Available at Gwent Archives.

Poggi, E. (1928) The Red Land of Gwent in Eastern Monmouthshire. *Economic Geography*, **4**, No. 1, 31-43.

Rackham, O. (1990) *Trees and Woodland in the British Landscape: The Complete History of Britain's Trees, Woods and Hedgerows.* revised edition, Phoenix Press, London.

Rackham, O. (2006) *Woodland.* Harper Collins, London.

RCAHMW (2017a): *Bettws, Charcoal Burning Site.* Royal Commission on the Ancient and Historical Monuments of Wales. Aberystwyth

RCAHMW (2017b) *Deri Woods Charcoal Burning Sites.* Royal Commission on the Ancient and Historical Monuments of Wales. Aberystwyth

RCAHMW (2017c) *St Mary's Vale; Deri Fach Charcoal Burning Site.* Royal Commission on the Ancient and Historical Monuments of Wales. Aberystwyth

RCAHMW (2017d) *Monmouthshire platforms.* Royal Commission on the Ancient and Historical Monuments of Wales. Aberystwyth

RCAHMW (2017e) *Llanelly blast furnace, near Clydach House, Llanelly*, Royal Commission on the Ancient and Historical Monuments of Wales. Aberystwyth

RCAHMW (2017f) *Wilden; Wildon Wire Works, Upper Mill, Govilon.* Royal Commission on the Ancient and Historical Monuments of Wales. Aberystwyth

Richardson, I. (2006) *Pollards and Platforms.* unpublished report.

Riden, P. (1987) *Gazetteer of Charcoal-fired Blast Furnaces in Great Britain in Use Since 1660.* Merton Priory Press, Cardiff.

Rippin, S. (2013) *The Charcoal Industry of Fforest Coalpit & the Grwyne Fawr Valley*. Abergavenny Local History Society, Abergavenny.

Ritchie, J. (1955) A natural hybrid in *Vaccinium. I.* The structure, performance and chorology of the cross *Vaccinium intermedium Ruthe*. New Phytologist, **54**, 49-66.

Rotherham, I.D. (2013) *Ancient Woodland: History, Industry and Crafts*. Shire Publications, Oxford.

Rotherham, I.D., Jones, M., Smith, L., and Handley, C. (2008) *The Woodland Heritage Manual: A Guide to Investigating Wooded Landscapes*. Wildtrack Publishing, Sheffield.

Steel, S. (1847) *A Report on the Sanitary Condition of the Town of Abergavenny, 1847*. James Hiley Morgan, Abergavenny.

Stout, T., MacDonald, A. and Watson, F. (2007) *A History of the Native Woodlands of Scotland, 1500-1920*. Edinburgh University Press, Edinburgh.

Trueman, A. (1921) The Iron Industry of South Wales. *The Geographical Teacher*, **11**, No. 1, 26-29.

Vrška, T., Janík, D., Pálková, M., Adam, D. and Trochta, J. (2016) Below- and above-ground biomass, structure and patterns in ancient lowland coppices. *iForest – Biogeosciences and Forestry*, **10**, 23-31.

Wade, G. (1909) *Monmouthshire*. Methuen and Co, London.

Warren, G., McDermott, C., O'Donnell, L. and Sands, R. (2012) Recent excavations of charcoal production platforms in the Glendalough valley, Co. Wicklow. *The Journal of Irish Archaeology*, **21**, 85-112.

Wheatley, H. (1913) Charcoal Ironworks. *Journal of the Royal Society of Arts*, **61**, No. 3175, 977-983.

White (1998) *Estimating the Age of Large and Veteran Trees in Britain*. Forestry Commission, Forestry Commission, Edinburgh.

Wiggins, H. (2006) Prehistoric defended enclosures in Gwent. *GGAT Report No. 78*, Glamorgan-Gwent Archaeological Trust Ltd, Swansea.

Williams, D. (1738) *The History of Monmouthshire*. Baldwin, London.

Archival sources
Commons Registration Act (1965) *In the Matter of Sugar Loaf Mountain Common, Llantilio Pertholey and Llanfoist Fawr Communities and Abergavenny Town, Monmouth District, Gwent,*
Gwent Archives (1950) *Abergavenny, Lord, manuscripts [1575x1600]-[c.1950] GB0218.D1583.*

Websites
British Geological Society (2008) *Digital Geological Map of Great Britain 1:25000 scale (DiGMapGB-25) data.* Version 2.18. Keyworth, Nottingham: British Geological Survey.
Cofiadurcahcymru (1998) *Archwilio The Glamorgan-Gwent Archaeological Trust Record.* [Online].
Embleton, A. (2016) *Grid Reference*, Version 2.2.1, mobile app. Available Google Play Store.
Glamorgan-Gwent Archaeological Trust (2017a) *001 Maesygwartha and Llanelly Iron Working Area.*
Glamorgan-Gwent Archaeological Trust (2017b) *HLCA 014 Govilon.*
Govilon Heritage (2017) *Iron Works.*
Grace's Guide (2014) *Blaenavon Ironworks.*
Langton, J. (2009) *Atlas and Maps.* http://info.sjc.ox.ac.uk/forests.
Natural Resources Wales (2011) *Ancient Woodland Inventory 2011.*
Ordnance Survey (1881) *County Series 1:2500, 1st Edition 1849-1899* [TIFF geospatial data], County/Tile: Monmouthshire. Published: Landmark Information Group, Using: EDINA Historic Digimap Service,
Ordnance Survey (1886) *County Series 1:10560, 1st Edition 1849-1899* [TIFF geospatial data], County/Tile: Monmouthshire. Published: Landmark Information Group, Using: EDINA Historic Digimap Service,
Ordnance survey (2017a) *MiniScale [TIFF geospatial data], Scale 1:100000, Tile(s): SO21.* Updated: Jan 2017, Ordnance Survey. Using: EDINA Digimap Ordnance Survey Service,

Ordnance survey (2017b) *1:25000 Scale Colour Raster [TIFF geospatial data], Scale 1:25000, Tile(s): SO21*. Updated: Mar 2017, Ordnance Survey. Using: EDINA Digimap Ordnance Survey Service,

Ordnance survey (2017c) *GB Counties- Past and Present*. [Online] Available at https://www.ordnancesurvey.co.uk/business-and-government/counties/

Portable Antiquities Scheme (2017) *Abergavenny Search*.

UK Soil observatory (2013) *UKSO Soils map viewer*.

Appendix 1: Source of data used in the estimation of tree and shoot ages

Tree species and type	Likely growth conditions	Average ring width (mm)	Assumed age at maturity (years)	Source
Oak standards (closed canopy)	Inside woodland	3.1	70	Average ring widths of Deri Fach clear-felled oak standards (x9), integrated with White's method (1998)
Oak standards (open woodland)	Poor or exposed ground	3	120	White (1998)
Oak stools	Inside woodland	1.5	N/A	Czech core samples (Vrška et al. 2016), WDTVA 2012
Shoots on oak stools	Inside woodland	3.1	70	Average ring widths of Deri Fach clear-felled oak standards (x9), integrated with White's method (1998)
Oak stubs	Inside woodland	1.03	N/A	Exmoor core samples (Richardson 2006). Age reduced by 25% to counter Richardson's likely overestimation in average ring width
Shoots on oak stubs	Inside woodland	3.1	70	Average ring widths of Deri Fach clear-felled oak standards (x9), integrated with White's method (1998)
Oak pollards	Poor or exposed ground	1.03	N/A	Exmoor core samples (Richardson 2006). Age reduced by 25% to counter Richardson's likely overestimation in average ring width
Shoots on oak pollards	Poor or exposed ground	3	120	White (1998)
Beech stubs	Inside woodland	3	120	White's data for beech standards (1998) increased by 30% as a rough guide to similar sized stubs (Elaine Butler, Pers. Comm.)
Shoots on beech stubs	Inside woodland	3	120	White (1998)
Beech pollards	Poor or exposed ground	4	60	White's data for beech standards (1998) increased by 30% as a rough guide to similar sized pollards (Elaine Butler, Pers. Comm.)
Shoots on beech pollards	Poor or exposed ground	4	60	White (1998)

Appendix 2: Features

Pollard diameters were measured by tape at a breast height (DBH) of 1.5 m or the narrowest point near to 1.5 m. Stub diameters were measured by tape at the narrowest point below the knuckle (top of the permanent trunk). Coppice stool diameters were measured by tape at the base (DAB) or the narrowest point near to the base.

1. Feature type - Platform

Feature number	GR	Size (m) length x width	Flora Using DAFOR System	Additional feature details
001	SO2748816651	6x5.5	Wood Sorrel A, Moss F, Leaf Litter D	
002	SO2763516687	6.5x5.5	Bilberry D	
003	SO2754516756	6.5x 6-7.5 (longer downslope)	Bilberry A, Leaf Litter S	At junction of paths
004	SO2747616781	6x5.5	Bilberry F	Path splits c.10m to SE
005	SO2745316727	5.5x5.5	Moss F	
006	SO2738116863	7x6	Moss O, Leaf Litter D	
007	SO2728016955	6x5.5	Bilberry D	Path splits 2m NW
008	SO2721517017	Not recorded	Bracken D Bilberry D	
009	SO2722017309	6x4.5	Bilberry D	
010	SO2726617181	9x5.5	Bilberry O	
011	SO2731517131	6x6.5	Bilberry D	
012	SO2739317063	7x5.5	Bilberry A Moss F	On track
013	SO2744416964	7.5x5	Bilberry O	Unmortared wall banking front
014	SO2758816916	7.5x5.5	Bilberry D	
015	SO2756516884	9x6.5	Bilberry D	
016	SO2776216733	6x4	Bilberry D	Split oak on back
017	SO2780916720	4.5x4	Bilberry D	
018	SO2780916720	Not recorded		
019	SO2787516616	6x4.5	Bilberry A	
020	SO2713217419	8.5x5.5		Poll on bank (gnarl, holl) Darker soil
021	Upslope c. 35m from SO2713217419	Not recorded		
022	SO2716517365	Not recorded		Black soil
023	SO2716817306	7x4.5	Bilberry D	Black path, 2 steps
024	SO2813916497	7x6	Grass A	

Feature number	GR	Size (m) length x width	Flora Using DAFOR System	Additional feature details
025	SO2789716785	8x5		
026	SO2746417100	7x6		
027	SO2753917121	5.5x4		
028	SO2764717027	7x5.5		
029	SO2782616819	8x6	Leaf Litter	
030	SO2783916833	6x2.5	Leaf Litter	Slight bank on downslope side
031	SO2773816837	7x5.5	Leaf Litter, Bilberry O, Sphagnum	
032	SO2770316840	7x6	Leaf Litter	
033	SO2759016922	8x6	Bilberry A	
034	SO2757816880	8.5x6	Bilberry A	
035	SO2749116999	7x6	Bilberry A	
036	SO2749717019	7x4.5	Bilberry A	
037	SO2741917134	7x5.5	Bilberry & Moss D, Bramble O	
038	SO2736517187	6.5x6	Bilberry A	
039	SO2739617233	Not recorded		
040	c.30m uphill from SO2730817264	Not recorded		
041	SO2819216380	6x4.5	Moss D	
042	SO2815616494	8.5x5.5	Moss A, A, Leaf A, Oak Sapling R	Black soil on exposed slope
043	SO2812816613	8.5x6	Leaf D, Moss A,	c.12m above path
044	SO2788216927	8.5x7	Leaf/ Moss/ Bramble A	
045	SO2758017132	9x6.5	Moss & Leaf D	c.10m S of stream, small track below
046	SO2748217195	8x6	Grass & Leaf D	
047	SO2739717256	10x6.5	Oaks 10-30 DBH D, Leaf D, Bilberry O	
048	SO2734717311	6x4.5	Leaf D	
049	SO2729017387	8x5.5	Bracken D, Bilberry O, Moss F	
050	SO2729917468	8x7	Leaf D	
051	SO2748116650	5.5 x 5.5		Charcoal fragments, slight cutting upslope, Path coming into S side

Feature number	GR	Size (m) length x width	Flora Using DAFOR System	Additional feature details
052	SO2801716870	6x5	Leaf D, Bracken F, Moss A	
053	SO2784617008	9x6	Leaf A, Bracken Or Fern F, Grass A, Bramble O, Bluebell O, Violet O	Stub at back 4m girth (slightly sloped tape)
054	SO2772917094	8.5x7	Bramble D, Wood Sorrel A, Violet O	
055	SO2769317059	7.5x6	Moss A, Bilberry O, O, Wood Sorrel F	c.10m from path
056	SO2768317163	7x8.5 (longer downslope)	Leaf/Soil D, Moss F, O, Wood Sorrel R	Black soil
057	c.30m belowSO27926 17048	Not recorded		
058	c, 70 below & slightly north of SO2792617048	Not recorded		
059	SO2779717107	8x6.5	Leaf D, Bramble A, Wood Sorrel A, Violet R	c.1m below enclosure fence
060	SO2760917246	8x6.5	Leaf D,	c.20m from stream
061	SO2753017255	8x6.5	Leaf D, Bilberry D, Hard Fern R (On Back Cutting)	
062	SO2780517281	8.5 x 5.5	Leaf D, Bilberry R	
063	SO2790717271	8.5 x 6	Grass D, Wood Sorrel O	
064	SO2789517096	7x2.5	Bracken O, Bramble F, Foxglove R	
065	SO2744216732	5.5x5		

Feature Type – Saw Pit

Feature number	GR	Pit dimensions (m) lxwxd	Mound dimensions (M) Lxwxh	Flora Using DAFOR System	Additional feature details
066	SO27563 16649	3x1x0.3	3x1x0.3	Pit: Leaf Litter D Mound: Moss D, Bilberry A	Mound on downslope side
067	SO27395 16827	4x1.5x0.4	4x1.5x0.5	50cm Dbh Oak	Mound on downslope side
068	SO27946 16773	6x2x0.45	6x2x0.45	Pit & Mound: Leaf Litter A, Grass A	Mound on upslope side
069	SO27403 17207	4x1x0.4	4x2x0.4	Pit: Leaf Litter D. Mound: Moss D	Mound on downslope side
070	SO27266 17469	6x1x0.6	6x1x0.6	Pit: Bilberries A, Bracken F Mound: Moss D, Leaf Litter A	Mound on downslope side
071	SO27246 17508	6x1x0.6	6x1x0.6	Pit: Bilberries A, Bracken Mound: Moss D, Leaf Litter A. F	Mound on downslope side
072	SO27743 17031	4x1x0.3	4x1.5x0.4	Pit: Leaf Litter D. Mound: Grass D	c.10m from path. Mound downslope
073	SO27513 17286	4x1x0.4	4x1.5x0.4	Pit & Mound: Bilberry D	Mound on downslope side
074	SO27762 17233	4x1x0.4	4x1x0.3	Pit & Mound: Leaf Litter D	Flat area (mound adjacent)
075	SO27875 17161	4x1x0.4	4x1x0.3	Pit & Mound: Leaf Litter D	Flat area (mound adjacent)

Feature Type – Hedge, Ditch, Bank

Feature number	Feature type	GR	Dimensions (m) width x height/ depth	Additional feature details
076	Hedge	SO2789016450	7.0 x 0.6 x 0.7	
077	Bank	SO2776316332	0.5 x 0.2	
078	Bank	SO2771216329	2 x 0.35	
079	Ditch	SO2771216329	0.6 x 0.2	
080	Bank	SO2648917696	4.0 x 1.2	
081	Ditch	SO2648917696	2.0 x 0.3	Adjacent to bank 080 (east side)

Feature Type – Stub, Pollard, (Coppice) Stool

Feature number	Feature type	GR	Diameter (cm) DBH/ DAB	Estimated Age (Years)	Maximum Diameter of Live Shoots (Cm) DBH	Flora Using DAFOR System	Characteristics indicating ancient/ veteran status
082	Oak stub	SO27003 17459	90	328	70		Hollow
083	Oak pollard	SO27687 16452	40	146	25		
084	Beech stub	SO27909 16378	156	445	50	Leaf Litter D, Moss On Stones A	Slight hollowing
085	Oak stub	SO27864 16454	90	328	40	Hard Fern O, Moss F	Slightly gnarly
086	Oak stool	SO27318 16888	125	417	50	Wood Sorrel F, Hard Fern R, Moss F, Fern O	Hollowing/ flat centre, dead wood in canopy & on floor
087	Oak stub	SO27073 17622	100	364	40	Wood Sorrel A	Dead wood in canopy & on floor, burls, slightly gnarly
088	Oak stub	SO27085 17486	159	579	50	Bracken D, Bilberry F	Hollowing, bilberry growing on knuckle, very gnarly
089	Oak stub	SO27114 17485	198	721	60	Wood Sorrel F, Bilberry F	Slightly gnarly, 1 bracket fungi
090	Oak stub	SO27130	198	721	50	Wood Sorrel	Extremely

Feature number	Feature type	GR	Diameter (cm) DBH/DAB	Estimated Age (Years)	Maximum Diameter of Live Shoots (Cm) DBH	Flora Using DAFOR System	Characteristics indicating ancient/ veteran status
		17473				A, Sphagnum Moss A, Opp. Saxifrage F, Hard Fern O	gnarly, hollowing until nearly split down 1 side, some bark loss, hard fern growing on branches
091	Oak stool	SO27129 17494	197	657	100	Wood Sorrel F, Sphagnum Moss A, Opp. Fern2 R, Hard Fern O, Bilberry A	Hollowing, a little dead wood in canopy & on floor, hard fern growing on branches
092	Oak stub	SO27132 17419	100	364	50	Leaf Litter D, Moss F	Gnarly, hollowing, bilberries growing on knuckle
093	Oak stub	SO27185 17290	125	455	70		Dead wood in canopy & on floor, burls, gnarly
094	Oak stub	SO27185 17290	108	393	70		Dead wood in canopy & on floor, burls, gnarly
095	Oak stub	SO27185 57295	60	218	30		Slightly gnarly, slight hollowing
096	Oak stub	SO27220 17309	100	364	30		Fern 2 growing on knuckle
097	Oak stool	SO27452 17001	111	370	35	Bilberry A	Hollowing
098	Alder stool	SO28089 16514	100	200	35	Grass A, Brambles R	Hollowing, burls, dead wood in canopy
099	Alder stool	SO28099 16510	150	300	40	Grass A, Moss A	Burls
100	Alder stool	SO27897 16785	126	252	40	Bramble O, Bluebell O, Dog Violet O, Wood Sorrel O	Hollowing, burls
101	Oak stool	SO27674 16942	185	617	55		Hollowing centre

Investigating Tree Archaeology

Feature number	Feature type	GR	Diameter (cm) DBH/ DAB	Estimated Age (Years)	Maximum Diameter of Live Shoots (Cm) DBH	Flora Using DAFOR System	Characteristics indicating ancient/ veteran status
102	Oak stub	SO27642 16922	90	328	35	Bluebells R, Wood Sorrel F, Wood Anemone O, Moss F	Hollowing, gnarly, burls, dead wood in canopy & on floor, ferns growing on tree
103	Beech stub	SO27630 16915	158	454	80	Leaf litter D, moss F	
104	Beech stub	SO27603 16976	100	228	20		Dramatically cut away on stream side, many burls, gnarly, dead wood in canopy, mossy, hollowing
105	Alder stool	SO27533 17051	123	246	30	Bramble F, Moss F, Opp. Saxifrage O, Wood Sorrel O, Mustard Sp. O	Gnarly, hollowing, dead wood in canopy, burls
106	Oak stub	SO27358 17175	170	619	50		Hollows, dead wood in canopy & on floor, bark loss
107	Oak stub	SO27340 17210	124	451	70		Hollow centre
108	Oak stub	SO27335 17207	121	441	70		Hollow, very gnarly
109	Oak stool	SO27332 17182	167	557	70	Bilberry D, Sphagnum Moss O, Wood Sorrel O, Wood Anemone R	Slightly gnarly base
110	Oak stub	SO27312 17206	134	488	50		Hollow, gnarly, bilberry growing on knuckle
111	Alder stool	SO27308 17264	217	434	40	Bramble F, Sphagnum Moss F, Opp. Saxifrage O, Wood Sorrel O, Bilberry O	Possibly part of a larger stool 280cm diameter. Slightly gnarly, hollowing, dead wood in canopy, burls

Feature number	Feature type	GR	Diameter (cm) DBH/ DAB	Estimated Age (Years)	Maximum Diameter of Live Shoots (Cm) DBH	Flora Using DAFOR System	Characteristics indicating ancient/ veteran status
112	Oak stool	SO27290 17302	167	557	35	Bilberry D, Sphagnum Moss O, Wood Sorrel O, Wood Anemone R	Gnarly, hollowing, dead wood in canopy, burls
113	Oak stool	SO27245 17387	150	500	50	Bilberry A	Hollowing centre,
114	Oak stub	SO28162 16629	139	506	50	Moss A, bilberry O, fern 2 O	
115	Oak stub	SO28017 16740	125	455	60		A little hollowing, gnarly, dead in canopy & on floor
116	Oak stub	SO28004 16778	120	437	60	40	
117	Oak stub	SO28007 16781	110	400			
118	Oak stub	SO27950 16853	162	590	80		Flat knuckle hollowing, bark loss
119	Oak stub	SO27888 16907	140	510	35	Moss D, Bramble O, Fern 2 O, Wood Sorrel O	Gnarly, flat knuckle, a little hollowing, dead in canopy & on floor
120	Oak stub	SO27746 16993	110	400	40		A little gnarly & hollowing
121	Oak stool	SO27578 17059	132	440	35		Dead wood in canopy
122	Oak stub	SO27595 17115	103	375	35		Burls, hollowing, gnarly, dead in canopy & on floor
123	Oak stool	SO27574 17071	163	543	70		Hollowing, dead in canopy & floor
124	Oak stub	SO28229 16616	117	426	70	Bilberry D, Fern 2 R	Hollowing, gnarly, dead in canopy & on floor
125	Oak stub	SO28227 16613	129	470	50	Bilberry D, Wood Sorrel O, Fern 2 R	A little hollowing, very gnarly, dead in canopy & on floor

Feature number	Feature type	GR	Diameter (cm) DBH/DAB	Estimated Age (Years)	Maximum Diameter of Live Shoots (Cm) DBH	Flora Using DAFOR System	Characteristics indicating ancient/ veteran status
126	Oak stub	SO28264 16496	140	510	100	Wood Sorrel O, Bluebell O	Hollowing, burls, dead in canopy & on floor, moss, ivy
127	Oak pollard	SO28242 16581	141	513		Bramble A	Hollowing, dead in canopy & on floor, a few burls
128	Oak stub	SO28229 16616	120	437	60		
129	Oak stub	SO28229 16616	100	364	40	Wood Sorrel A	Very gnarly, a little hollowing, bilberries growing on knuckle, dead wood in canopy
130	Oak stub	SO28202 16707	189	688	90	Moss D, Bracken O, Wood Sorrel O	A lot of hollowing, very gnarly, dead in canopy & on floor, moss
131	Oak stool	SO28191 16707	183	610	50		Hollowing & dead wood on floor
132	Beech pollard	SO28045 16860	120	285	50		Gnarly for beech, a lot of hollowing
133	Oak stub	SO28093 16708	159	579	80	Moss D, Bracken F, Bilberry O	Gnarly, mossy, flat knuckle, hollowing
134	Singled oak stub	SO27785 17054	151	/	60		Very gnarly, Singled shoot on swollen base
135	Oak stub	SO27760 17104	127	462	40	Wood Sorrel A, Lesser Celandine A	Very gnarly, hollowing
136	Oak stub	SO27661 17050	121	441	35		Gnarly
137	Oak stub	SO27663 17053	120	437	35		Gnarly
138	Oak pollard	SO27666 17227	134	488	100		
139	Oak pollard	SO27797 17129	100	364	30		
140	Beech pollard	SO27794 17126	130	327	100		Hollowing
141	Oak stool	SO28021 16916	125	417	60		
142	Oak stool	SO28024 16919	125	417	40		

Feature number	Feature type	GR	Diameter (cm) DBH/DAB	Estimated Age (Years)	Maximum Diameter of Live Shoots (Cm) DBH	Flora Using DAFOR System	Characteristics indicating ancient/ veteran status
143	Oak stool	SO28027 16922	125	417	40		
144	Beech pollard	SO27622 17221	172	544	80	Bracken D, Bilberry A	Very hollow-split open with broken branches sprawling onto ground,
145	Oak stub	SO27610 17227	100	364	30	Leaf Litter D	Dead wood in canopy, hollowing
146	Oak pollard	SO27522 17271	158	575	70		Dead wood in canopy, hollowing, flat knuckle
147	Oak pollard	SO27533 17288	100	364	40		Dead wood in canopy
148	Beech pollard	SO27753 17264	140	373	60		A little hollowing, fluting
149	Beech pollard	SO27773 17300	130	327	50		
150	Oak pollard	SO27762 17233	150	546	70	Wood Sorrel F	Gnarly
151	Oak stub	SO27875 17147	100	364	40		Gnarly, Hollowing, Dead Wood In Canopy
152	Oak pollard	SO27901 17211	135	492	40		
153	Beech pollard	SO27953 17300	162	487	80	Grass D, Wood Sorrel F	Hollowing, fluting
154	Beech pollard	SO27937 17104	160	476		Grass D, Wood Sorrel A, Dog Violet F, Foxglove F	Hollowing, fluting, dead in canopy & the floor, flat knuckle
155	Beech pollard	SO28078 16907	163	492	80		
156	Beech stub	SO27950 16790	100	228			
157	Beech stub	SO27940 16780	100	228			
158	Alder stool	SO28077 16566	150	300	40		Large burl

Investigating Tree Archaeology

Feature number	Feature type	GR	DBH/DAB Diameter (cm)	Estimated Age (Years)	Maximum Diameter of Live Shoots (Cm) DBH	Flora Using DAFOR System	Characteristics indicating ancient/ veteran status
159	Alder stool	SO27900 16770	120	240	45	Bramble O, bluebell O, dog violet O, wood sorrel O	
160	Alder stool	SO27890 16800	110	220	35		
161	Alder stool	SO27890 16790	100	200	30		
162	Alder stool	SO27870 16800	90	180	30		
163	Alder stool	SO27830 16860	120	240	30		Gnarled, dead in canopy
164	Alder stool	SO27810 16860	110	220	35		Gnarled, hollow
165	Alder stool	SO27760 16900	100	200	40		Gnarled, burls
166	Alder stool	SO27830 16860	90	180	30		Gnarled, dead in canopy
167	Alder stool	SO27674 16942	70	140	25		
168	Alder stool	SO27679 16937	85	170	30		
169	Alder stool	SO27679 16948	100	200	40		
170	Alder stool	SO27528 17056	100	200	25		Gnarled, roots visible
171	Alder stool	SO27459 17087	100	200	30		
172	Alder stool	SO27455 17088	110	220	25		
173	Alder stool	SO27459 17095	120	240	25		
174	Alder stool	SO27439 17176	80	160	30		Gnarled
175	Alder stool	SO27444 17177	120	240	30		Gnarled, burls
176	Alder stool	SO27351 17201	100	200	35		
177	Alder stool	SO27351 17209	120	240	35		
178	Alder stool	SO27315 17269	100	200	25		Dead in canopy, gnarly
179	Alder stool	SO27300 17270	110	220	25		Gnarled, burls, hollowing

Appendix 3: Non-feature trees recorded by estimated location and diameter

Diameters were estimated through a visual comparison with a 1m ranging pole. The locations assigned are approximate (within 15 m), based on estimated distance from a transect or recorded location

Feature type	Approximate GR	Approximate diameter (cm) DBH/ DAB	Estimated age (years)
Beech pollard	SO2795017240	150+	423+
Beech pollard	SO2796017220	150+	423+
Beech pollard	SO2798017220	150+	423+
Beech pollard	SO2799017210	150+	423+
Beech pollard	SO2801017200	150+	423+
Beech pollard	SO2781017280	150	423
Beech pollard	SO2781017260	120	285
Beech pollard	SO2767017180	100	209
Oak pollard	SO2798016800	113	411
Oak pollard	SO2750917116	100	364
Oak pollard	SO2736017260	80	291
Oak pollard	SO2722017544	100	182
Oak pollard	SO2821016630	70	127
Oak pollard	SO2765517196	100	364
Oak pollard	SO2765017170	100	364
Oak pollard	SO2767017210	120	437
Oak pollard	SO2788517150	89	324
Oak pollard	SO2787517138	100	364
Oak pollard	SO2788017145	90	328
Oak pollard	SO2787617150	80	291
Oak pollard	SO2790117211	135	491
Oak pollard	SO2794017050	100	364
Oak pollard	SO2815016750	100	364
Oak stool	SO2712017400	150	500
Oak stool	SO2712017403	150	500
Oak stool	SO2712317402	150	500
Oak stool	SO2712017400	100	333
Oak stool	SO2711717414	100	333
Oak stool	SO2737717100	80	267
Oak stool	SO2750516932	120	400
Oak stool	SO2750016937	100	333
Oak stool	SO2745217010	100	333
Oak stool	SO2745717095	100	333
Oak stool	SO2790516575	100	333
Oak stool	SO2803016710	125	417
Oak stool	SO2802016715	90	300
Oak stool	SO2775016930	125	417
Oak stool	SO2757017085	80	267

Investigating Tree Archaeology

Feature type	Approximate GR	Approximate diameter (cm) DBH/ DAB	Estimated age (years)
Oak stool	SO2800816869	125	417
Oak stool	SO2802716882	125	417
Oak stool	SO2797516835	100	333
Oak stool	SO2798016845	100	333
Oak stool	SO2798516855	100	333
Oak stool	SO2799016885	100	333
Oak stool	SO2799516875	100	333
Oak stool	SO2800516865	100	333
Oak stool	SO2801516859	100	333
Oak stool	SO2802516860	125	417
Oak stool	SO2789816967	100	333
Oak stool	SO2783017010	150	500
Oak stool	SO2775717031	80	267
Oak stool	SO2754017240	125	417
Oak stool	SO2793017060	100	333
Oak stub	SO2713217419	100	364
Oak stub	SO2712017410	100	364
Oak stub	SO2717517285	80	291
Oak stub	SO2718017291	120	437
Oak stub	SO2718517297	120	437
Oak stub	SO2728917181	100	364
Oak stub	SO2728517185	80	291
Oak stub	SO2806016670	110	400
Oak stub	SO2801716740	120	437
Oak stub	SO2801016751	120	437
Oak stub	SO2801 016780	120	437
Oak stub	SO2798016800	113	411
Oak stub	SO2797016820	110	400
Oak stub	SO2787016880	120	437
Oak stub	SO2790016910	80	291
Oak stub	SO2766016980	110	400
Oak stub	SO27640 16990	110	400
Oak stub	SO2757617049	120	437
Oak stub	SO2757517050	80	291
Oak stub	SO2757817061	85	309
Oak stub	SO2757717072	100	364
Oak stub	SO2757917083	100	364
Oak stub	SO2757817074	80	291
Oak stub	SO2757617065	120	437
Oak stub	SO2757817056	110	400
Oak stub	SO2757917077	80	291
Oak stub	SO2757817068	90	328
Oak stub	SO2756017060	80	291
Oak stub	SO2751017070	80	291
Oak stub	SO2745017160	80	291
Oak stub	SO2744017160	80	291
Oak stub	SO2748017180	100	364

Feature type	Approximate GR	Approximate diameter (cm) DBH/ DAB	Estimated age (years)
Oak stub	SO2746017210	115	419
Oak stub	SO2735017260	80	291
Oak stub	SO2733017300	100	364
Oak stub	SO2800216860	150	546
Oak stub	SO2802216878	125	455
Oak stub	SO2806216781	125	455
Oak stub	SO2805016782	125	455
Oak stub	SO2807216773	125	455
Oak stub	SO2806516770	125	455
Oak stub	SO2799516861	80	291
Oak stub	SO2799516850	125	455
Oak stub	SO2798516845	100	364
Oak stub	SO2788016961	100	364
Oak stub	SO2788516968	100	364
Oak stub	SO2789116958	120	437
Oak stub	SO2789416963	110	400
Oak stub	SO2790116980	150	546
Oak stub	SO2790816974	140	510
Oak stub	SO2791516982	130	473
Oak stub	SO2784617010	127	462
Oak stub	SO2779817025	100	364
Oak stub	SO2768017190	125	455
Oak stub	SO2788017160	110	400
Oak stub	SO2812016830	120	437
Singled oak stub	SO2821016410	95	/
Singled oak stub	SO2821516405	70	/
Singled oak stub	SO2819016430	90	/
Singled oak stub	SO2819516436	75	/
Singled oak stub	SO2819516430	90	/
Singled oak stub	SO2818016460	95	/
Singled oak stub	SO2818016466	70	/
Singled oak stub	SO2806016680	80	/
Singled oak stub	SO2807516694	80	/
Singled oak stub	SO2779016930	110	/
Singled oak stub	SO2756017080	80	/
Singled oak stub	SO2801216872	150	/

Stunted Oaks at Burbage nr Hathersage, Derbyshire, May 2013

Chapter 15. Life and Death of Wooden Artefacts: a Review of the Evidence for Early Medieval Woodcraft

Kevin Tillison
University College Dublin, Irish Research Council Government of Ireland Postgraduate Scholar

Abstract

In early medieval Ireland (A.D. 400-1100), the significance of woodcraft is exemplified in the Early Irish Laws, which suggested woodworking and woodworkers had distinct categories with variations of social status based on specialisation. Modern archaeological investigations have expanded our long-held understanding about the early medieval period and have provided a large corpus of effectively recorded and classified material to examine. Before it is possible to facilitate new research involving wood and woodcraft, it is necessary to collate the archaeological data relating to wooden artefacts, evidence for woodworking, and the diverse contexts in which they are found, thus allowing for a better understanding of wood and woodcraft to be gained. This paper represents the preliminary research from an on-going PhD project that includes a systematic review of the Early Medieval Archaeology Project's findings, from which 37 rural sites in Ireland with evidence for woodworking and/or worked wood were identified. To-date, the archaeological data and discussion on approximately 1000 small wooden finds, and other products related to woodworking have been collated from their diverse sources into one structured form in order to examine the wooden material. Future work will include the review of the Drumclay Crannog, Co. Fermanagh assemblage and the urban assemblages from Waterford and Cork with further comparison to five international assemblages.

Introduction

Despite organic artefacts' importance throughout the past, archaeological evidence relating to these objects, like wooden artefacts, is less likely to preserve in the archaeological record and is less frequently the focus of material culture studies. Fortunately, Ireland's unique environment provides a rare glimpse into the life of wooden artefacts across the island in a variety of contexts and by relation provides key insights into the life of past peoples. The archaeological data associated with evidence for woodworking, worked wood, and related artefacts required a collation to better understand its significance to early medieval peoples. Therefore, a systematic review was undertaken to identify the currently available archaeological evidence relating to woodcraft in order to work towards a better understanding of wood and woodcraft in early medieval Ireland.

The word woodcraft, for the purposes of this study, encapsulates small wooden finds, evidence for woodworking and the woodworkers. Woodcraft can also include structural woodworking or non-portable wooden material, but carpentry of this form will be not a focus of the thesis related to this paper. Specifically, this research is designed to examine early medieval assemblages that include wooden artefacts (small finds or portable objects) and/or evidence of woodworking from 38 rural secular sites and two urban sites (total 40 sites in Ireland), with comparisons to five contemporary international assemblages. Of particular interest, is exploring the life of the wooden objects, with a more in-depth focus on wooden vessels, whilst also investigating the people who interacted with these artefacts.

Research Background

There is a long tradition in research, specifically in archaeology, of collating materials in order to gain further insights into past peoples' lives. In Ireland, researchers like Wood-Martin (Wood-Martin, 1886) saw the significance of evidences being accumulated during his era, and in this case, placed a focus on lake-dwelling or *crannógs*, taking it upon themselves to collate the research or data which at the time was spread among

Proceedings, Catalogues and Journals. For example, the Royal Irish Academy Proceedings are full of accounts of individuals finding archaeological material in a variety of places during the nineteenth century, which in turned, built up a large corpus of evidence for structures and artefacts (e.g. Anon, 1870; Anon, 1874; Molloy, 1870; Wakeman, 1870; Gray, 1883; Fitzgerald, 1898). Although wooden objects were not the primary focus of Wood-Martin's research, the waterlogged nature of *crannógs* meant a significant number of wooden artefacts were concurrently brought together.

Major collations of sites with wooden material did not occur again for many years, however, many significant sites were excavated during this lull. Several of these examples were produced from the work carried out by The Harvard Archaeological Mission (e.g. Hencken *et al.*, 1935; Hencken *et al.*, 1941; Hencken *et al.*, 1950). These archaeological excavations arguably established Irish archaeological studies in a politically charged time and established more systematic techniques for archaeological investigations (O'Sullivan, 2003). However, in the case of *crannógs* (where wood preservation is more common), these site-types were not necessarily excavated particularly well, as evident from the subsequent re-interpretations mostly regarding the chronologies of the sites (e.g. Newman, 2002; Newman, 1997; Newman, 1986; Johnson, 1999; Lynn, 1985). The reports produced by Hencken and others remain heavily referenced despite some of the shortcomings of these excavations and still provides valid information regarding the early medieval period. The Harvard team also did not shy away from the use of historical sources and folklore when investigating the archaeology of Ireland and the utilisation of multidisciplinary research produced important insights into the significance of site like Lagore *crannóg*, Co. Meath, which is considered a royal site based on such evidence. Although considered antiquarian by some, there is validity behind the use of historical sources as well as Irish and international ethnographies or folklife studies, when used appropriately in conjunction with archaeological evidence.

Although several significant catalogues or collations of information were published during the twentieth century (e.g. Raftery, 1983; Eogan, 1983), with regard to wooden objects specifically, a long period of time elapsed before another significant study was produced. Potentially, the re-vitalisation or possibly the start of a conscious effort to collate data and discussion on wooden artefacts began in Britain with John Coles et al.'s publication in Proceedings of the Prehistoric Society (Coles et al., 1978) as well as the establishment of wetland archaeology during this same period. This new trend continued in the form of several PhD projects carried out by Morris, Earwood, and later, Comey (Morris, 1984; Earwood, 1990; Comey, 2002). The latter projects led to successful PhD degrees and later resulted in monographs relating to the work carried out (Earwood, 1993; Morris, 2000; Comey, 2010). These past research projects give validity to approaching the study of wooden artefacts by working towards gathering information into a single form, thus allowing for more informed comparative analyses.

Part of the issue is that this work has not been continuous. As a result, a similar type of study or review has not been carried out in many years and therefore current understandings do not include evidence from more recent archaeological investigations. This is especially true due to the dramatic increase in the pace, scale and intensity of archaeological excavations in Ireland between *c.* 1992 and 2008. The numerous archaeological investigations in Ireland, over this period, resulted in a large increase in the quantity of artefactual material (O'Sullivan *et al.*, 2008), including wooden artefacts. This newly discovered large corpus of material requires integration into the discussions and interpretations about the early medieval period. These types of reports have in recent years remained in their original unpublished forms despite providing information on wooden species' identifications and object classifications. Since there has not been in depth, repeated, and updated research on wooden artefacts, it has created problems in gaining a better understanding of objects made of wood. Thus, providing a gap which will be addressed through the course of the thesis related to this paper, i.e. an updated collation of archaeological data on wooden objects, woodworking evidence, and related material in Ireland.

Preliminary Findings

Research undertaken by the Early Medieval Archaeology Project (EMAP) was used as a starting point and basis for the database created as part of this project in order to facilitate the collation of data relating to small (portable) wooden finds. EMAP formed an overarching investigation and analysis of the history, character and results of early medieval archaeological excavations in Ireland. This resulted in several reports and publications, thus creating a strong foundation for more detailed analysis of material culture, such as wooden artefacts.

One of the reports was a gazetteer of rural secular sites with evidence for several types of craft production and industrial activity practiced during the early medieval period, including evidence for woodworking (Kerr *et al.*, 2012a, 2012b). Woodworking was not a major priority for EMAP, but it does highlight some excavated rural sites with small wooden finds and specialised woodworking tools. From this list of 317 sites, 37 were identified with evidence for woodworking and/or worked wood (Table 1). EMAP's sources of data were derived from both published and unpublished literature, consisting mainly of excavation reports. Archaeological evidence for woodworking is classified as direct and indirect. Direct evidence is described as the waste material or unfinished product that can be interpretive as the activity (e.g. woodworking) occurring at the site. For example, direct evidence for woodworking is interpreted as, wood chips, rough-outs, and woodturning cores. Artefacts, at least small finds, are not necessarily direct woodworking evidence because these types of objects are portable, meaning they did not have to be created at the site where they were found. Indirect evidence is described as the specialised tools used for a specific craft. For example, indirect evidence for woodworking can be interpreted as, drawknives, croze, and saws. Worked wood for the purposes of the thesis associated with this paper included non-structural, small (portable) wooden finds found in early medieval Irish contexts.

Table 1: The forms of evidence for woodworking and/or worked wood found in sites across early medieval Ireland, i.e. direct and indirect.

Site Name	County	Site Type	Woodworking Evidence
Antiville	Antrim	Souterrain	Indirect
Ballinderry 1	Westmeath	Crannog	Neither
Ballinderry 2	Offaly	Crannog	Direct
Ballyaghagan 1	Antrim	Souterrain	Neither
Ballymacash	Antrim	Uni-Enclosure	Neither
Baronstown	Meath	Non-Circular site	Both
Cahercommaun Fort	Clare	Cashel	Indirect
Carraig Aille 1	Limerick	Cashel	Indirect
Carraig Aille 2	Limerick	Cashel	Indirect
Carrigatogher	Tipperary	Multi-Enclosure	Neither
Castlefarm	Meath	Cemetery/Settlement	Indirect
Clea Lake	Down	Crannog	Indirect
Collierstown 1	Meath	Cemetery/Settlement	Neither
Deer Park Farms	Antrim	Raised-Enclosure	Indirect
Dooey	Donegal	Other	Both
Dowdstown 2	Meath	Non-circular Enclosure	Neither
Dressogagh	Armagh	Multi-Enclosure	Neither
Feltrim Hill	Dublin	Cashel	Indirect
Garryduff 1 & 2	Cork	Uni-Enclosure	Indirect
Johnstown 1	Meath	Cemetery/Settlement	Indirect
Killederdadrum	Tipperary	Uni-Enclosure	Indirect
Killickaweeny	Kildare	Uni-Enclosure	Indirect
Knowth	Meath	Raised-Enclosure	Indirect
Lagore	Meath	Crannog	Direct
Larrybane	Antrim	Other	Indirect
Lisleagh 1	Cork	Multi-Enclosure	Neither
Lissue	Antrim	Uni-Enclosure	Indirect
Lough Faughan Crannog	Down	Crannog	Indirect
Mounty Offaly	Dublin	Cemetery/Settlement	Direct
Moynagh Lough	Meath	Crannog	Neither
Newtownlow	Westmeath	Crannog	Neither
Rathtinaun	Sligo	Crannog	Neither
Raystown	Meath	Non-Circular site	Direct
Roestown 2	Meath	Non-Circular site	Indirect
Seacash	Antrim	Uni-Enclosure	Neither
Sluggary	Limerick	Multi-Enclosure	Indirect
Woodstown 6	Waterford	Other	Neither

The preliminary review of the 37 Irish sites resulted in a collation of data and discussion on approximately 1000 wooden artefacts and related objects.

Future work

This PhD project described here is still in its preliminary collation stages. Once complete, the collation stage will allow for a determination of the archaeological evidence for the processes wooden objects went through before their depositions. The typical processes are *making, using,* and *depositing* of an object, in addition to more unique processes such as *repairing, recycling* and *repurposing*. Furthermore, the collation stage will allow for the identification of the archaeological contexts of woodcraft that further support how artefacts were *made, used* and *deposited*, while also supporting other objectives of this thesis.

One such objective is exploring potential sources for gaining a better understanding of the people who interacted with wooden artefacts, particularly the *makers* or craftspeople. The archaeological evidence and archaeological contexts determined through the collation stage will be used as a foundation for further comparison with multidisciplinary research and data, such as historical sources, and Irish and international ethnographic literature. Although disciplines, such as ethnography, do not provide a direct link to early medieval peoples, archaeological remains are not consistently inscribed with the social aspects of people's lives and alternative sources provide a potentially more informed perspective than a purely theoretical approach. Therefore, as part of this project, it is necessary to establish criteria for the use of non-archaeological sources when attempting to gain better understanding of woodcraft, for example, manufacturing processes, functional purposes, depositional practices, the social identity of craftspeople and household assemblages in various temporal and spatial contexts.

A further investigation of woodcraft traditions will occur concerning the possibility of an Irish assemblage type and by relation understanding the set of objects people required in early medieval Ireland. It is necessary to have previously extrapolated evidence such as typology, morphology, chronology, and distribution, in order to make Irish material comparable to other spatial and temporal contexts. The assemblages found in Ireland will be compared to five international early medieval assemblages to compare and contrast the wooden artefacts. In addition, a review of the National Folklore Collection in University College Dublin will occur to determine common sets of wooden objects people used in later periods within Ireland, to create a better sense of what objects could be considered necessary for a household.

Overall, the research design for this PhD project will involve systemically reviewing the available archaeological evidence found in Ireland relating to woodcraft. Then, a forensic approach will be used to analyse woodcraft by building the surrounding multi-proxy evidence to create the most probable interpretations. Followed by, a comparative analysis of different Irish sites and between Irish and international sites. Furthermore, throughout the study, arguments will be strengthened by using multi-disciplinary research in order to create more informed insights and produce a more holistic study of woodcraft and the life of wooden artefacts.

References

Anon. (1870) 'Donation of finds from Ballydoulough Crannogs, County Fermanagh'. *Journal of the Royal Society of Antiquaries of Ireland*, **11**, 569.

Anon. (1874) 'Donation of oak paddle from Drumdarragh crannog, near Enniskillen'. *Journal of the Royal Society of Antiquaries of Ireland*, **13**, 314–315.

Coles, J.M., Heal, S.V.E. and Orme, B.J. (1978) 'The Use and Character of Wood in Prehistoric Britain and Ireland', *Proceedings of the Prehistoric Society*, **44**, pp. 1–45.

Comey, M. (2002) *Medieval stave built wooden vessels from Ireland and Russia*. Unpublished PhD thesis, University College London, London.

Comey, M.G. (2010) *Coopers and Coopering in Viking Age Dublin*. Dublin: National Museum of Ireland (Medieval Dublin excavations 1962-81, Ser. B).

Earwood, C. (1990) *Domestic wooden artefacts from prehistoric and early historic periods in Britain and Ireland: their manufacture and use. Archaeology*. Unpublished Ph.D. thesis. University of Exeter.

Earwood, C. (1993) *Domestic wooden artefacts in Britain and Ireland from Neolithic to Viking times*. Exeter: University of Exeter Press.

Eogan, G. (1983) *The hoards of the Irish later Bronze Age*. Dublin: University College.

Fitzgerald, W.L. (1898) 'An Ancient Footway of Wooden Planks across the Monavullagh Bog'. *The Journal of the Royal Society of Antiquaries of Ireland*, **8**(4), 417–418.

Gray, W. (1883) 'Crannoge canoe from Lough Mourne, County of Antrim'. *Journal of the Royal Society of Antiquaries of Ireland*, **16**, 371–372.

Hencken, H. O. *et al.* (1935) 'Ballinderry Crannog No. 1', *Proceedings of the Royal Irish Academy. Section C: Archaeology, Celtic Studies, History, Linguistics, Literature*, **43**, 103–239.

Hencken, H.O., Price, L. and Start, L.E. (1950) 'Lagore Crannog: An Irish Royal Residence of the 7th to 10th Centuries A.D.'. *Proceedings of the Royal Irish Academy. Section C: Archaeology, Celtic Studies, History, Linguistics, Literature*, **53**, 1–247.

Hencken, H.O. and Stelfox, A.W. (1941) 'Ballinderry Crannog No. 2'. *Proceedings of the Royal Irish Academy. Section C: Archaeology, Celtic Studies, History, Linguistics, Literature*, **47**, 1–76.

Johnson, R. (1999) 'Ballinderry crannóg No. 1: A reinterpretation'. *Proceedings of the Royal Irish Academy. Section C: Archaeology, Celtic Studies, History, Linguistics, Literature*, pp. 23–71.

Kerr, T. *et al.* (2012a) *Industry Activity on Rural Secular Sites in Ireland, A.D. 400-1100: Site Gazetteer A-G*. Early Medieval Archaeology Project (EMAP). UCD/QUB.

Kerr, T. et al. (2012b) *Industry Activity on Rural Secular Sites in Ireland, A.D. 400-1100: Site Gazetteer H-Z.* Early Medieval Archaeology Project (EMAP). UCD/QUB.

Lynn, C.J. (1985) 'Lagore, County Meath and Ballinderry No. 1, County Westmeath Crannogs: Some Possible Structural Reinterpretations'. *The Journal of Irish Archaeology*, **3**, 69–73.

Molloy, K. (1870) 'Notice of discovery of timber structure in bog near Clonmacnois'. *Journal of the Royal Society of Antiquaries of Ireland (Journal of the Historical and Archaeological Association of Ireland, Vol. 1- Fourth Series, 1870-71)*, **11**(1), 279.

Morris, C.A. (1984) *Anglo-Saxon and medieval woodworking crafts: the manufacture and use of domestic and utilitarian wooden artifacts in the British Isles, 400-1500 AD.* Unpublished PhD thesis, University of Cambridge, Cambridge.

Morris, C.A. (2000) *Craft, industry and everyday life: Wood working in Anglo Scandinavian and Medieval York.* In: P.V. Addyman and York Archaeological Trust (eds). *The archaeology of York, Vol.17, The small finds.* Published for the York Archaeological Trust by the Council for British Archaeology, York.

Newman, C. (1986) *The archaeology of Ballinderry Lough.* Unpublished MA thesis, University College Dublin, Dublin.

Newman, C. (1997) 'Ballinderry Crannóg No. 2, Co. Offaly: The Later Bronze Age'. *The Journal of Irish Archaeology*, **8**, 91–100.

Newman, C. (2002) 'Ballinderry Crannóg No. 2, Co. Offaly: Pre-Crannóg Early Medieval Horizon'. *The Journal of Irish Archaeology*, **11**, 99–123.

O'Sullivan, A. (2003) 'The Harvard Archaeological Mission and the Politics of the Irish Free State'. *Archaeology Ireland*, **17**(1), 20–23.

O'Sullivan, A. et al. (2008) *Early Medieval Ireland: Archaeological Excavations 1930-2004.* Early Medieval Archaeology Project (EMAP). UCD/QUB.

Raftery, B. (1983) *A Catalogue of Irish Iron Age antiquities.* Veröffentlichung des Vorgeschichtlichen Seminars Marburg. Sonderband, 1, Marburg.

Wakeman, W.F. (1870) 'Iron tools and canoe discovered at the Crannog of Cornagall, Co. Cavan (note)'. *Journal of the Royal Society of Antiquaries of Ireland (Journal of the Historical and Archaeological Association of Ireland, Vol. 1- Fourth Series, 1870-71)*, **11**(2), 461–5.

Wood-Martin, W.G. (1886) *The lake dwellings of Ireland: or, Ancient lacustrine habitations of Erin, commonly called crannogs*. Hodges, Figgis & Company.

A besom maker at work, binding a head. Courtesy of Ian D. Rotherham

Chapter 16. Relict Woodlands in the South Pennines and Dark Peak – reconstructing the evidence from ecological indicators and archival sources

Ian D. Rotherham
Sheffield Hallam University

Summary

Detailed landscape histories are changing perceptions of the nature of Domesday environments with implications for conservation and future site management. Bringing together sources from ecological sciences, from historical research, from cartographic evidence, and from archaeology, increasingly, we are now able to present time-lines of environmental change for specific sites. Furthermore, the individual locations are placed within a conceptual framework of the wider landscape and this is in turn related to the socio-economic and political drivers acting throughout history. Building on the work of historians such as David Hey and Melvyn Jones for example, and ecologists such as Donald Pigott and Penny Anderson, there is emerging consensus of opinion on the origins of rural landscapes in the English uplands and particular on the woodlands and other treed areas. Indeed, the landscape evolution of ecologically distinct zones such as heaths, moors, bogs, and woods, is now drawn into a coherent whole by concepts such as 'shadow woods' which place ecological histories into a socio-economic timeline of common origins. This chapter examines the approach in the south Pennines. This is an area on which David Hey focussed many of his countryside history studies, and in particular some of his last published works on the Peak District moors and on ancient woods.

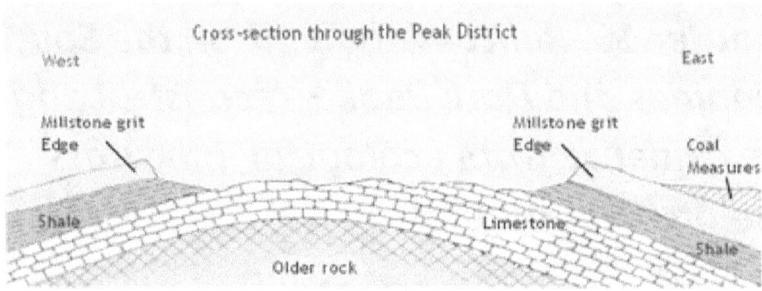

Figure 1. A cross-section through the geology of the Peak District

The study area

The Pennine Chain of hills runs down the spine of England from southern Scotland with land generally at between 500 and 1,000 feet in altitude and terminating in the Dark Peak of the Peak District. In this southern zone the higher ground is mostly flat-topped plateaux underlain with coarse millstone grit. As the land falls eastwards, the geology is a mix of sandstones, shales and coal seams. The soils are mostly acidic with some base-flushing where permeable sandstones meet impermeable shale, and agriculture has been limited by altitude and exposure, soil acidity and low nutrient status and in some areas by waterlogging. The higher-level settlements have been mostly agricultural, but the lower-level landscapes characteristically mix farming and industry. Coal-mines were frequent as the mineral outcrops close to the land surface, and there are numerous stone quarries for sandstone (for building works) and for ganister (for the refractory industry). The vegetation and woodlands of the study area were described by Linton (1903), Moss (1913), and then by Tansley (1949) for example, in his epic volume on British vegetation. The general background to the southern part of the region was detailed by Edwards (1962) and its vegetation brought up to date by Anderson and Shimwell (1981). These accounts have tended to focus on the Peak and Pennines at the southern end of the Pennine chain, and few works provide a more holistic account of the region.

However, there have been pioneering studies (e.g. Conway, 1947, 1949; Woodhead, 1929) on the palaeo-ecology of the region which resonate with the wider region and provide insight into vegetation changes over time. Because of this research we know a considerable amount about vegetation change both historically and prehistorically. Atherden (1992) brought much of this material together in an account that provides a broad synthesis and overview of the ecology on upland environments such as in the Peak and Pennines.

It was in this wider context that the works of David Hey (e.g. 2008, 2014, 2015, and 2017) provide excellent reviews and case-studies of the historical aspects of these upland landscapes. Local histories also help (e.g. Bygones of Bradfield for example (undated) or Lea Wood Heritage Community Project, 2014)).

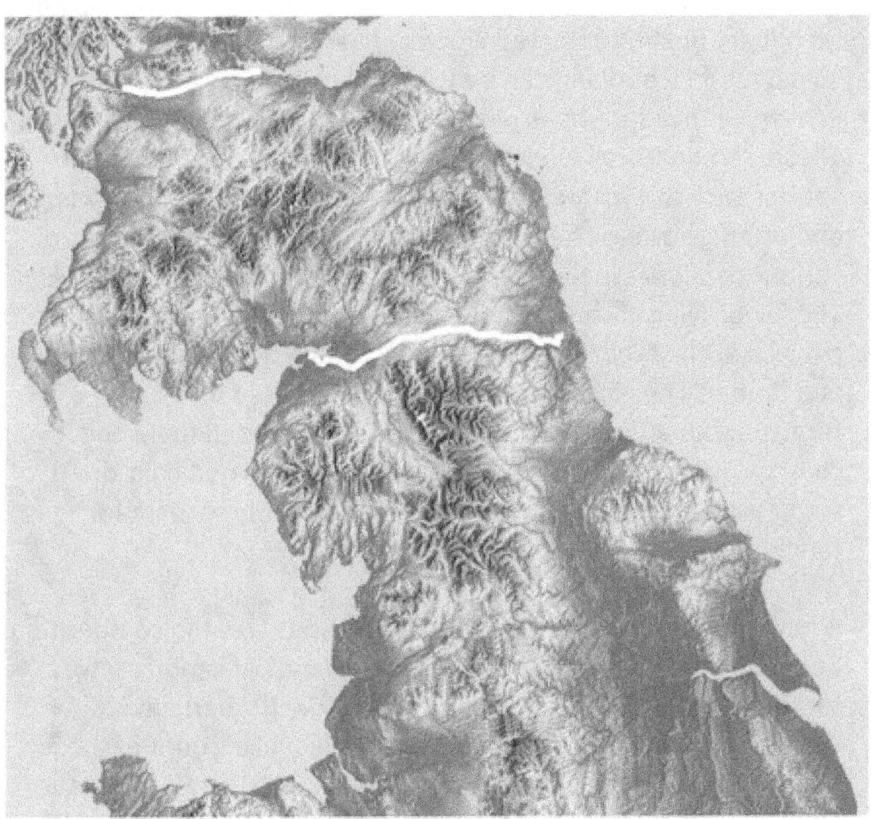

Figure 2. The study area lying at the southern end of the great Pennine chain

An introduction to woodlands in the South Pennines and Dark Peak

With the underlying geology dictating landform and land-use, gritstone and sandstone edges outcrop to face west along the eastern flank of the Dark Peak. Other edges face north or south on either side of the river valleys which cut through the Pennines from South Yorkshire into West Yorkshire. In terms of understanding the woodland heritage of the region, this topography is significant as it is below these edges on the boulder-strewn slopes that most woods occur. They also clothe the gulleys and smaller valleys which run from the edges into the lower valleys. The woodlands mix 'ancient' woods (i.e. pre-1600 AD) mostly dominated by oak (*Quercus petraea* and hybrids), and secondary birch-dominated woods of varying ages. Wet areas which retain woodland can be especially interesting for their ecology with alder (*Alnus glutinosa*) mixed with willows (*Salix* sp). These 'semi-natural' woods mix with deciduous plantations of species such as sycamore (*Acer pseudoplatanus*) around farms and often grown as shelter-belts, and commercial plantations of various conifers especially around upland water-supply reservoirs. The lower-lying ancient woods were historically managed as coppice-with-standards for industrial production of small wood and timber. The higher levels were often utilised by local farmsteads but also by industry. Products included fuelwood, charcoal (part-burnt wood), whitecoal or chopwood (kiln-dried wood used in lead-smelting), timber, and of course, bark for tanning.

A major factor in these woodland landscapes was the competition between different fuel-uses and the demands of various actors for these resources (Rotherham *et al.*, 2004; Rotherham and Egan, 2005). Whilst there is no overall regional account of these woodlands, authors such as Jones (2000, 2009, 2012), Anderson and Shimwell (1981), Rotherham and Jones (2000), Lewis (2019), and Smith (2010), provide selected case-studies.

Investigating Tree Archaeology

Figure 3. Ancient woodland vegetation in a coal measures wood

The importance of the fuel economy in shaping landscapes

Issues of fuel use were discussed with regard to woodland by Rotherham and Egan (2005), and in terms of wider issues of fuelwood, charcoal, and coal, by Rotherham (2005). These and the associated socio-economic matters are major drivers in woodland use and management over time.

Upland areas such as the English Pennines and particularly the Peak District, the Yorkshire Dales, the North Yorkshire Moors, much of Wales and large areas of Scotland have seen their landscapes changed dramatically through fuel exploitation (Rotherham, 2005). In these landscapes the interactions between peat and turf fuel, mineral coal, and wood have been influential. For parts of the Peak District and South Pennines as demonstrated by Ardron *et al*. (1998), there was more medieval peat cut (*c*.34 million cubic metres), than from the Norfolk Broads at the same time (Ardron, 1999). Most peat exploitation was in the early medieval period with lower-lying sites often exploited and progressively destroyed during the sixteenth, seventeenth and eighteenth centuries. Destruction was associated with parliamentary and private 'enclosures' of heath, moor, common, bog and 'waste'.

However, the exhaustion of a fuel supply or competition from other users for this or an associated resource (such as demand for wood for industrial charcoal affecting communal fuelwood in early industrial England), could represent a crisis for local communities. The potential issues are well demonstrated by the situation in the South Pennines. Here an interesting example of competing uses and their impacts was demonstrated by farming communities of the Derbyshire and South Yorkshire Pennines in the 1700s (Bevan, 2004; Rotherham et al., 2004; Rotherham, 2005). With their traditional fuels a mix of local wood from the valleys, and of peat or turf from adjacent moorland. Away from the coalfield such as in the Derbyshire Derwent Valley, mineral coal was expensive because of the difficulty in transporting it to this isolated area. When intensive production of industrial charcoal for metal-smelting affected their fuelwood resource farmers petitioned the landowner for better roads. These were to enable coal to be imported into the Upper Derwent Valley more cheaply. Farmers were burning a mix of peat and wood for fuel, harvested according to traditional common rights probably back to before the medieval period. However, with the rise of industry, woods that had been less important since the disestablishment of the Royal Forest of the High Peak in the 1600s became valuable to supply much-need charcoal for local iron- and lead-smelting. Then, as eighteenth-century industrial production rose the woods were increasingly in demand to supply fuel to nearby forges served by packhorse routes. Landowners now saw their woodlands as valuable commodities to be protected for useful exploitation rather than uncultivated land to be left for the use of local peasants. The situation triggered issues of fuel availability, transport infrastructure, and costs. At the same time, Britain was becoming industrialised and urbanised, with coal to become 'king', and better roads revolutionising transportation. Improvement of transport was considered the key to resolving an acute fuel crisis. However, for the wooded landscape the result was the protection and managed exploitation of sites which in some cases meant their survival through to the present-day. Such woods were precious resources and carefully protected but their descendants are not 'natural' but semi-natural or eco-cultural, a result of people interacting with nature over millennia.

Ancient woods

A specifically ecological approach to woodlands types and their classification is taken by the National Vegetation Classification (Rodwell, 1991), and this is the system adopted by most plant ecologists. However, the NVC is of limited help in understanding historical changes and the influences of changing drivers within specific woods. The ending of traditional utilisation (Rotherham, 2007, 2008) may be a major determinant of woodland status and so may fluctuations of grazing herbivores (both numbers and types) (Anderson and Radford, 1994; Rotherham and Derbyshire, 2011).

Ancient woodland in the UK is taken to be that originating before 1600 AD (Peterken, 1981) or 1700 AD (Rackham, 1986). If a site is evidenced as pre-dating such times, then it is assumed to be 'ancient' since there was little plantation of forestry before then. So, in Britain, 'ancient' woodland (Rackham, 1986; Peterken, 1981) is that which has existed since at least 1600 AD, and if a wood was present in 1600, it is believed likely to have been there for some considerable time previously. Ancient woodland also provides living record of past land management practices and countryside, through features such as wood-banks, old pollards and coppice stools, remnant charcoal pits, ore furnaces and kilns, and ancient trackways. There is a complication however, in what we understand by 'woodland' and there are two broad types of ancient woods identified in Britain:

1. That continuously wooded since 1600 AD and composed of native tree species not obviously planted. This is known as semi-natural ancient woodland.

2. That continuously wooded since 1600 AD but where former tree cover has been replaced with planted trees (often conifers or exotic broadleaved species). This is known as replanted ancient woodland.

However, there is a further complication which is discussed later and this is the separation between 'woods' which are enclosed and managed as coppice or coppice-with-standards (see Jones, 2009) and wood-pastures which are unenclosed and historically included tree management alongside grazing livestock. The typical examples of the latter are unenclosed royal forests and medieval deer-parks. Nevertheless, the evidence of Domesday (1086), is that the bulk of pre-Norman feudal woodland was present as wood-pastures and many were wooded commons. This is important in understanding the woodlands of the Dark Peak and the southern Pennines. The role of grazing herbivores in woodland can be hugely significant (Pigott, 1983; Mitchell and Kirby, 1990; Kirby *et al.*, 1995; Peterken, 1996; Rackham, 1976, 1980, 2003; Hester *et al.*, 1996).

This process of identifying ancient woods is relatively straightforward for the typical woods of the region. As described by Jones (2009) for example, many sites are evidenced from archival sources and from old estate maps *etc*. As a general rule, the first edition Ordnance Survey maps (generally around 1830 to 1850) are taken as a starting point in the search for ancient woods. More robust and older evidence is then sought. Potential sources if they exist include old estate maps, estate records and accounts, bills of sale, and other documentation (see Rotherham *et al.*, 2008; Rotherham, 2013b). The evidence for woodlands and wood-pastures in historic landscapes can take us back to the Domesday account (1086 AD) to provide insight into woodland resources at a manorial level though this is spatially non-specific (see Jones, 2009; Rackham, 1986). Whilst at both extremes of the historic timeline, i.e. first edition Ordnance Survey in the 1800s on the one hand, and Domesday around 1100 AD on the other, the evidence in-between is very patchy. Some sites can be incredibly well-documented (see Lewis, 2019 for examples) whilst for others the evidence is limited or even non-existent.

In the absence of documentation however, evidence of long-term woodland uses of countryside can be gleaned from sources such as place-names and this can be very informative (Jones, 2009;

Rotherham, 2013b, 2017). Not only is the evidence physically imprinted into our environment, but woods and wooded landscapes are also recorded in place-names, settlement names, and field-names such as Wood End, Wood Lane, Hagg Side, Hollins End, Endowood, Woodseats, Woodthorpe, Willowgarth, Owlerton, and the like. Woodseats, for example, would be 'the cottages deep in the wood', and Clayroyd a 'woodland clearing with clayey soil'. From early medieval times, woods were themselves named: Park Spring or Parkwood Springs (the park coppice wood), West Haigh Wood (the enclosed wood), Newfield Spring (the coppice wood by the new field), and many others. Family names also reflect our wooded past with Underwood, Woodward, Hurst, Frith, Wood, Woodman, Turner, Collier, Greenwood, Barker, Tanner, Forester, Warren, Warrender, Stubbs, and Parker being just a few examples.

Influenced by the work of Rackham (1976, 1980, and 1986) the woodland research of Jones (2000, 2009, and 2012) is very informative in terms of the history and utilisation of woods in the study region. In this context too, Hey (2008, 2015, and 2017) provides detailed historical insights. Some examples are given below from David Hey (2008) and which indicate the intensity of management of some of the region's woodlands and therefore their associated economic value.

So, in 1642 it was noted that the woods of the Cavendish Estates in Nottinghamshire and Derbyshire were producing both timber and underwood for the manufacture of poles, handles, pit-props, and charcoal. Most of the woods were managed as rotational coppice-with-standards to supply ironmasters and lead smelters. There were 4,000 cartloads of timber, 600 cartloads of ash wood, 3,000 cartloads of coppice wood, 2,000 cartloads of log wood, 40 loads of poles or 'grove timber' for the lead mines, 5,000 cartloads of cordwood or stackwood, 500 cartloads of charcoal, and 1,000 horseloads of white coal. For sites such as Linacre Woods there were leases for activities such as 'coaling' and the necessary free passage for horses and carts, and reference to *'pittes and kylnes for white Coal and Charcoale'*, and *'with sufficyent turffe, braken and hillinge.......for the necessary Coalinge'*. White coal or chopwood was kiln-dried wood used in the lead-smelting process. It was especially valuable since it burnt cooler than charcoal and could be used to control the temperature of a lead-smelt. Cutting of woodland turf to cover the charcoal clamps and white coal kilns depleted woodland soils and had major impacts on ancient woodland indicator plants. These types of historical evidence provide a real insight into the functioning of medieval and early industrial woodlands.

Figure 4. Charcoal burners in the English Lake District (IDR)

In this context it is worth seeking other sources of evidence as proxies for hard documentation or map-based materials. This is where the idea of 'botanical indicators of ancient woodlands' comes in (see Jones, 2009 for example). A detailed review of the approach was undertaken by Glaves *et al.*, 2009a, b, and c). This has been developed further and into a sophisticated tool for landscape-level interpretation of woodland origins (Rotherham, 2011).

The general idea is that some animals and plants have their occurrence (distribution and abundance) restricted or facilitated by specific environmental factors or variables. Analysis of occurrence or absence may provide information not only about individual species, but more generally about communities of animals and plants, the environment, and about site history. Species at a site need to be considered in terms of:

1. Associated species;
2. Known environmental factors – geography, geology, soil, topography, aspect *etc*;
3. Known history of the site and its management;
4. The known status of the species in the region and in sites with similar environmental factors and constraints.

Lists of so-called indicator species are not considered definite or necessarily reliable but are an attempt to collate ideas and information into usable coherent forms. Indicators may provide information on:

1. Long-term habitat continuity.
2. Environmental quality e.g. soil-, water- or air-pollution and fragmentation or isolation.
3. Environmental conditions e.g. soil type, wetness, micro-climate or aspect.
4. Human impacts and management history.

The ideal indicator should:

1. Be relatively conspicuous and easily identifiable.
2. Be widespread and relatively abundant in suitable environments.
3. Exhibit a range of tolerance to adverse conditions varying in intensity.
4. Be relatively long-lived (individuals, colonies, or populations).
5. Be not too mobile since they must tolerate adverse conditions or die. For indicators of antiquity, minimal mobility is preferred.

All indicators need careful assessment for:

1. Local context and distribution.
2. Other indicators: A range of species or taxa is more reliable than a one-off.
3. Status at a site: Expert ecological opinion may be necessary to ascertain this. This applies if identification or genuine 'wild' occurrence is in question.
4. Other historical or ecological information.
5. Caution in interpretation.

There are two distinct groups of indicators providing information on the history and potential conservation status of wooded landscapes. These are broadly 1) those such as invertebrates and other taxonomic groups associated with dead wood in veteran trees, and 2) the plants, especially in the ground flora believed to indicate antiquity or habitat continuity. The trees are themselves often the best indicators, though this is frequently overlooked.

Indicators are used to identify or confirm ancient woodland status because they help in reading the landscape, current ecology and management, and history. Since some animals and plants have their occurrence in a specific niche restricted or facilitated by particular environmental factors or variables, certain species are found mostly in ancient woodlands (Peterken, 1974, 2000; Spencer, 1990). In terms of indicators in woodland and forest, there are two key considerations:

1. The species habitat requirements and specificity to woodland or forest.
2. The habitat continuity and antiquity of the forest or woodland (i.e. its ancientness).

In the application of ancient woodland indicators there are several objectives:

1. enhanced understanding of environmental change in woodlands and wider landscapes;

2. the setting of priorities for woodland conservation and management (age and continuity being important conservation considerations);
3. an attempt to unify approaches of ecologists, historians, and archaeologists in analysing and evaluating woodlands and forests.

Current approaches to the use of ancient woodland indicators are based on interlinked ecological principles:

1. The ecological (or autecological) characteristics of ancient woodland indicator species:
   a. Plant strategy theory: Grime's comparative plant ecology approach (Grime *et al.*, 2007).
   b. The species autecology approach developed by Donald Pigott *etc.* (see Beswick & Rotherham (eds), 1993).
   c. Ellenberg's indicators (see Hill *et al.*, 1999).
2. Historic timelines for sites and regions:
   a. Continuity of woodland and its environmental characteristics.
3. Spatial and temporal issues:
   a. Including changes in environment between and within woodlands.
4. Effects of woodland clearance and re-establishment on species and especially indicators, including:
   a. The rate at which species are lost.
   b. Species re-colonisation ability.

and

5. Changing perceptions of landscape and woodland history, particularly following the work of Frans Vera (Vera, 2000), and his view of the dynamic nature of landscape and ecology.

The ability of plants to tolerate and survive shade or to recolonize a site having been lost (Vickers *et al.*, 2000) are important in any assessment as an indication of antiquity or continuity.

The uses of plant ecological indicators for identifying ancient woodlands

Following from the above, it is suggested that through knowledge of plant distributions and ecology of wooded sites, the occurrence of certain species can *'indicate'* the antiquity of a wooded site and to a degree its continuity as a wood (e.g. Peterken, 1974, 2000). However, the definition of *'continuously wooded'* considers areas of open ground within a wood, and open, canopy-free areas occurring over relatively short periods. This approach is useful and pragmatic. However, a difficulty with understanding indicators is that the affinity to woods of many of these species varies greatly with geology and hence soils and / or drainage, and especially with climate and microclimate. In Britain, many plants found only in woods in inland sites in eastern England for example, are far less conservative on the coast or in western or northern zones. Their ability to re-colonise into a new wood from *refugia* is a key issue and again varies considerably.

Figure 5. Wood anemone is a good indicator of ancient woodland in the study region (IDR)

To compound the problems there are many so-called *'regional lists'* of good indicators mostly based on intuitive assessment and experience of known and respected experts. These are pragmatic tools to read the landscape rather than precise scientifically derived evidence, and their use and interpretation necessitates care and caution. The danger is in interpretation to present these uncritically as universal 'truths'. Indeed, they are not truths as such, but are incredibly useful and helpful tools as a part of a wider *'toolkit'* in the woodland assessor's armoury. An example of a plant which in the UK is taken as a high-grade indicator of ancient woodland is *Anemone nemorosa* (wood anemone), yet across the North Sea in Norway, it grows as a weed on motorways and similarly disturbed sites. Understanding and careful interpretation (described as 'intelligent interrogation' (Rotherham, 2011)) are the key to successful application of the approach.

Making these lists more helpful has involved careful assessment their merits and consideration of evidence for the ecological and historical basis of regional environmental variations. This assists the formulation of more robust and transparent evidence-based lists tested and used at regional levels.

To be an ancient woodland indicator the species must firstly be a plant capable of growing in a 'woodland environment' (Crawford, 2006, 2009; Rackham, 1986; and Rotherham and Wright, 2008). This raises questions of definition of for example, what we mean by 'woodland'. Shade-bearing or shade-tolerance is often an important factor in determining whether species can be regarded as ancient woodland indicators, but this is interpreted by some authors as shade dependence, which is somewhat different. Some species normally found in open situations may occur in woodlands and are considered a coincidence of past management therefore not indicative or diagnostic of ancient woodland or woodland continuity. Nevertheless, these plants can provide information on past management within woodland which may have been more open at some point. However, there are serious complications with assumptions about habitat-type, aspect, and geographic location, since many 'woodland' plants can survive without a tree canopy. This is especially so on north-facing slopes, western Atlantic sites, and if there is abundant water and shade;

such as rocky upland cloughs. At the same time, many plants typical of coppice woods cannot tolerate long periods of stock-grazing or other damaging management and can easily be eliminated from a site. They may never return, at least not for many decades or even centuries. However, many woodland plants can survive and tolerate periods of shade but do well when there are pulses of sunlight for a few years. Essentially the shade generated by a tree canopy may prevent tall, competitive plants from overtopping and excluding the woodland indicators. During the sunny times of a woodland glade created through treefall or an open area associated with coppice management, the flowers of the woodland ground floor burst into life to flower and set seed. If this happens only once in 25 years or even 200 years, then that is enough for survival. Furthermore, many woodland ground floor plants have evolved to take advantage of the period in spring and early summer before the tree canopy closes and the soil becomes droughted. In doing this, these plants are adapted to avoid shade and drought and form the typical vernal flora of the ancient woodland ground floor (Rotherham, 2013 b, c, and 2017).

These assumptions underlie most British botanical indictor lists derived either intuitively by local experts or from regional surveys (Glaves *et al.*, 2009 a, b, and c). Current research casts doubt on some aspects of this approach in terms of assumed ecological attributes. Nevertheless, the principle of the lists if interpreted correctly is generally sound. Pasture woods and wooded commons are one end of a spectrum of site types, and medieval coppices are the other. Understanding the type of 'woodland' becomes significant and such plant lists have a role to play but in the context of anciently 'wooded landscapes' (Glaves *et al.*, 2009a, b, & c) rather than 'woods'.

The ecological niche and regional lists
Along with the above, many species have a niche-space characterised by particular growing requirements of pH, moisture, slope, and aspect, and impacted on by interactions with other species. They may compete well, or poorly, depending on the local conditions. Furthermore, woodland conditions may change

over time and this may be a rotational or cyclical pattern such as in managed coppice woodland. Here the canopy is regularly and systematically removed during the harvesting to return during the re-growth phase of each coppice compartment. Similarly felling and regeneration or re-planting can take place in a standard wood but over a longer timescale, and in natural woodland the fall of a great tree will temporarily create a glade with increased sunlight.

These factors combine to make problematic the derivation of simple regional species-lists to be reliably applied to identify those woodlands which are ancient and those more recently established on previously non-wooded sites. However, if sensible limitations are noted, and it is accepted that these are only 'indicators', the suite of plants growing in and around a wood can be hugely informative. Deciding and questioning exactly what these plants might 'indicate' is important but often overlooked; many so-called 'indicators' of ancient woodland sites being plants of 'undisturbed' ground. In this context, the intimate relationship between coppice wood, wooded common, wood pasture, and heath, is increasingly recognised (Rotherham, 2017). In many cases these plants are ecological markers of a lack of macro-disturbance and associated eutrophication. These plants are useful indicators of the history of a wood in its landscape, but they do not necessarily imply total coverage by tree canopy.

The generally accepted method of determining which species are 'ancient woodland indicators' has been to analyse species lists from documented woodlands of known historic origins (Glaves *et al.*, 2009 a, b and c). These lists are then compared with ones from woodlands known to have more recent origins, and the resulting lists are refined by 'expert opinion'. In some cases, the lists have been derived solely in this way. It can be argued that ancient woodland indicator species should be those that are restricted to recorded ancient woodland sites and be absent from recently wooded sites. Unfortunately, this is an overly simplistic view and may result in a very circular argument. Attempts to produce robust indicator lists are unable to provide an infallible system of identifying ancient woodlands. Any lists produced are often accompanied by caveats that they should only be used as 'tools' to assist in the determination of ancient woodland status (Rotherham, 2011).

When trying to identify ancient woodland sites it is useful to sum the number of ancient woodland indicators to enhance the level of confidence. It is also possible to weight the species according to their reliability as indicators (Rotherham, 2011). There is a general increase in confidence with an increase in the number of ancient woodland indicators (Rose, 1999; Rose and O'Reilly, 2006). However, some authors have found that this approach potentially gives a false impression of antiquity or at least a lack of disturbance (see Glaves *et al.*, 2009a). This is for various reasons such as:

1. **The size of the woodland:** A small ancient wood may contain for example fifteen ancient woodland indicator species, and a larger but younger recent wood might contain the same number. Site history and complexity are therefore important. Larger woods may 'acquire' fragments of older woodland over time, but these are now incorporated into a generally younger wooded site. Alongside the total number found it is worth looking in detail at individual species and their reliability as indicators. The context of the wood, spatial, geographical, historical and ecological, will also influence expectations. Therefore, on base-rich soil the expected numbers will be much higher than species-poor acidic sites though they may be equally ancient.

2. **Internal environmental variations (habitat diversity):** Ancient woodlands without significant internal habitat variation may contain the same number of ancient woodland indicator species as younger woodland with greater internal variation. However, in the latter case the key indicator species of ancient woodland continuity will be absent.

3. **Biogeographical variations in species status:** The potential range of species in woodland can vary across

the country due to a mix of environmental and historical factors. Because of this, relatively fewer species are needed to assign 'ancient' status to a wood on the eastern side of Britain than the west. This is due to the western Atlantic influences that are conducive to many of the species concerned. (Glaves *et al.*, 2009a, b, & c)

A typical regional English botanical indicator list for ancient woodlands is given in Table 1 as an example. This list was developed for the Peak National Park firstly by Penny Anderson, and then by subsequent Peak Park ecologists. It has been applied in the South Pennines / South Yorkshire / North Derbyshire region by Ian Rotherham and colleagues and modified accordingly. It can be used in a wider range of situations but subject to the provisos as given and is applied with caution in the context of regional and other variations.

As noted by Rotherham (2011), there is considerable interest in being able to identify 'ancient' woods (e.g. Rackham, 1976, 1980, 1986, 2006; Peterken, 1981, 1996). However, it is argued that many such approaches to wooded landscapes are fundamentally flawed by a lack of understanding of the historic context of the sites and of their ecologies. Research in the UK and Europe (Glaves *et al.*, 2009a, b, & c) sought to address these issues to provide a robust interrogation of forest and woodland dynamics to better inform contemporary management and conservation. A methodology providing a robust framework and evidence-base for assertions of antiquity and continuity of woodland in the landscape was developed as a model into which historical and ecological information can be placed (Rotherham, 2011). The approach enables issues of woodland antiquity and ecological continuity to be more critically assessed and relies on objective scientific data and 'intelligent interrogation' of the accumulated information.

Table 1. An Example of Ancient Woodland Botanical Indicator Species for the English Peak District Gritstone Area

Acer campestre*	Frangula alnus	Primula vulgaris*
Adoxa moschatellina	Gagea lutea	Prunus padus
Agropyron caninum	Galium odoratum	Prunus avium
Allium ursinum	Geranium sanguineum	Pyrola minor
Anemone nemorosa	Geum rivale	Ranunculus auricomus
Aquilegia vulgaris*	Helleborus viridis	Rhamnus catharticus
Brachypodium sylvaticum	Hordelymus europaeus	Rosa arvensis
Bromus ramosus	Hyacinthoides non-scripta	Rubus caesius
Campanula latifolia	Hypericum pulchrum	Rubus saxatilis
Campanula trachelium	Ilex aquifolium	Sanicula europaea
Cardamine amara	Lamiastrum galeobdolon	Scirpus sylvaticus
Cardamine impatiens	Lathraea squamaria	Solidago virgaurea
Carex laevigata	Lathraea squamaria	Sorbus torminalis
Carex pallescens	Lathyrus montanus	Stachys officinalis
Carex digitata	Lithospermum officinale	Stellaria holostea
Carex remota	Lonicera periclymenum	Stellaria neglecta
Carex strigosa	Luzula pilosa	Tamus communis
Carex sylvatica	Luzula sylvatica	Taxus baccata (where native)
Chrysosplenium alternifolium	Lysimachia nemorum	Thelypteris oreopteris
Chrysosplenium oppositifolium	Melica uniflora	Tilia cordata or platyphyllos
Circaea x intermedia	Mercurialis perennis	Trollius europaeus
Cirsium heterophyllum	Milium effusum	Ulmus glabra
Conopodium majus	Myosotis sylvatica	Veronica montana
Convallaria majalis*	Narcissus pseudonarcissus*	Viburnum opulus*
Corydalis claviculata	Orchis mascula	Vicia sepium
Daphne laureola	Oxalis acetosella	Vicia sylvatica
Daphne mezereum	Paris quadrifolia	Viola palustris
Dipsacus pilosus	Phyllitis scolopendrium*	Viola reichenbachiana
Dryopteris carthusiana	Polygonatum multiflorum	⊕ Carex pendula
Dryopteris pseudomas	Polygonatum odoratum	⊕ Carpinus betulus
Epipactis helleborine	Polypodium vulgare (s. lato)	⊕ Malus sylvestris
Equisetum sylvaticum	Polystichum aculeatum	⊕ Poa nemoralis
Equisetum telmateia	Polystichum setiferum	Moehringia trinerva – but occurs in plantations too
Festuca altissima	Potentilla sterilis	

⊕ Often introduced;* only included if they occur well within the wood and do not appear to have been planted.

Investigating Tree Archaeology

Figure 6. Wood sorrel is a persistent indicator especially on more extreme sites (IDR)

A key idea to emerge from on-going research is that of the 'Act of Commons' or 'Statute of Merton' (1235) represents a watershed in the spatial fixing of 'woods' in the English post-Domesday countryside. Enclosed from commonland, mostly wooded common, such named woods if they survive today are identifiable by so-called 'botanical indicators'; these are 'ancient' woods. The act stands as a tipping point between the open, fluid Saxon landscape and the fixed, feudal countryside of the Normans. Viewed in this light the indicators may be considered to take us back to the pre-wood phase of the countryside of wood pasture and wooded common.

Central to the methodology is the use of records of plants known to be long-term associated with woods, but also bringing to bear information on ancient trees, soils and other sediments, and from documentation. Soil horizons in woods and former woodland sites for example, if undisturbed, can provide good evidence of long-term woodland use. Being able to identify and age, even approximately, ancient trees such as old, worked coppice-stools for example, can present unequivocal confirmation of site antiquity. Work currently in progress in the UK and in Europe (Rotherham *et al.*, in prep), provides evidence for such 'worked' trees as being anything from 400 to 900 years old; thus taking a site timeline back well before the 1600 AD point for an ancient wood. However, the commonly used 'indicators' of woodland sites are the typical flowering plants and ferns of wooded countryside.

Main Types of Evidence for 'Ancient' Woodland and Continuity of Woodland Cover (from Rotherham, 2011; and Rotherham *et al.*, 2008)

1. More than 2ha in extent and recorded on the 'Ancient Woodland Inventory' – but smaller fragments may still be ancient but excluded from the Inventory.
2. Shown as woodland on early estate maps (pre-1600 AD) or estate maps from the seventeenth century and subsequent to that.
3. Shown as woodland on maps from seventeenth- and eighteenth-century map series or before.
4. Pre-1600 AD manorial and estate records refer to woodland or describe woodland management activities.
5. Management accounts and surveys that refer to the site as woodland or describe woodland management or processes for the site from the sixteenth century onwards.
6. Present on Ordnance Survey (OS) first series maps (early nineteenth century), and OS maps since.
7. Woodland names on older series as well as modern Ordnance Survey maps derived from old place-names or descriptions of woodland management.
8. Woodland location along or next to old parish boundaries or adjacent to commonland or heath.
9. Woodland topography, for example a site is located on steep slopes, valley sides, or along streams (i.e. generally land unsuitable for arable agriculture).
10. Woodland shape, for example irregular or sinuous boundaries or those not fitting regular enclosure patterns of surrounding field boundaries of the seventeenth century (or later).

11. Woodland with well-developed external boundary banks and ditches, and especially with old or veteran trees growing on them; internal boundaries not straight.

12. Woodland with archaeological features linked to traditional woodland management, for example charcoal hearths, old kilns of various types.

13. Features relating to non-woodland activities only associated with post-1600 AD period.

14. Canopy structure typical of ancient woodland type with old or large coppice stools, veteran trees, old pollards, standing dead wood.

15. Woodland with 'ancient woodland indicator' species (botanical, mycological, entomological).

16. Series of aerial photographs showing woodland cover over the same area may provide information about any possible twentieth century re-planting. LiDAR imagery can also support this.

Evidence from the above can be combined to confirm woodland continuity and determine whether a site may be classed as 'ancient' according to the accepted definitions. Although the robustness of some types of evidence is less certain but even so it can still be applied to support, confirm, or indicate woodland continuity (Kirby, 1988, 1984, 2002/03, 2004, 2008). When applying an indicators approach, several sources of information are used in combination. These may include more-or-less robust evidence carefully interrogated and used to demonstrate antiquity, continuity, or gaps in continuity. Confidence in site designation as ancient woodland is ultimately linked to two factors: 1) the evidence which indicates woodland continuity or show a clear gap in woodland cover; 2) the reliability of evidence of continuity of a break in woodland cover. For most woods, only some of the evidence types will be available and interpretation may be a matter of subjective judgment based on objective information. This is then taken to decide on balance as indicating whether a wood is ancient or not.

Field survey

Reading the landscape for clues to its history is an acquired skill. Yet everyone does this even if at a superficial level. Merely walking through a bluebell wood, we connect it to antiquity and history. Refined and linked to detailed knowledge of species ecology, to understanding of woodland archaeological features (often humps and bumps), and the findings underpinned by map and archive interpretation, and we have a powerful tool. However, of the various approaches to help find an ancient wood or a woodland ghost, plant indicators are the easiest, quickest and often, as living connections to the past, the most exciting (Rotherham, 2007; Rotherham & Ardron, 2006; Rotherham & Wright, 2008).

Challenges in terms of woodland fieldwork include ecological complexity and often limited resources for survey and assessment. These may combine to make sites difficult to fully assess or evaluate. With time, resources and even competence often restricted ecologists often rely on indicator species to provide information on the nature and quality of a site (Rose & O'Reilly, 2006; Rose, 1999). The findings can guide nature conservation evaluations, identify priority areas for management or protection, and be used for site monitoring.

Ancient woodland indicators have been used individually to indicate site antiquity but are best applied as part of a broader approach. This involves reading the landscape, understanding history of occurrence, and relating it to other evidence (Hermy *et al.*, 1999; Crawford, 2006, 2009). Furthermore, by considering detailed studies of individual sites but set in a wider geographic spatial region, we can examine and illustrate these issues. For example, we can consider the evidence used to identify old and ancient coppice woods. Other questions then arise such as what do ancient coppiced woodland indicators tell us about the pre-coppice wood history and how far back can they 'indicate'? Woodland history and usage change substantially over time, and the type of high forest which we now associate with ancient woodland, may have been quite different historically. Such closed canopy woods may have been woodland pasture with a more open canopy (Rotherham, 2013a; Rotherham et al., 2013). Ancient woodland indicators may therefore be related to environmental conditions (light, humidity *etc*) associated with contemporary high forest and not to the conditions found in that same woodland at some point in the past. Human management practices, chance and catastrophic events can each affect the species found in woodland. Indeed, there is a need to determine what we mean by 'woodland' and to define the environmental conditions associated with that. For example, does a 'wood' need to have trees, and if so how many trees and how far apart? This may seem an odd question, but in wood pastures, it raises serious issues of definition (Rotherham, 2011, 2017).

Such woodland historical and archaeological features can modify the woodland environment and ecology and affect the species found. So, for example, different species may be found in sunken tracks and charcoal hearths. In attempting to unravel the story of a wood, there is a need to relate such history and archaeology to the woodland ecology. In this context, what can indicators tell us about the environment? All plants, animals and fungi provide information about the environment, and are *potentially indicators* of something. The main problem is in knowing *what* they 'indicate', specifically what do ancient woodland indicators indicate? A key characteristic attributed to many ancient woodland indicator species is poor dispersal and colonization ability, and therefore a poor ability to re-colonise after woodland clearance (Pigott, 1993; Rackham, 2006). However, there is a need for more data on colonisation rates into new woodlands. Such rates vary between species and with climate and soils, but many 'indicator' species move 0.5m – 1.5m per year (Vickers, Rotherham, & Rose, 2000). There are some wider implications in the use of ancient woodland indicators including:

1. Regional character and distinction in indicators, including what are the differences in specificity of species to ancient woodlands in upland and lowland areas, in the

more continental climates in the south east and more oceanic north west *etc.*?

2. What about indicators of broader historical landscape with trees (treescapes) and other types of wooded landscape including parks and heaths?
3. What are the implications of the Vera hypothesis (Vera, 2000) (and the contention that historically Britain was not covered in dense forest) for our assumptions regarding ancient woodland indicators?
4. What about woodland shadows in the landscape, i.e. the survival of woodland indicator species after woodlands are cleared?

There are preconceptions associated with the use of ancient woodland indicators, specifically the historical static image of unchanging medieval coppice woodland. With current research and new insights, these need to be revised in order to relate to a more dynamic changing wooded landscape where fluxes in land use and climate have modified woodland and its surroundings. Many so-called 'ancient woodland indicators seem to give good and reliable information on a site that was medieval or early industrial coppice in Britain. However, it is unclear what they tell beyond this or how they relate to the more fluid vision of the landscape.

Archival and map-based evidence
It is important to remember that much evidence such as old maps and documents were written for specific purposes, and the absence of evidence may not necessarily mean that the woodland did not exist at the time. In other words, absence of evidence is not evidence of absence.

Documentary sources can be particularly helpful in identifying potentially ancient woodland sites, and in some cases for confirming ancient status (Rotherham *et al.*, 2008; Goldberg & Kirby, 2003/04; Castle *et al.*, 2008). Maps and other historical evidence can help identify the age and continuity of woodland

and should be the starting point for any study of woodland history and archaeology. The ecology and landscape of woodland and the surrounding broader landscape both directly and indirectly determine the species found in that woodland. This is through the way they influence the available niches and associated land uses (the latter in turn modifying the environment). Archaeological features in a wooded landscape can be very useful in understanding site history and can be divided into:

1. The archaeology *of* the woods, linked to the historic uses of that woodland, including charcoal hearths, wood-banks, worked trees *etc*, and

2. The archaeology *in* the woods, which covers all archaeology not directly linked to the woodland and its uses, for example agricultural remains from historic periods when the woodland was largely cleared of trees.

This was an approach that I coined some years ago to help separate out the ways in which archaeology can aid an understanding of ancient woods.

An evidence-based interpretation of the relict woodlands of the South Pennines and Dark Peak

Turning our attention to the Dark Peak, the Domesday account (1086) is especially informative as noted in Rotherham (2017). According to Melvyn Jones (pers. comm.) the Domesday account for Derbyshire shows that wood pasture was widespread. Of the 252 manors listed, 118 had wood pasture but only 35 had *silva minuta* (coppice woods). And wood pasture was very extensive. Close to the study area, Edale with outliers at Aston, Shatton and Tideswell among others had more than 13,000 acres of wooded commons in 1086. And even closer to the core site, Hathersage (with outliers at Bamford, Hurst, Offerton, and Stony Middleton) had 4,032 acres of wood pasture. Yet fast-forward 700 years, and Burdett's 1791 map of Derbyshire has only one wood in north-east of Derbyshire west of Sheffield (and this was at Padley which is part of the study area). There was nothing whatsoever at

Hathersage or in Edale. The contemporary Ancient Woodland Inventory shows a good number of ancient woodland sites around the lower parts of the study area (*c.* 100 metres above sea level) but none on the higher ground (*c.* 300 to 400 metres above sea level).

Figure 7. Shadow woods bluebells indicating long-standing wooded common and wood-pasture (IDR)

'Shadow Woods' and the search for lost landscapes

In order to better understand this regional woodland heritage, it is first necessary to be more precise about the nature of a 'wood' as opposed to merely woodland. This is discussed in more detail by Rotherham (2013c, 2017) and definitions are provided. Importantly a key question relates to the origins of enclosed 'ancient woods' and particularly the nature of the countryside within which enclosure took place. Following from the discussion above, coppice woods mostly originated after Domesday though some go back to the preceding Saxon countryside. The 'woods' were enclosed and named and then managed over centuries as simple coppice or else coppice-with-standards; those surviving today are our 'ancient woodlands'. Botanical indicators of ancient woodlands provide robust evidence of antiquity and continuity often back to these medieval landscapes, but not as is often assumed, to some semi-mythical 'wildwood'. Consideration of the Domesday account provides evidence that this enclosure to woods was from the extensive wood pasture of the time, and areas remaining unenclosed were then mostly a mix of royal forest, and of wooded commons. In seeking to unravel this tangled history of our countryside we have addressed the nature of 'woods', 'lost woods', ghost woods', and 'shadow woods' (Rotherham, 2017, 2018).

Some definitions:

Woods: These are treed sites enclosed from the wider countryside, named and managed over subsequent centuries. The sites were protected from large grazing herbivores at least during the early years of the coppice cycle or after major tree-felling. This approach to tree management originated with the Romans and some woods occurred in the Saxon landscape, but most originated in the two to three centuries following the Conquest.

Lost woods: Enclosed woods often suffered damage, loss or destruction over the centuries following their establishment. So lost woods are sites which were enclosed and named but were subsequently removed or lost by conversion to farmland, by urban development or under infrastructure such as roads, or simply by opening-up and reversion to a grazed landscape (See for example, Lewis, 2019). Some ancient woods, such as Gardom's Coppice in the Peak District, still exist in the countryside but have in effect been 'lost' from memory and even from maps. This ancient wood now shrouded by secondary birch growth has over 1,000 veteran coppice trees that had been overlooked by surveyors.

Ghost woods: When woods are lost, then destruction may be total, and a site can be completely removed. However, in many cases the ghost of a lost wood can be seen in the landscape with physical features like woodbanks, walls, charcoal hearths, lanes *etc*. In many cases, veteran trees and ancient woodland botanical indicators mark the area of a past wood now etched into the modern landscape. Even in intensively farmed or highly urbanised areas, the indicators survive alongside field-names and place-names associated with woodland use.

Shadow woods: The concept of 'shadow woods' as lost Domesday landscapes is one of the exciting results from the on-going research. These are remnants of the once extensive Domesday wood pastures which persisted unenclosed into the medieval as wooded commons. In other words, it was from these landscapes that our woods originated and remarkably, having survived periods of medieval enclosure and especially the intensive parliamentary enclosures, some areas remain. These were initially identified by the processes described earlier using detailed field surveys of indicators, soils and other evidence. Not being 'woods' these sites often have limited documentary evidence associated with them; though some Peak District moors were described in nineteenth-century maps as 'wood pastures'.

Lost Woods & Shadows

Perhaps the biggest issue in terms of shadows and ghosts is that of being able to see them, to recognise them, and then to understand them. First, we need to see them in the landscape. It has been an interesting experience to go in search of lost landscapes, of hidden ecologies, and forgotten histories. Yet once you begin to see the evidence and to read the signs, a whole new landscape comes to life. It is there all the time, but we simply fail to see it (Rotherham, 2018).

Conclusions

In major debates on countryside origins from pre-medieval landscapes and ecologies (e.g. Vera, 2000), it is often the case that history has been largely overlooked. Yet the work of local historians such as David Hey and Mel Jones has changed our awareness of key processes in the landscape. Furthermore, if we consider the (albeit) broad-brush account of Domesday (1086 AD) this provides a glimpse into the nature of anciently treed landscapes. Taking this approach combined with botanical indicators and issues of comparative plant ecologies (Grime *et al.*, 2007), and of fluctuating herbivore impacts, then a new vision of upland treescapes is emerging (Rotherham, 2017, 2018).

Equally exciting and derived from this new approach to woodland history is that in many places in Britain you can discover a local landscape the ecology of which touches backwards to Domesday and beyond. However, unlikely as this may seem, the recent discovery (which I have yet to publish with colleagues from the Czech Republic) that some of our coppice oak trees often dismissed by conservation agency colleagues as of little interest, may in fact be from 600 to 1,000 years old, or more, lends even greater credence to the claims of antiquity and continuity. Some of these connections may be through areas of unenclosed commonland, even if neglected. Others might be remnants in ancient, massive lane-banks or field boundaries around your parish. Even in more urban sites, the local riverside or streamside might hold signs and evidence of unenclosed ancient woods or ghost woods.

The most fascinating areas so far discovered are the surviving ancient wood pastures that have recently been identified. This is remarkable stuff and the research indicates that a wider search in suitable countryside, urban or rural, will be productive. If we are correct that these are remnants of the unenclosed wood pastures of Domesday, and with links back to Vera's vision of an ancient landscape, then this is amazing stuff.

Figure 8. Dog's mercury which is a good indicator of anciently wooded sites on acid soils (IDR)

Bibliography

Anon. (undated) *Bygones of Bradfield Volume III, Then and Now*. Bradfield Historical Society, Bradfield, Sheffield.

Anon. (2014) . Lea Wood Heritage Community Project, Archaeological Research Services Ltd., and partners, Bakewell.

Anderson, P. (1978). *The Longshaw Estate, Hathersage. Ecological Survey. Unpublished technical report to the Peak Park Joint Planning Board and the National Trust*. Bakewell: Aldern House.

Anderson, P., & Radford, E. (1994). Changes in vegetation following reduction in grazing pressure on the National Trust's Kinder Estate, Peak District, Derbyshire, England. *Biological Conservation*, **69**(1), 55–63.

Anderson, P., & Shimwell, D. (1981) *Wild Flowers and other Plants of the Peak District*. Moorland Publishing, Ashbourne.

Ardron, P.A. (1999) *Peat Cutting in Upland Britain, with Special Reference to the Peak District*. Unpublished PhD Thesis, University of Sheffield, Sheffield.

Atherden, M. (1992). *Upland Britain: A Natural History*. Manchester University Press, Manchester and New York.

Beswick, P. & Rotherham, I.D. (Eds.) (1993) Ancient Woodlands - their archaeology and ecology - a coincidence of interest. *Landscape Archaeology and Ecology*.

Bevan, W. (2004) *The Upper Derwent 10,000 years in a Peak District Valley*. Tempus Publishing Ltd, Stroud, Gloucestershire

Castle, G., Latham, J. & Mileto, R. (2008) Identifying Ancient Woodland in Wales – The role of the Ancient Woodland Inventory, historical maps and indicator species. Countryside Council for Wales. *Contract Science Report No. 819*.

Conway, V.M. (1947) Ringinglow Bog, near Sheffield. I. Historical. *Journal of Ecology*, **34**, 149-181.

Conway, V.M. (1949) Ringinglow Bog, near Sheffield. II. The present surface. *Journal of Ecology*, **37**, 148-170.

Crawford, C.L. (2006) A provisional ancient woodland indicator plant list for Scotland. *Native Woodlands Discussion Group Newsletter*, 31 (2), Autumn 2006. Downloadable from *www.tnrc.co.uk*.

Crawford, C.L (2009) Ancient woodland indicator plants in Scotland. *Scottish Forestry*, 63(1), 6-19.

Edwards, K.C. (1962) *The Peak District*. Collins New Naturalist No. 44, London.

Farey, J. (1811 – 17) *A General View of the Agriculture and Minerals of Derbyshire*. 3 volumes, The Board of Agriculture, London.

Glaves, P., Rotherham, I.D., Wright, B. Handley, C. & Birbeck, J. (2009a) *A Report to the Woodland Trust. Field Surveys for Ancient Woodlands: Issues and Approaches.* Hallam Environmental Consultants Ltd., Biodiversity & Landscape History Research Institute, and Geography, Tourism & Environment Change Research Unit, Sheffield Hallam University, Sheffield.

Glaves, P., Rotherham, I.D., Wright, B. Handley, C. & Birbeck, J. (2009b) *A Report to the Woodland Trust A Survey of the Coverage, Use and Application of Ancient Woodland Indicator Lists in the UK.* Hallam Environmental Consultants Ltd., Biodiversity & Landscape History Research Institute, and Geography, Tourism & Environment Change Research Unit, Sheffield Hallam University, Sheffield.

Glaves, P., Rotherham, I.D., Wright, B. Handley, C. & Birbeck, J. (2009c) *A Report to the Woodland Trust Field Surveys for Ancient Woodlands: Issues and Approaches* Hallam Environmental Consultants Ltd., Biodiversity & Landscape History Research Institute, and Geography, Tourism & Environment Change Research Unit, Sheffield Hallam University, Sheffield.

Goldberg, E. & Kirby, K. (2002/3) Ancient woodland: guidance material for local authorities. *English Nature*, Peterborough.

Grime, J.P., Hodgson, J.G., & Hunt, R. (2007*) Comparative Plant Ecology. A Functional approach to common British species*. Second Edition. Castlepoint Press, Dalbeattie.

Hermy, M., Honnay, O., Firbank, L, Grashof-Bokdam, C. & Lawesson, J.E. (1999) An ecological comparison between ancient and other forest plant species of Europe, and the implications for forest conservation. *Biological Conservation*, **91**, 9-22.

Hester, A. J., Mitchell, F. J. G., & Kirby, K. J. (1996). Effects of season and intensity of sheep grazing on tree regeneration in a British upland woodland. *Forest Ecology and Management*, **88**(1–2), 99–106.

Hey, D. (2008) *Derbyshire: A History*. Cambridge University Press, Cambridge.

Hey, D. (2014) *A History of the Peak District Moors*. Pen & Sword, Barnsley.

Hey, D. (2015) *A Manorial Landscape at Holmesfield*. In: *Essays on Derbyshire History presented to Gladwyn Turbutt*. Derbyshire Record Society, Chesterfield, 1 – 20.

Hey, D. (2017) *Ancient Woods of the Dronfield District*. Books at the Barn, Dronfield.

Hill, M.O., Mountford, J.O., Roy, D.B. & Bunce, R.G.H. (1999) *Ellenberg's indicator values for British Plants*. ECOFACT 2a Technical Annex. Centre for Ecology and Hydrology, Wallingford.

Jones, M. (2000) *The Making of the South Yorkshire Landscape*. Wharncliffe Books, Barnsley.

Jones, M. (2009) *Sheffield's Woodland Heritage*. 4th Edition, Wildtrack Publishing, Sheffield.

Jones, M. (2012) *Trees and Woodland in the South Yorkshire Landscape: A Natural, Economic and Social History*. Wharncliffe Books, Barnsley.

Kirby, K.J. (1984) *Forestry Operations and Broad-leaved Woodland Conservation*. Nature Conservancy Council, Peterborough.

Kirby, K.J. (1988) *A Woodland Survey Handbook*. Nature Conservancy Council, Peterborough.

Kirby, K.J. (2002/03) *Ancient Woodland: guidance material for local authorities*. English Nature, Peterborough.

Kirby, K.J. (2004) *Table of Ancient Woodland Indicator Plants*. In: Rose, F. (2006) *The Wildflower Key*. Penguin Books, London.

Kirby, K.J. (2008) Woodland indicators – some experiences from Natural England, *Proceedings of a Woodland Indicator Workshop Held on 14 May 2008*, Sheffield, Biodiversity & Landscape History Research Institute, Sheffield.

Kirby, K.J., Thomas, R.C., Key, R.S., McLean, I.F.G., & Hodgetts, N. (1995). Pasture-woodland and its conservation in Britain. *Biological Journal of the Linnean Society*, **56**, 135–153.

Lewis, H. (2019) Interactions between human industry and woodland ecology in the South Pennines. Unpublished PhD, University of Bradford, Bradford with University of Hull and Sheffield Hallam University.

Linton, W.R. (1903) *Flora of Derbyshire*. Bemrose & Sons Ltd, London.

Mitchell, F. J. G., & Kirby, K. J. (1990). The impact of large herbivores on the conservation of semi natural woods in the British uplands. *Forestry*, **63**(4), 333–353.

Moss, C.E. (1913) *Vegetation of the Peak District*. Cambridge University Press, Cambridge.

Peterken, G.F. (1974) A method for assessing woodland flora for conservation using indicator species. *Biological Conservation*, **6**, 239-245.

Peterken, G.F. (1981) *Woodland Conservation and Management*. Chapman & Hall, London.

Peterken, G.F. (1996) *Natural Woodland – ecology and conservation in northern temperate regions*. Cambridge University Press, Cambridge.

Peterken, G.F. (2000) Identifying ancient woodland using vascular plant indicators. *British Wildlife*, 11, 153-158.

Pigott, C. D. (1983). Regeneration of oak-birch woodland following exclusion of sheep. *Journal of Ecology*, **71**(2), 629–646.

Pigott, C.D. (1993) The History and Ecology of Ancient Woodlands. *Landscape Archaeology and Ecology*, **1**, 1-11.

Rackham, O. (1976) *Trees and Woodland in the British Landscape*. J. M. Dent & Sons Ltd, London.

Rackham, O. (1980) *Ancient Woodland: its history, vegetation and uses in England*. Edward Arnold, London.

Rackham, O. (1986) *The History of the Countryside*. Dent, London.

Rackham, O. (2003) *Ancient woodland: its history, vegetation and uses in England*. (2nd ed.), Castlepoint Press, Colvend.

Rackham, O. (2006) *Woodlands*. HarperCollins New Naturalist No. 100, London.

Rodwell, J.S. (ed.). (1991). *British Plant Communities: Vol I: Woodlands and Scrub* (Vol. 1). Cambridge University Press, Cambridge.

Rose, F. (1999) Indicators of Ancient Woodland; the Use of Vascular Plants in Evaluating Ancient Woods for Nature Conservation. *British Wildlife*, **10** (4), 241-251.

Rose, F. & O'Reilly, C. (Eds.) (2006) T*he WildFlower Key* (Revised Edition). Frederick Warne, London.

Rotherham, I.D. (2005) Fuel and Landscape – Exploitation, Environment, Crisis and Continuum. *Landscape Archaeology and Ecology*, **5**, 65-81.

Rotherham, I.D. (2007) The implications of perceptions and cultural knowledge loss for the management of wooded landscapes: a UK case-study. *Forest Ecology and Management*, 249, 100-115.

Rotherham, I.D. (2008) *The Importance of Cultural Severance in Landscape Ecology Research*. In: Dupont, A. & Jacobs, H. (eds.) *Landscape Ecology Research Trends*, ISBN 978-1-60456-672-7, Nova Science Publishers Inc., USA. Chapter 4, pp 71-87.

Rotherham, I.D. (2011) *A Landscape History Approach to the Assessment of Ancient Woodlands*. In: Wallace, E.B. (ed.) *Woodlands: Ecology, Management and Conservation*. Nova Science Publishers Inc., USA, 161-184.

Rotherham, I.D. (ed.) (2013a) *Trees, Forested Landscapes and Grazing Animals: A European Perspective on Woodlands and Grazed Treescapes*. EARTHSCAN, London. 412pp.

Rotherham, I.D. (2013b) *Ancient Woodland: History, Industry and Crafts*. Shire Publications, Oxford, 64pp.

Rotherham, I.D. (2013c) *Searching for Shadows and Ghosts*. In: Rotherham, I.D., Handley, C., Agnoletti, M. & Samojlik, T. (eds) (2013) *Trees Beyond the Wood – an exploration of concepts of woods, forests and trees*. Wildtrack Publishing, Sheffield, 1-16.

Rotherham I.D. (2017) *Shadow Woods: A Search for Lost Landscapes*. Wildtrack Publishing, Sheffield.

Rotherham, I.D. (2018) *The Magic and Mysteries of Ecclesall Woods*. In: Atherden, M. Handley, C. & Rotherham, I.D. (eds) (2018) *Back From The Edge: The Fall and Rise of Yorkshire's*

Wildlife. Second expanded edition published by Wildtrack Publishing, Sheffield, 85-102.

Rotherham, I.D. & Ardron, P.A. (2006) The Archaeology of Woodland Landscapes: Issues for Managers based on the Case-study of Sheffield, England and four thousand years of human impact. *Arboricultural Journal*, **29** (4), 229-243.

Rotherham, I.D., & Derbyshire, M.J. (2012) Deer in and around the Peak District and its urban fringe. *British Wildlife*, **23** (4), 256-264.

Rotherham, I.D., Egan, D. & Ardron, P.A. (2004) Fuel economy and the uplands: the effects of peat and turf utilisation on upland landscapes. *Society for Landscape Studies Supplementary Series*, **2**, 99-109.

Rotherham, I.D. & Egan, D. (2005) *The Economics of Fuel Wood, Charcoal and Coal: An Interpretation of Coppice Management of British Woodlands.* In: Agnoletti, M., Armiero, M., Barca, S. & Corona, G. (eds) *History and Sustainability*. European Society for Environmental History, 100-104.

Rotherham, I.D., Handley, C., Agnoletti, M., & Samoljik, T. (eds) (2013) *Trees Beyond the Wood – an exploration of concepts of woods, forests and trees.* Wildtrack Publishing, Sheffield.

Rotherham, I.D. & Jones, M. (2000) Seeing the Woodman in the Trees – Some preliminary thoughts on Derbyshire's ancient coppice woods. *Peak District Journal of Natural History and Archaeology*, **2**, 7-18.

Rotherham, I.D. & Wright, B. (2008) Searching for the Ghosts: how a forester reads the woodland landscape. *World of Trees*, **16**, 40-41.

Rotherham, I.D., Jones, M., Smith, L. & Handley, C. (eds) (2008) *The Woodland Heritage Manual: A Guide to Investigating Wooded Landscapes.* Wildtrack Publishing, Sheffield

Smith, P.E. (2010) An Assessment of Woodland History and Archaeology: A Case Study Approach. Unpublished MPhil Thesis, Sheffield Hallam University, Sheffield.

Spencer, J. (1990) Indications of antiquity: some observations of the nature of plants associated with ancient woodland. *British Wildlife*, **2**, 90–102.

Tansley, A.G. (1949) *The British Islands and their Vegetation. Cambridge University Press, Cambridge.*

Woodhead, T.W. (1929) History of the vegetation of the South Pennines. *Journal of Ecology*, **17**, 1 – 34.

Vera, F.H.W. (2000) *Grazing Ecology and Forest History.* CABI Publishing, Oxon.

Vickers, A.D., Rotherham, I.D. & Rose, J.C. (2000) Vegetation succession and colonisation rates at the forest edge under different environmental conditions. *Aspects of Applied Biology*, **58**, 351-356.

Biographical notes:
Ian Rotherham is Professor of Environmental Geography at Sheffield Hallam University and has written extensively on the ecology and history of ancient woodlands. Along with academic papers and books he also writes and broadcasts for the popular media. He chairs a number of national and international research committees for bodies such as the International Union of Forest Research Organizations, the British Ecological Society, and the European Society for Environmental History. He is a leading author on countryside environmental history.

Chapter 17. The Oaks of Lincoln Cathedral

Andy Alder
Woodscapes Consultancy

Abstract
This chapter focuses on the timbers of Lincoln Cathedral, those already in place dating back to 966 AD; new timber already stockpiled; and trees growing and being planted in dedicated woodlands that are ready to replace the building timbers in the future. The research combined fieldwork and desktop research. It shows a hidden side of the building where 75% of the woodwork is original. Whilst undertaking the research, we also recorded an art installation taking place in the Chapter House, hewing wooden beams using traditional tools and methods.

Figure 1: Lincoln Cathedral exterior and interior roof

Chronology
The timeline for the development and phases of building and renewal is set out below giving a brief chronology of Lincoln Cathedral and its oaks, used for timbers and small wood.

- 1072: Work starts on the Cathedral
- 1124: Cathedral is ravaged by a great fire
- 1185: An earthquake causes damage
- 1237: The Central Tower collapses- due to experimental building techniques

- 1238: Henry III gives 30 oaks for building works
- 1268: A Royal gift of 10 oaks from Sherwood Forest
- 1284: Edward I gives 12 oaks to make shingles
- 1290: Edward I gives another 4 oaks for building work
- 1311: The Central Tower is replaced (Tallest building for 238 years at 160m)
- 1420: The western towers are raised by 200 feet
- 1548: The Central Tower spire is blown down
- 1610: Lincoln mapped by John Speed
- 1761: The roof of the Chapter House is redesigned as the roof was described as 'greatly decayed' – completed by 1800
- 1807: The West Tower spires are removed
- 2018: 75% of the roof timbers are still original

Figure 2: Roof timbers in Lincoln Cathedral roof space (A. Alder 2018)

Dating of Roof Timbers

A Dendrochronology survey of the Cathedral's timbers was undertaken over a period of 20 years by Laxton *et al.* who published their report in 2001. Samples were taken of over 500 oak timbers from nine different roofs in the Cathedral. In each case the tree-ring dates, in conjunction with other evidence, were used to date the constructions and repairs to the roofs. Loss of sapwood and, in the early-modern period, use of seasoned timbers, made accuracy in dating difficult. However, they identified three distinct periods of oak-felling:

    c.1192-1280 (medieval construction)
    c.1500-c.1570 (post medieval repairs)
    c.1660-c.1750 (early modern repairs).

The oldest recorded beam is dated c.966AD, so was therefore approximately 100 years old in 1066. It was discovered that 75% of the roof beams are original, with the largest being 15m in length. According to Cathedral records, in the past, the lead roof covering the timbers has been renewed every 250 years and this may partly account for the preservation of the roof timbers.

Cathedral Treen

Where timbers from the roof are replaced wood from the old beams is often reused and turned into new products. The old timbers have been used by local craftsmen to make wooden artefacts such as small bowls marketed under the name of 'Cathedral Treen'. Some parishes commissioned larger pieces to make church fittings such as wall cupboards.

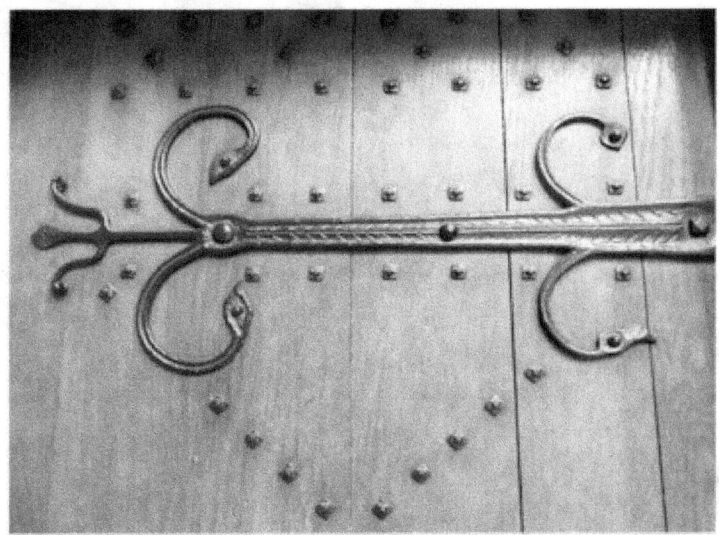

Figure 3: Oak door in Lincoln Cathedral (A. Alder 2018)

Some views of the Lincoln Cathedral roof.

The series of photographs (Figures 4 to 8) below gives an idea of the detailed methods used in constructing the strong timber frame within the roof. It highlights some of the carpentry techniques which are still used today.

Figure 4: Makers marks and brace joint detail (A. Alder 2018)

Figure 5: Tree Nail construction and use in joints (A. Alder 2018)

Figure 6: Template and joint details (A. Alder 2018)

Figure 7: Joint detail and tools used by the carpenters (A. Alder 2018)

Figure 8: The view from the roof of Lincoln Cathedral (A. Alder 2018)

Conservation and the future

A leather-bound "Book of Oaks" contains the names of all those who have pledged, planted, grown and promised oaks for supplying timbers to Lincoln Cathedral. A stone replica of the book stands in Monks Wood, Lincolnshire. In Aisthorpe, 3,000 oak trees have also been planted. The first trees are likely to be selected for the Cathedral early in the twenty-second century. The oak trees that have been planted and are destined for the roof are felled when they reach the right size – 200mm thick and 8-10 metres long. New timbers must be stored and dried within the Cathedral's environment for several years before they can be used as illustrated in Figure 9.

Figure 9: Timber stored in the Cathedral roof space for future use and repair (A. Alder 2018)

Art Installation: Hewing in the Chapter House

In November 2017, an art installation took place in Lincoln Cathedral's Chapter House to celebrate the 800th anniversary of the historic Charter of the Forest. This was a companion document to the Magna Carta signed on November 6th, 1217.

The Charter of the Forest asserts the rights of the common people to get subsistence from the forest, such as estovers and subsistence wood products, restricting the amount of land that the King could claim as Royal land. Every church was required to read out the Charter four times a year in designated services.

The 800th anniversary art installation involved wood workers hewing timber beams using traditional tools over a weeklong period, in the Chapter House. One special feature was the sound of metal against wood which using the acoustics of the Chapter House were amazing to hear. Figures 10 to 12 illustrate the illustration in progress.

 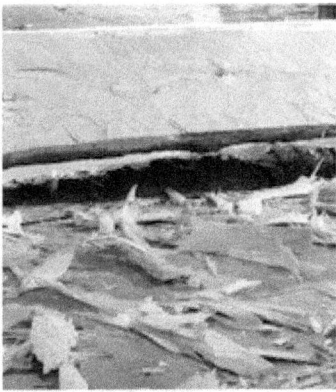

Figure 10: Alan Ely and Shaun Farrell hewing in the Chapter House (A. Alder 2017)

Figure 11: Hewing in the Chapter House (A. Alder 2017)

Figure 12: Hewing in the Chapter House (A. Alder 2017)

Figure 13: Timbers in situ in the roof space (A. Alder 2018)

Conclusion

The roof timbers of Lincoln Cathedral appear to be in safe hands, with the future protected by dedicated trees – from little acorns mighty cathedrals grow.

Acknowledegements

The Author would like to thank everyone who made the field work possible and, also to Alan Ely and Shaun Farrell for their work in the art installation and keeping these skills alive for the future.

References

Rackam, O. (2006) *Woodlands* Collins, London.

Laxton, R., Litton, C., & Howard, R (2001) *Timber: Dating of the Roof Timbers at Lincoln Cathedral* English Heritage Research Transactions, HMSO, London.

Short Contributions

The Diversity and Origin of Modified Tree Forms: with Reference to Type Specimens Found in the UK and Case Studies from the Gleadless Valley, Sheffield

Paul Ardron,
Independent Consultant

This paper explored and attempted to classify the many and varied forms of trees modified by past human activity. Some of these trees have resulted from specific woodland-based industries; others have been shaped and impacted by a variety of forces, not all necessarily anthropogenic. Type specimens from case study sites including the Gleadless Valley, Sheffield and Upper Derwent Valley, Derbyshire were cited along with examples from other locations around the UK. The focus was on tree forms other than coppice and pollards; although certain variants of these types were discussed. Upland trees in particular, often subject to extremes of weather and other geophysical forces combined with more *ad hoc* human influences, have sometimes developed particularly dramatic and distinctive forms.

****

Timber Use and Selection at Must Farm: Construction, Life and Destruction of a Late Bronze Age Settlement

Mike Bamforth
University of York

Recent excavations by Cambridge Archaeological Unit (funded by Forterra and Historic England) at the Late Bronze Age pile dwelling of Must Farm, Peterborough, have provided a rare glimpse into life on the edge of the fens. The settlement came to an end, possibly not long after its construction, in a catastrophic conflagration / fire event. Although the settlement has been partially truncated by quarrying, five circular, wooden, stilted-structures supported by earth-fast driven piles, a section of raised wattle walkway and an encircling palisade were excavated from the muds of the palaeochannel they were constructed above. Interrogating the wood and timber selected to build the settlement and craft so many of the artefacts used by the inhabitants will be one of the key elements to understanding this enigmatic site. Analysis of the carpentry used, and timber selected alongside traces the catastrophic fire has charred into the wood at Must Farm are providing a wealth of information about the construction, use and destruction of the settlement.

****

Trees of National Special Interest - Past History, Safeguarding Present and Future Values

Jill Butler
Woodland Trust

Some trees stand out from all others as very special or remarkable. This may be due to their age, size or condition, as a collection of trees of historic or biodiversity value or their association with nationally important people or events. Most of these will be important to science because they give us insights into past lives and activities i.e. tree archaeology.

Excavated oak sub-fossils from the gravel beds of the River Trent near Nottingham provide evidence of pollarding in the UK 4,400 years ago. Some living pollard oaks may predate the date when England became a recognised state in 927. The practice of pollarding has continued throughout the intervening period until today and is associated with historic landscapes: wood-pastures, old hedgerows and old orchards. It is a European wide, deeply historic practice that provided the many products for everyday life for people and their domesticated stock.

Ancient yews are often associated with places of worship which long pre-date the Romans. Ancient open-grown oaks and other species of tree are often found in mediaeval deer parks where they were essential for mast production for the deer and also as vantage points for the hunt. Their roles are depicted in Mediaeval Books of Hours and other artefacts. Other trees, such as the Parliament Oak, the Capon Tree, Newton's Apple Tree, and the Tolpuddle Martyrs' tree, to name a very few, have associations with celebrities or uprisings or cultural events.

Sadly, despite their value as national icons, they can be extremely vulnerable. Even in the nineteenth century, the Boscobel or Royal Oak is said to have been destroyed by tourists all too keen to take a souvenir away with them. The Pontfadog Oak blew over a few years ago and a similar fate befell the Buttington Oak in 2018 – both lost due to poor root structure. Others are threatened by development, such as at Aldermaston Court in West Berkshire where there was a significant campaign to save the trees.

Although archaeology can be protected e.g. by Scheduled Ancient Monument designation and trees may be protected by Tree Preservation Orders (TPOs), much can still be lost even as we start to become more interested and aware. However, TPOs do not differentiate trees of national status, they are most often used in the protection of trees in local development situations. More recently, there have been calls for a statutory designation of Tree of National Special Interest with agreed criteria that distinguish those trees that tell us more about history, our past lives and activities. As such, the stories about their value as tree archaeology would demonstrate to owners their value to society as a whole and ideally be eligible for management grants where necessary – inspiration and inducement. The Woodland Trust and Ancient Tree Forum would wish to see all ancient trees designated in this way and also the many collections of ancient and other veteran trees to make their values more visible to society, owners, policy makers, advisors and grant aiders.

****

The ICOMOS Principles for the Conservation of Wooden Built Heritage

Doug Evans
ICOMOS-UK Wood Committee

Ever since the ICOMOS International Wood Committee was established in 1975, the need for a set of conservation principles has been a continuous theme in the Committee's ongoing discussions and activities. The first *"Principles for the Preservation of Historic Timber Structures"* were adopted by ICOMOS at the General Assembly in Mexico in October 1999. In a session of the nineteenth General Assembly of ICOMOS held in Delhi on 15th December 2017 a new and updated *"Principles for the Conservation of the Wooden Built Heritage"* were adopted as an ICOMOS doctrinal text. The presentation looked at the main reasons that led to the revision of the Principles including: to recognise a wider variety of wooden heritage including its intangible side; to better recognise the diversity of cultural heritage and the subsequent diversity of approaches, and therefore to reflect the Nara Document on Authenticity (Japan 1994); and to update and adapt its content to present day concerns, knowledge and processes.

****

The Missing Ingredient: The Materiality of Alcohol Fermentation in Early Medieval Ireland

Jessica Gleman,
University College Dublin

Alcohol fermentation has been utilised by societies across the globe over several millennia, despite differences in societal structures, cultures, economies and broader food-ways. In early medieval Ireland (AD 400-1100), alcohol, particularly ale, was central to social gatherings and ceremonies, from the inaugurations of kings to the payment of labourers. This poses the questions, how was alcohol made, presented and shared in Ireland's past?

The production and storage of ale requires a suite of suitable objects and containers – the brewing kit. Whilst alcoholic fermentation is frequently discussed in terms of consumption and ritual, there is far less consideration given to the container itself, and the relationships between the contents and vessels used in fermentation and storage. Vessels have an observable effect on beverages and the fermentation process –today these effects are mostly associated with aging alcohols to add flavour complexity. This project examines evidence of fermentation in early medieval Ireland by exploring ale through a multidisciplinary approach, drawing upon historical writings, folklore, archaeological science, material culture and international ethnographies, along with scientific analysis to compare wooden vessels of different materials and the analysis of how fermentation affects the vessel (use-alteration) and vice versa.

The selection of materials is influenced by the interplay between brewing, the brewer and cultural choices. In contemporary society, the emergence of the craft-beer movement demonstrates a new appreciation of the brewer and their creative outlet. This project will investigate choices made by early medieval brewers, particularly, vessel material selection, and the wider concept of the craftsperson. International studies on fermentation have developed useful scientific approaches and ethnographies, but such approaches have not been applied to early medieval evidence, especially in Ireland. The project will therefore utilise an international approach to better understand brewing and associated material culture in early medieval Ireland.

****

Dugout boat finds in Britain as records of ancient great trees from prehistory to the late medieval period

Damian Goodburn,
London Museum of Archaeology

The paper covered such finds as records of moderately to very, large trees in the past landscapes of several regions of Britain from eastern Scotland, through Wales to South-east England. It was informed by a number of relatively recent studies indicating the variations in the parent trees used through time and space. Several of the examples used were subjects of experimental reconstruction which informed this work.

****

Tanneries and Treescapes

Christine Handley[1] & Ian D. Rotherham[2],
[1]SYBRG ; [2]Sheffield Hallam University

The relationships between supply and demand for wood, timber and bark across markets, geographical areas, and time-periods are complex, but there are common themes. These relationships have influenced the form, structure and management of woodlands; and their legacies can be seen today. Bark was sometimes described as a waste by-product of other wood and timber industries. However, it is clear that with the high economic value of the tanning industry as a whole, and the central role of leather goods in society for centuries, the impact on woodlands in some areas of the country, to ensure a ready and steady supply of mostly oak tree-bark for tanning varied but could be highly significant. From an early twenty-first century and Western perspective, it is difficult to appreciate the central role that leather and woodland products once had. Furthermore, even the memories of past, traditional uses have often been lost (see for example, Rotherham, 2007; Rotherham *et al.*, 2008)). They were fundamental to everyday lives and their economic influence shaped the way societies developed.

Problems of supply of tree-bark, rich in tannins, to meet the demand for leather were eventually solved by finding alternative reliable sources of tanning agents. However, this did not start to have a significant impact until later in the nineteenth century; until then the woodland resource had to be used. Interestingly though, some writers on rural craft industries do not seem to recognise tanning as such (e.g. Green, undated, late 1800s). On the whole, earlier writers have not considered in detail how bark was exploited in different circumstances, and the way this has affected the present woodland resource. These issues were started to be addressed in outline in this poster.

****

Sweet chestnut in Britain: archive review, dendrochronology and DNA analysis

Rob Jarman[a]*, Gill Campbell[f], Frank M. Chambers[a], Zoë Hazell[f], Claudia Mattioni[e], Andy K. Moir[b,c], Karen Russell[d], & Julia Webb[a]
[a]Centre for Environmental Change and Quaternary Research, University of Gloucestershire, Cheltenham, UK; [b]Tree-Ring Services, Mitcheldean, UK; [c]Institute for the Environment, Brunel University, Uxbridge, London, UK; [d] K Russell Consulting Ltd, Leighton Bromswold, Huntingdon, UK; [e]Consiglio Nazionale delle Ricerche, Istituto di Biologia Agroambientale e Forestale, Porano, Italy; [f]Historic England, Fort Cumberland, Portsmouth, UK.
*lead author

This paper presented evidence from three integrated studies of the historical ecology of sweet chestnut *Castanea sativa* in Britain, to indicate techniques useful in investigative tree archaeology.

Our review of all the published archaeological and palaeoenvironmental records described as sweet chestnut found in Britain (thirty-five finds of wood, charcoal, pollen and nuts for the pre-Roman period through to AD 650) has revealed that some finds are misidentifications, some are not identifiable or not dateable, and others are food and artefacts considered imported. Three recently analysed records might possibly derive from sweet chestnut growing in Britain before AD 650, but their provenances are indeterminate. Several written records geographically locate specific trees and their produce, dating from AD 1113 (Goldcliff Priory, Mon.) and AD 1145–54 (Castiard and Flaxley Abbey, Glos.): they indicate sweet chestnut trees/groves established before the twelfth century AD and are the earliest definitive evidence of sweet chestnut growing in Britain.

Our DNA analysis of over 750 sweet chestnut trees/stools across Britain and Ireland has revealed a single overall genepool, part of a larger genepool covering areas of France, Spain, Portugal and Italy regarded as refugia during the Last Glacial Maximum. Clusters within the British and Irish genepool distinguish the oldest trees from the youngest, and the trees of historic parks, gardens, and ancient woodlands from those of plantations and open countryside. Interpretation of these results is under review. The DNA analysis examined individual trees / stools for clonality, to determine their antiquity and geospatial characteristics. Some 'enormous' stools are in fact conglomerates of several plants, but some of <16 metres girth are single plants. Several iconic collapsed and layered trees have been genetically mapped, identifying their sequential growth phases over hundreds of years. Some geospatially separate clonal trees evince, for the first time, vegetative propagation from one location to another.

Our dendrochronological analysis of living trees, fallen deadwood and previously cut stumps has provided a tree-ring chronology for sweet chestnut in southern Britain, presently spanning AD 1660–2014. This was constructed from 54 growth-ring sequences from 28 trees, sampled from 15 sites in historic landscapes and ancient woodland across southern England and south-east Wales. Twenty-three trees cross-matched to form a master *Castanea* chronology and cross-dated with oak *Quercus* reference chronologies from Britain and Northern France, confirming absolute dates for specific trees and their contextual landscapes. Measurable growth-ring sequences were extracted from long-dead fallen trees and stumps, with pith and sapwood surviving in trees >250 years old lying dead for <60 years. The results indicate the potential to dendrochronologically determine sweet chestnut wood (with >50 growth-rings) in archaeological or historical contexts.

DNA and dendrochronological analyses enable the histories of individual trees/stools and their landscape contexts to be more accurately described.

****

The history of wood pasture and tree uses in Herefordshire from documentary sources and digital mapping

David Lovelace
Ancient Tree Forum

Digital methods and equipment have dramatically increased the accessibility of primary historical sources for local historians. Free and open source software for mapping, analysis and data handling is now as powerful and functional as any proprietary equivalent and can be used by anyone with a bit of patience. Aerial photography, LiDAR and GNSS / GPS are free resources for landscape study and field work. Selected sites throughout Herefordshire, including the Forest of Deerfold, Bringewood Chase, Croft Estate and the woods of the Wye Valley were used to illustrate how digital methods have helped gain insights into their histories.

****

Roundwood age and diameter: useful criteria in recognizing past woodland management?

Welmoed Out[1], Kirsti Hänninen[2], Katarina Čufar[3], O. López Bultó[4], & Caroline Vermeeren[2]
[1]Moesgaard Museum, Department of Archaeological Science and Conservation; [2]BIAX Consult; [3]University of Ljubljana, Biotechnical Faculty, Department of Wood Science and Technology; [4]Autonomous University Barcelona, Department Prehistory

European wood and pollen data sets from periods as early as the Mesolithic and Neolithic have been interpreted as indicative of woodland management such as coppicing and pollarding. Particularly, finds consisting of large quantities of long, straight branches or stems at archaeological sites often raise hypotheses about woodland management. While it is highly likely that people affected their surroundings in such a way that they benefitted the quality and quantity of wood, leaves and/or fruits of various trees, direct and representative evidence of the intentionality of such practices in prehistory is available for few regions and periods only.

To study woodland management in the past, a first important question is actually whether it is possible at all to obtain evidence of this former woodland management. While various methods based on archaeological wood assemblages are available, this method focuses for practical reasons on branch or stem age/diameter of uncarbonized, waterlogged wood.

This paper presented an overview of a method that has been designed to investigate whether the study of branch/stem age and diameter of uncarbonized wood allows us to detect woodland management in the past. A model has been developed that predicts the branch age and diameter of managed and unmanaged trees. It is assumed that managed trees tend to produce long, straight branches that grow relatively fast and that branches of unmanaged trees are less straight, grow slower and thus are older when they reach the same diameter.

Measurements of branches and stems of managed and unmanaged hazel, alder, ash and willow have been collected and used to test and adjust the model. The results show that wood of managed and unmanaged trees can be distinguished to a certain extent, particularly when a representative number of measurements is available. The model and data from modern-day trees can be used to interpret the archaeological wood assemblages. Here, data from three archaeological case studies were presented: the Early Neolithic lakeshore settlement of La

Draga in Catalunya, Spain; the late Neolithic pile-dwelling at Stare Gmajne in Slovenia (Eneolithic according to Slovenian terminology); and a single Late Neolithic structure with unknown function at Ronæs Skov, Denmark. A challenge for future research is to collect large quantities of measurements of branch and stem age and diameter from archaeological sites.

****

Incorporating cultural and palaeoecological data to further understand historic woodland usage

Suzi Richer

Woodlands often have a complex history, both in terms of how people have used them and how they have evolved floristically. This complexity and the interconnections between the various elements are often lost in the research process due to the necessary specialisation along disciplinary lines. Using a case study of Shrawley Wood, Worcestershire, UK, the paper illustrated how it is possible to not only bring these individual stands together, but how they can be woven together to bring the complex history of the woodland to life. Using oral history, palaeoecology, archaeology, and woodland management, we can start to refine our understanding of the development of the woodland, the products that came from it and the people who lived there.

****

The changing nature of trees for timber framed buildings - a Wealden perspective

Joe Thompson
Sussex Oak and Iron

The evidence in surviving buildings, from *circa* 1300 to 1900, shows a change in the nature of the trees, and the methods and techniques of converting them into timbers for timber framed buildings. This is an aspect of vernacular archaeology that has had limited investigation, but which can inform the history of woodlands as well as buildings. The seminal work by Oliver Rackham, mainly from an East Anglian viewpoint, established the framework for the fieldwork and subsequent analysis. This presentation reviewed and presented new evidence regarding the species, sizes, grade and conversion of trees, gathered in the Weald; a region of Southern England, famed for its timber. The author has worked with timber framed buildings since 1990 and regularly teaches both practical and theoretical workshops on this subject, primarily at the Weald and Downland Museum in West Sussex.

****

The changing nature of woodlands: the dendrochronological evidence

Cathy Tyers
Historic England

Dendrochronology is generally perceived solely as a scientific dating technique that provides independent dating evidence in relation to when a structure or object was constructed or modified, hence informing the understanding and significance of that structure or object. This process involves the recording of various characteristics of the timbers during both the assessment of dendrochronological potential and the subsequent analysis stage. The information recorded relates directly to the trees utilised and hence can be exploited to reveal not only the date of felling of the trees but also information about the sources of those trees, be they woodlands or more open environments. Two key but basic pieces of data, namely approximate age of tree at felling and average ring width (average growth rate), are used to demonstrate temporal changes and geographical differences in the character of historic timber trees. The examples provided highlighted the potential of this ever increasing body of information to enhance our understanding of the historic treescape and potentially reveal differences in environmental and anthropological influences across regions and how these affected the use and selection of timber in historic structures and objects.

The presentation aimed to flag up both the existence and the potential of this information that is basically an under-utilised by-product of the dendrochronological dating process that is so widely applied to historic assets.

****

The conference and associated events were organised by *South Yorkshire Biodiversity Research Group* (The South Yorkshire & UK Econet) **www.ukeconet.org** with the *Landscape Conservation Forum, Sheffield Hallam University, Historic England, the Ancient Tree Forum, the Vernacular Architecture Group,* **and other partners**

South Yorkshire Biodiversity Research Group is a non-for-profit, voluntary organisation established in the 1990s. The Group organises, runs, and delivers community-based, citizen-science training throughout South Yorkshire and beyond with national activities in partnership with major universities and other key stakeholders. Our work involves: a) Connecting people with nature; b) work with lesser known plants, animals and organisms; and c) raising awareness of large-scale conservation of natural environments on land to help counter the effects of damaging human activities. (The latter are achieved in partnership with major projects on re-wetting the Humberhead Levels, on restoring the Pennine peat bogs and moors, and through our research work on 're-constructing nature', and on 'rewilding' the landscape).

South Yorkshire Biodiversity Research Group provides a forum for the dissemination of information on biodiversity, landscape and environmental conservation issues. We work with a broad range of stakeholder groups, individuals, schools and colleges, including hard-to-reach groups within the community. We welcome new paretners and participants.

The *Landscape Conservation Forum* (LCF) was initiated in Sheffield in 1987 following the seminar *'The Future of the Historic Landscape'* that accompanied the *'Landscapes Through Time'* exhibition at the then Sheffield City Museum.

The Forum involves archaeologists, ecologists, planners and others operating in the Sheffield and Peak District area and welcomes participation in heritage conservation from the professional and voluntary sectors.

The LCF aims to integrate heritage conservation. Its objectives are to:

- **Promote greater understanding between professionals**
- **Establish joint approaches to casework**
- **Create a unified input to conservation management and strategic resource planning**
- **Promote integration of heritage conservation into interpretation and education.**

www.ingramcontent.com/pod-product-compliance
Lightning Source LLC
Chambersburg PA
CBHW052044220426
43663CB00012B/2439